Radical Islam

NEVER SUBDUED II

A True Story

FRANKLIN HOOK

Copyright © 2015 Franklin Hook
All rights reserved.

ISBN-13: 9781508634898
ISBN-10: 1508634890
Library of Congress Control Number: 2015904767
CreateSpace Independent Publishing Platform
North Charleston, South Carolina

HIS001030 HISTORY/AFRICA/NORTH
HIS057000 HISTORY/MARITIME HISTORY & PIRACY
HIS000000 HISTORY/GENERAL
HIS036000 HISTORY/UNITED STATES/GENERAL
HIS27000   HISTORY/MILITARY/GENERAL
HIS037050 HISTORY/MODERN /18TH CENTURY
HIS037060 HISTORY/MODERN /19TH CENTURY

Cover Art: The scene depicts the action of February 9, 1799, when the *USS Constellation*, commanded by Captain Thomas Truxton, captured the French frigate *L'Insurgente*. The image file photo is a work of a sailor or employee of the U.S. Navy taken or made as part of that person's official duties. As a work of the U.S. federal government, the image is in the Public Domain. The image has been flipped horizontally to accommodate a normal American book cover. The artist is unknown, but considering the error in the number of stripes in the flag, it was not likely a member of the U.S. Navy.[1] It is not a work of British artist James Hardy III, who painted a similar scene titled, *USS Constellation* vs French *L'Insurgente*.

1 Note extra stripes on the American flag.

DEDICATION

For Patricia K. and Dorann A.

CONTENTS

Preface and Acknowledgments		ix
Introduction	A True Story	xv
Prologue 1	October 19, 1469, A Day That Changed the World	xix
Prologue 2	Setting the Stage October 13, 1775, A Paper Navy	xxxi

Part I

Chapter 1	Thomas Jefferson, a New Sheriff in Town	3
Chapter 2	العاهرة ابن من, an Arabic Oath	13
Chapter 3	Tribute or War? Was Kipling Right?	23
Chapter 4	Our Country Right or Wrong- Stephen Decatur	39
Chapter 5	The Easy Way to Make General	61
Chapter 6	A Desert Where No Christian Ever Sat His Foot	81
Chapter 7	Is Treason Motivated by Design or Weakness?	91

PART II

Chapter 8	Seeds of War-the Chesapeake-Leopard Affair	105
Chapter 9	War of 1812 – Triumphs and Tragedies	121
Chapter 10	Decatur – Again! And Again!!	143
Chapter 11	Decatur & 10 Commandments of Muslim diplomacy	157
Chapter 12	Reflections	185
Epilogue	What Happened to the Main Characters	191
Index		253

Nail Our Flag To The Mast

Nail our flag to the mast! That all nations may know
It floats over freemen who'll defend it,
We'll ne'er haul it down, though o'erwhelming, the foe,
though the smoke may enshroud, though the war-hail may rend it.

When the smoke clears away at the close of the fray,
Our flag, though in tatters, we'll proudly display and
E'en though we sink, still unconquered at last,
We'll sink 'neath the wave our flag nailed to the mast.

Nail our flag to the mast! tis the flag of the free:
While the deeds of our fathers are hallowed in story,
Our standard a terror to tyrants must be,
To freeman a beacon of honor and glory.

Spite of wind and rain on its folds, not a stain,
Our flag shall forever untarnished remain;
In peace or in war, from the first to the last,
Dear country, speed on, with flag nailed to the mast.

From Rhymings by Howard Wainwright, 1860[2]

---

[2] Library of Congress

PREFACE and ACKNOWLEDGEMENTS

This is a story about pirates, real pirates in real places. Specifically it is a true story about the Pirates of the Barbary Coast who harassed merchant shipping throughout the Mediterranean in the 18th and 19th centuries. More specifically it's about our founders including George Washington, Thomas Jefferson, John Adams, Alexander Hamilton, Benjamin Franklin, and many others with historical name recognition, and how they reacted to extortion on the high seas with virtually no assets at their disposal.

The story also relates to the consequences of religious intolerance and involves Christians, Jews, Muslims and Fundamentalists of all three religions on all sides. It relates entirely to the present day. This true narrative history will present the facts. You be the judge.

My curiosity was first piqued when I was doing research for my first historical narrative, *Never Subdued,* which involved Muslims of the southern Philippines, some of whom were pirates. I discovered that these characters were labeled Moros by the Spanish invaders because they were Muslims. Robert A. Fulton, author of *Moroland,*[3] referring to the attempted subjugation of the Philippine Moros by Spanish conquistadors in 1564, said this: *"To their consternation and rage, they discovered that many of the people they sought to subjugate were Muslims of the same religion and beliefs of their ancient enemies from the Barbary Coast of present-day Morocco."*[4] I at first thought that the Barbary Coast pirates or their descendants had immigrated to the Philippines, but author Fulton in a personal communication straightened me out:

"There is no known or even suspected historical migration of people from the Barbary Coast to the Philippine Islands, or the rest of SE Asia for that matter. Rather the people who came to be called the Moros in the Phil-

---
3 Fulton, Robert A, Tumalo Creek Press, Bend, Oregon, 2007.
4 Franklin Hook, Never Subdued, 2011, Create Space p 176.

ippines were descendants of certain former pagan tribes who were of the dominant Malay Race that exists in SE Asia. There is and was no North African physical connection or heritage between the two. While the spread of Islam within the current Middle East during the 8th Century was primarily by military conquest, in SE Asia it happened six centuries later, in about the 14th Century, occurring peacefully for the most part. Rather Islam spread gradually to the region through the aegis of active proselytization by Muslim traders from South Asia, the present day countries of India and Pakistan, who were opening new trade routes to the region and establishing small trading enclaves, marrying into the local communities.

"In other words, Muslims did not come from North Africa and settle down in SE Asia; SE Asians were converted and persuaded to accept Islam by "preachers" coming from outside the region. The same can be said about how Christianity came to the [Philippine] islands 200 years later, by Spanish and Portuguese sailors and soldiers, many of who were deeply religious and often even part-time priests. But, unlike as happened in Latin America, it happened much more often out of persuasion than raw force of arms.

"They came to be tagged by the Spanish with the name "Moro", only because the Spanish called anybody, anywhere who was a Muslim, a "Moro" whether they resided in North Africa or anywhere else. It was a pejorative which, ironically, down through the centuries came to be accepted as a badge of honor."[5]

Of course I learned quite a bit about the Moros during my original research, but many questions remained. Why, for example, had some of these practitioners of the Muslim religion turned to piracy? Why was there such hostility to the Spanish and currently also to the Jews? Why were they such fanatics in following certain passages in the Koran,[6] especially those suggesting that murder and violence is an acceptable part of the culture?

I don't claim to be an expert on the Koran or the Muslim religion, but perhaps there are significant parallels with the Christian Bible and

---

5 Fulton, Robert A, personal communication 3/12/2015.
6 Also spelled Qur'an'

the Torah[7] of the Hebrews that would explain fundamentalist thinking. Emmett Fox, one of the outstanding spiritual leaders of the last century, has stated that the Bible teaches by using many symbols, allegories, and parables and if one does not understand that, he or she will never understand the Bible. Fox also said that certain words in the Bible have different meanings than their literal interpretation. For example the word fear in the Bible *"if taken literally has misled many people because the truth is that fear is entirely evil and it is indeed the only enemy we have."*[8] Fox thought that the word fear in many places in the Bible really means reverence.

Another word, wrath, Fox said should be interpreted as "great activity" because the phrase *the wrath of God* puzzles many students of metaphysics since God is supposed to represent love and not anger. Likewise the word salvation means "health, harmony, and freedom", and the word wicked means "bewitched" or "under a spell," and so on and so forth for many other words. Fox said vengeance means vindication, repentance means to change one's mind and the word Christ means spiritual truth about any person, situation or thing.[9]

Dr. Fox also indicated that interpreting allegories and parables[10] in Bible stories as literal truth can also get you into trouble. For example, he said that God knows everything at all times and does not need to test us. If you interpret as literal the passage in Genesis where God told Abraham to prepare to kill Isaac, then that would be an error. Fox indicated that it was Abraham's idea of God that led him to prepare to kill Isaac and it was his higher self, i.e., his indwelling Christ that saved him from that tragedy. Of course Dr. Fox's explanation appeals to me because I am thinking what kind of a God

---

7 *The Torah and the first five books of the old testament of the Christian Bible are the same.*

8 *Fox, Emmett, Make Your Life Worthwhile, Harper & Row, New York, 1946, p 58*

9 *Ibid, pages 58-70.*

10 *Webster defines allegory as the representation of spiritual, moral, or other abstract meanings through the actions of fictional characters and parable as a short allegorical story designed to illustrate some truth, religious principle or moral lesson.- Random House Webster's College Dictionary.*

who is supposed to be all Love, would instruct one of his own to kill his own son?

Of course there are other ways to interpret the passage in Genesis referred to above. Some ministers believe the passage is an allegory, but interpret it to refer to God presenting his own son, Jesus, as a sacrifice for our sins, in other words allowing the killing of his son.

Might there be parables and allegories in the Koran as well? More than one Islamic scholar says there are. The *As-Salāmu Alaykum Wa Rahmatullahi Wabarakathuhu*[11] website internet blog[12] flatly states that the Koran uses the principle of comparison through allegory.

Dr. Umar Azamba BA, PHD,[13] Manchester, U.K., points out that parables and allegories are used throughout the Koran as well, even those passages said to be dictated directly to Mohammed by the Almighty.

The point is, if fundamentalist Muslims ignore the teachings of the Koran by allegory and parable and interpret some of the passages that seem to be advocating violence, even killing and slaughter of nonbelievers as a literal order from Allah then we know the problem can possibly be solved by education, as formidable a task as that may seem. The same can be said of the far right wings of the Christian religion regarding both the Old and New Testaments and the Torah of the Hebrew religion. In the meantime negotiators from the West could likely benefit from knowing some common sense rules such as the nonreligious 10 Commandments of Muslim Diplomacy. These were offered previously in my book *Desert Storm Diary*[14] and are also found in chapter 11 of this publication.

As always there are many people to thank for their assistance when submitting a manuscript for publication. I relied heavily on previous meticulous historians and researchers such as Ian W. Toll, author of *Six Frigates;* Karen Armstrong, *The Battle for God;* Donald R. Hickey, *The War of 1812;* Richard Zacks, *The Pirate Coast;* and much older pub-

---

11 An Arabic phrase meaning approximately "Peace, mercy, and blessings be with you."
12 Islamic Web Site, http://islamicresponse.blogspot.co.uk/2008/07/purpose.html
13 http://www.dr-umar-azam.com/parables_in_the_holy_quran.html
14 Hook, Franklin- Fall River Publishing, 2012

lications such as a *History of the United States Navy from 1775 to 1893*, published in 1894 and written by Edgar Stanton and R.C. Smith.

The digitization of other older publications like William Eaton's journal or Commodore Preble's diary by Google, various universities or government agencies and the Library of Congress have also been invaluable. For a complete list please refer to the bibliography including Internet sources.

There are numerous websites also listed in the bibliography which I used in research for this manuscript. Among the most frequently visited included the multiple sources of the Jefferson Monticello Websites, the Department of the Navy and Army websites, the Library of Congress and many others.

Among those individuals to whom I am once again grateful include Robert A. Fulton of Bend Oregon who is the author of *Moroland* and *Honor for the Flag: The Battle of Bud Dajo*, and who once again screened the manuscript and offered critical advice, the second time I have been honored with his expertise and analysis. I am once again also favored with the editorial assistance of Roxane Brodnick, of San Simeon, California, who corrects my errors with a knowledge which is consistently amazing to my uneducated eye for print.

Not to be excluded from my thanks are the amazing book production experts from Create Space, Charleston, South Carolina, including those who designed the cover, and my son, Paul Hook of Mill City, Oregon, computer nerd *extraordinaire* and part-time cartographer. Last but not least my thanks go to my publicists and designers of the *Never Subdued* (and all my other) web pages, the Robert Sharp and Associates Agency of Rapid City, SD.

Franklin Hook, Spring 2015.

A TRUE STORY
INTRODUCTION

Dear Reader,
The book is divided into two parts separated by the first and second Barbary wars. The hiatus between the Barbary Wars was caused by the United States having to deal with hostile actions by both the French and British navies, which resulted in an undeclared war (the Quasi-War) with France and a declared war (the War of 1812) with Great Britain. Although both of these wars had little to do with our dispute with the Muslim dominated North African Barbary States, the near freezing of U.S. commerce by a British blockade of our ports preceded by the seizing of American merchant vessels and cargoes by the French, forced the fledgling nation of the United States to ignore its relations with the Barbary Coast, at least for a period of time.

If the reader is well-versed in the Quasi-War and the War of 1812, repeating the facts presented here may be time-consuming. If however one is not familiar with these conflicts as was I, reading about them will not only explain the nations' delay in dealing with the extortion by the Barbary Pirates, but will help you understand why and how our leaders and military heroes developed the courage and resolve to be successful against them. One can speculate why the Barbary Corsairs ceased to be a problem for the United States after 1815, but there is no doubt that American shipping commerce thrived all over the world after the second Barbary war. Was it just because of the U.S. Navy and Decatur's heroic feats or was there more involved? Author Robert Fulton suggests:

"I strongly suspect that it was directly related to the subsequent steady conquest of North Africa by France, Italy, and the UK; which

in turn was enabled first by enormous increases in European population, (nearly five-fold in the 19th century), versus stagnation in the Muslim states accompanied by major advances in marine and military technologies by those same European powers (think steam, coal, and manufacturing standardization). The balance of power dramatically changed and rendered the pirate and slave economies of the Barbary Coast unsustainable, threw their politics into disarray, and rendered them impotent. They may not have been subdued in the conventional sense but most certainly found themselves effectively obsoleted by a changing world. For the United States, the problem simply went away."[15]

There is no doubt in my mind that Robert Fulton has significant points, but there's also no doubt in my mind that the U.S. Navy and Stephen Decatur's resolve and heroics triggered the change in the balance of power in North Africa and the Mediterranean.

I was born during the Great Depression and grew up in a patriotic America during World War II followed by the space age of the late 1950s and 1960s with all of its associated scientific discoveries and advancements. Until recently I never knew an America with a timid foreign policy and a bureaucratic government that has grown so large as to be not only dictatorial, but anti-capitalistic. It is also a government that is so irresponsible with its spending that our nation is now threatened with bankruptcy.

Sure, we had our antiwar protesters during Vietnam, and our share of terrorists like the Weather Underground and Timothy McVeigh. But we had nothing like the current young generation has had to face since September 11, 2001. It is my hope that narrative histories like this one will help educate our youth and show them that other generations in our nation have had to face similar situations against similar culprits and found a way to overcome the threats.

Even many people among older generations like mine may not know that for years we paid ransom and other extortion demands and treasure, such as ships and other equipment, to hostile governments and pirates in order to avoid violent conflict or war. Some might ar-

---

15 Fulton, Robert A, *personal communication of May 5, 2015.*

gue that we do the same thing today with foreign aid which lands in the hands of dictators and thieves instead of its intended targets of relief. That may be, but perhaps true stories like this one will educate our youth so that future members of our Congress vote in America's best interest instead of their party's or their own.

This story is a narrative history, and like my first volume, *Never Subdued*, it involves some imaginative but logical conversations amongst the principal participants. Some of the conversations can be documented in available records such as the Thomas Jefferson papers, diaries and the Congressional Records. One particular conversation of importance is documented in Alexander McKenzie's biography of Oliver Hazard Perry concerning his battle flag transfer during the Battle of Lake Erie. The words of that conversation, recorded by a participant who was there, were edited by the author to a more modern parlance. Others are purely from my imagination, but in a real situation with a known outcome. It is my belief that this technique presents a better teaching platform for true history, makes the story real, which it is, and presents facts which are more likely to be retained by the reader.

So sit back dear reader and relax. Read on and enjoy a true history with real heroes, real villains, and real outcomes. Find out what really changed the balance of power in North Africa and the Mediterranean. I believe you will come to realize how fortunate our nation is to have had founders and military leaders and heroes with realistic and practical knowledge and wisdom. I think you will also confirm if you didn't already know that they were men and women of courage and foresight, although not without personality flaws whose actions sometimes bordered on jealousy or political gain. Hopefully our nation can return to at least some of their positive values.

PROLOGUE 1

A Day That Changed The World- October 19, 1469.
Barbary - "foreign lands" (especially non-Christian lands), from Latin barbaria. Meaning 'Saracens living in coastal North Africa'- In European languages [the term 'Barbary'] from the first [has] been treated as identical with Latin barbaria; Byzantine Greek -barbaria land of barbarians"
- The Online Etymology Dictionary

It was Tuesday, October 19, 1469, a day that some historians would call "the day that changed the world."[16] For Isabella, the daughter of John II of Castile and Isabella of Portugal, it was her wedding day. Isabella had been betrothed to her second cousin, Ferdinand of Aragon, since the age of six. The betrothal was abrogated more than once during the previous dozen years of Isabella's young life. Finally, after much political intrigue, the betrothal resulted in a royal wedding.

After several abrogations Isabella had put her foot down and refused to marry any one of a number of candidates returning her troth to Ferdinand of Aragon, with whom she had fallen in love. So on this day the 18-year-old bride and her 17-year-old husband were wed and thus began a reign that would unite all of the dominions of Spain and elevate the nation to a dominant world power.[17]

The ceremonies took place in the ancient city of Valladolid the capital of the Northwest Spanish province of the same name. The city is built around the confluence of two Rivers, the Pisuerga and

---

16 Stiadi, Edwin, http://www.edwinsetiadi.com/2011/05/19-october-1469-day-that-changed-world.html
17 ibid

the Esgueva, and was once the province of Islamic warriors in the 700s A.D.

Near the end of the seventh century a Muslim army of Moros reinforced with other Arabs from Egypt and the Arabian Peninsula had invaded the Iberian Peninsula, that huge chunk of land that juts out of southwestern Europe into the Atlantic Ocean. The invading Muslims conquered this land then occupied by the Visigoths, the western faction of the Goths which were Germanic tribes who settled the areas from the Black Sea to the Iberian Peninsula. The area then became known as Al Andalus, was completely under Muslim control and covered nearly the entire Iberian Peninsula later to become primarily Spain and Portugal.[18]

This whole area known as Al Andalus was controlled by Damascus, the Syrian capital of the Islamic world. What that means is that the caliphs in Spain and Portugal had little to say about Islamic policy and were directed by the government in Damascus. The major cities in Al-Andalus were Córdoba in the south and Valladolid, meaning the city of Al-Walid,[19] further north.[20]

By the year 1400 the Iberian Peninsula consisted of three kingdoms: Portugal on the Atlantic coast, Aragon, a small kingdom bordering France on the Mediterranean Sea, and Castile, a rural kingdom in the middle. The southern part of the Iberian Peninsula remained under Muslim control as it had been for seven centuries.

After their marriage in 1469, Isabella and Ferdinand, incorporated a number of Spanish dominions into their kingdom, thus increasing their reach and power base. At first religious freedom was left alone by the royal couple who appreciated the many contributions that

---

18 *Spanish Fiestas* web site, Moors in Spain http://www.spanish-fiestas.com/history/moors/

19 *Al-Walid was a Caliph who ruled the city at the time.*

20 *Spanish Fiestas* web site, Moors in Spain http://www.spanish-fiestas.com/history/moors/

the Islamic religion and culture had made to scientific advancement. These included among others:
- An Astrolabe. A device similar to a sextant that could measure the position of the stars and planets.
- Streetlights
- Running water
- The founding of the first Spanish University at Valencia in 1209.

The Moors had also occupied Al Andalus (Spain) for over 800 years, thus there was the inevitable influence on language, education, science, mathematics, and medicine.

"Words beginning with 'al,' for example, are derived from Arabic. The Moors were also advanced in medicine, science, and astronomy, and Arabic words such as algebra, alcohol, chemistry, nadir, alkaline, and cipher entered the language. Even words such as checkmate, influenza, typhoon, orange, and cable can be traced back to Arabic origins."[21]

While the Muslims were in power citizens of other religions were allowed to practice their faith but were required by the Muslims to pay a tax in order to do so. Christians and Jews who took advantage of this policy were called *"dhimmi."*[22] Even though Muslims had been in power since the time of their invasion, the power base had gradually lessened as the Christian dominions and kingdoms of the remainder of the Iberian Peninsula expanded so that by the year 1300 Muslims controlled only Granada, a tiny area in southern Spain.[23] The power base of the Iberian Peninsula, however, was going to further dramatically change, and it could be related directly to the introduction of the Spanish Inquisition in the city of Valladolid in 1478.

One Internet source stated that in 1478 the Pope (Sixtus IV) gave the Spanish king, Ferdinand V, (nine years after his marriage to Isabella) power to initiate the Spanish Inquisition during which people were

---

21 Kohen, Elizabeth. (original source) 2003. *Cultures of the World: Spain*. New York, NY: Benchmark Books. Quoted Internet source, http://facts.randomhistory.com/interesting-facts-about-spain.html.

22 Croy, Anita. 2010. *Countries of the World: Spain*. Washington D.C.: National Geographic

23 Walbert, David, *Spain and America: From Reconquest to Conquest*, NC Digital History http://www.learnnc.org/lp/editions/nchist-twoworlds/1677

tortured to prove they were true Christians. Thousands of converts fled Spain as the Inquisition spread fear across Europe. This particular source stated that 5,000 victims of the Inquisition were killed in the first 50 years.[24] Karen Armstrong says the count was much higher with some 13,000 Jewish converts (conversos) alone executed in the first 12 years.[25] The Inquisition was not abolished until 1834.

Actually the Spanish Inquisition, starting in 1478, most likely delayed the inevitable result of the expulsion of both Jews and Arabs from Spain because the Christians were squabbling amongst themselves. The biggest squabble was the war of Castilian succession which started about 1475 after Henry IV of Castile died in 1474. The war was fought between the supporters of Henry's half-sister, Isabella, and his daughter Juana. Isabella however was the one that was successful mostly because her army was more aggressive than Juana's, which was led by her husband Alfonzo, who was also much older (43) and was also her uncle. Political intrigue, intermarriage, and politics however did play a part since there was a rumor that Juana was not Henry IV's daughter, but in fact was the daughter of Beltran de la Cueva, said to be Joan of Portugal's lover. Joan was Henry IV's second wife and his widow. It sounds like a soap opera, but it was all real.

"During the Reconquista,[26] Muslim states fell one by one to Christian kingdoms invading from the North. The major cities of Cordoba, Seville, and Toledo fell from the [years of] 1000s to the 1200s. The Murabitun and Muwwahidun (Almoravid and Almohad)[27] movements from North Africa helped slow the Christian tide, but disunity among the Muslims eventually led to continued loss of land.

"One Muslim state – Granada – was able to escape conquest by Christians in the 1200s. After the fall of Cordoba in 1236, the rulers of the Emirate of Granada signed a special agreement with the Kingdom of Castile, one of the most powerful Christian kingdoms. Granada had agreed to

---

24 Cultures of the World, Spain http://facts.randomhistory.com/interesting-facts-about-spain.html

25 Armstrong, Karen, The Battle for God-Random House, 2000, page 7, Ballantine Books, Div. of Random House, 2000.

26 Meaning the re-conquest of the Iberian Peninsula in its entirety by the Christians.

27 Jewish Virtual Library: Those who advocate the unity of Allah, Moroccan Berbers from Tinmel in the Atlas Mountains. http://www.jewishvirtuallibrary.org/

become a tributary state to Castile. This meant they were allowed to remain independent as the Emirate of Granada, but in exchange for not being invaded by Castile, they had to pay a yearly sum (usually in gold) to the Castilian monarchy. This created a detrimental situation for the Muslims of Granada as they paid regularly to strengthen their enemies."[28]

Some would argue that the tribute paid by the Muslims was a tit-for-tat for the *dhimmi* tax, called *jizya*, paid by Christians and Jews of previous generations to the Muslims so they could practice their own religion without other penalty. No matter what you call them, both policies produced revenue for the power base of whoever was in charge at the time, and no matter who started the policies they would, as you will see, be reflected in international crisis negotiations for centuries to come.

1492 was a big year of expansion of territory and power for Ferdinand and Isabella. On January 2, of that year the city of Granada, the last Muslim fortress and foothold in southern Spain, was attacked and surrendered to the Army of Ferdinand and Isabella who were responding to a Muslim raid on the southern coastal town of Zahara de la Sierra, a municipality in the province of Cádiz, Andalusia, Spain. The Castilian royals apparently felt the annual tribute paid in gold by the citizens of Granada as insurance to avoid invasion was voided by the Muslim invasion of Zahara, regardless of from where the raiders came.

On March 31 that year, 1492, Ferdinand and Isabella issued the Edict of Expulsion for all Jews under their domain who would not convert to Roman Catholicism. The offer was baptism or expulsion. The edict was a move by the royal couple to unify their nation under one religion, and came with the blessing of the Vatican. A similar edict and choices would be declared for the Muslims seven years later in 1499.[29]

According to the Treaty of Granada drawn up in 1492 after the victory of Castilian forces over the city, the Muslims, who were now citizens of Castile instead of the emirate of Granada, could continue

---

28 Alkhateeb, Firas, Lost Islamic History website, http://lostislamichistory.com/granada-the-last-muslim-kingdom-of-spain/

29 Armstrong, Karen, The Battle for God, page 3. Ballantine Books, Div. of Random House, 2000

to practice their religion and abide by their own laws as well as speak their own language. However, seven years later in 1499 the articles of that peace treaty would be broken when Cardinal Cisneros forced mass conversions of Muslims, and burned all religious texts written in Arabic. His actions forced the First Rebellion of the Alpujarras[30] and resulted in the killing of one of his Prelate Officers.

Things escalated from there with the burning of priceless books. The new "converts" were then subjected to the Spanish Inquisition with its apparently endless executions and were forced to lead a double life in order to practice their Islam in secret. By 1526, the remaining Moors who had not fled were given a choice between baptism and exile.[31]

In that same year of 1492, Ferdinand and Isabella financed Christopher Columbus, an Italian explorer from Genoa, Italy, to search for a new route over the oceans to India. Columbus took his instructions from Isabella in the city of Valladolid. We all know the result of that expedition when Columbus sailed in the month of August and landed on one of the islands in the Bahamas by mistake but discovered (or rediscovered?) the New World in the process. For Spain it meant almost immediate world power status and riches.[32]

The religious intolerance of the Iberian Peninsula extended into the Middle Ages. Philip III carried it further by expelling Moriscos, who were Christians of Moorish ancestry because many practiced Islam in secret.[33] Phillip III did this by decree on April 9, 1609.[34] Moranos[35] (Jewish converts to Christianity) and Moriscos (Islamic con-

---

[30] Alpujarras- The etymology of 'alpujarra' is unclear, though the most credible suggestion is that it derived from the Arabic word al-bugsharra, meaning 'sierra of pastures'. - http://www.spainforpleasure.com/tag/andalucia-2/. In this case it refers to the region including Granada where the revolts took place.

[31] Armstrong page 3

[32] Boase, Roger, History Today, Vol 52, Issue 4, 2002. http://www.historytoday.com/roger-boase/muslim-expulsion-spain

[33] Gonzales, Matthew, Morisco Expulsion 1609: http://mattgonzalez8947.umwblogs.org/about/

[34] Carr, Matthew, (Orig. source) cited by Alkhateeb, Firas, http://lostislamichistory.com/spains-forgotten-muslims-the-expulsion-of-the-moriscos/

[35] Also spelled Morranos.

verts to Christianity) were derogatory terms as far as the Christians were concerned, equivalent of calling them pigs or little pigs.[36] Over the next few years, in what theoretically could have represented national karma, Phillip's reign saw the decline of Spain as a significant European power.

To summarize, when Isabella exiled the Jews and the Moors from Spain in order to solidify her country with the Roman Catholic religion, the consequences would be felt around the world for centuries to follow. When they were kicked out of Spain most of the Moriscos,[37] who were followers of Mohammed, i.e. Muslims, took refuge on the north coast of Africa. It wasn't long before some of these exiles took up a new occupation, piracy, including a form of indenture or slavery for those sailors captured for whom they could not get ransom. As the descendants emigrated throughout the Middle East the culture and at least some of its lawless practitioners grew in number and prospered. Its effects have never been subdued or eradicated to this day. Witness the pirates operating off the coast of Somalia and now the metastasis of ISIS in the Middle East and North Africa.

Of the estimated 200,000 Jews who were living in Spain at the time of the exile, only about 70,000, or less than half, converted to Roman Catholicism. The majority of those exiled, about 80,000, fled to Portugal where they could practice their religion peacefully. Another 50,000 fled to the Ottoman Empire mostly along the northern coast of Africa, where they were warmly welcomed. At that time Muslims and Jews got along relatively peacefully; both groups were, after all, Semites and descendants of Abraham. The seeds of dissent, however, may have been planted (again)[38] when the Jews in the Iberian Peninsula were forced to pay the tax called *jizya* for being non-Muslims (infidels). The policy was enacted since they were considered *dhimmi*

---

36 Armstrong page 7.
37 Encyclopedia Britannica
38 Jizya was levied in the time of Muhammad on vassal tribes under Muslim control and protection, including Jews in Khaybar, Christians in Najran, and Zoroastrians in Bahrain. -Wikipedia

along with the Christians. Some historians might date the isolation of the Hebrews from practicing Muslims much earlier:

"*The Umayyad caliphs (661–750) [A.D.], however, faced with increasing financial difficulties, demanded the jizya from recent converts to Islam as well as from the dhimmis. This discrimination against converts was a cause of the Abū Muslim rebellion (747) [A.D.] in Khorāsān and helped to precipitate the downfall of the Umayyads.*"[39]

In fairness it should be noted that the jizya tax was an important part of revenue throughout much of Muslim history. It was also a humanitarian tax, paid only by men and only by those with sufficient funds. Exemptions included the old, the crippled, the blind etc.

Two distinct differences resulted from the Jews' expulsion as compared to the Muslims' exile. Former Roman Catholic Nun, Karen Armstrong, author of *The Battle for God, A History of* Fundamentalism,[40] points out that as the Christians took over more and more of the Islam communities of the Iberian Peninsula they brought their anti-Semitism with them. Even back in the 1300s Christians attacked Jewish communities, dragged the citizens to baptismal fonts and under penalty of death forced their conversions. Even up to the time of Ferdinand and Isabella there were Christian riots against the upwardly mobile Moranos, who were Jewish converts to Christianity, and whose property was often confiscated and the owners either killed or driven out of town.[41]

Even Jews, who fled to Portugal, although they initially had an exemption of almost 10 years from the Spanish Inquisition, eventually fell to its atrocities as did the others. Anti-Semitism was rampant throughout Christian Europe, which is a story in itself. Only those Jews who fled to the Ottoman Empire were exempt from the open persecution by the Christians. They were however subject to the Islamic jizya tax and were considered second class citizens or *dhimmi*.

The first distinct difference in the long-term result of the Jewish expulsion and exile from Spain, as compared to the Muslim's deportation,

---

39 Encyclopaedia Britannica http://www.britannica.com/EBchecked/topic/304125/jizya

40 Armstrong, Karen, The Battle for God, Ballantine Books, Div. of Random House, 2000, page 7.

41 Ibid

is that although for the most part the Hebrews withdrew into their religion as did the Muslims, their reaction was different. Some, especially those who had immigrated to Portugal, became atheists. For a very detailed explanation of the Jewish reaction to exile, read Karen Armstrong's book. According to Armstrong they had gone through secularism or rejection of their faith, to atheism, to rationalism in which reason alone was sufficient to live, to nihilism a philosophy close to anarchy, to pluralism in which there is a belief in more than one basic cause, and finally the privatization of faith. The bottom line is that regardless of their ecclesiastic tendency, the Jews, for the most part, became self-sufficient and upwardly mobile in their economic status. Whenever their success appeared to be benefiting themselves more than their persecutors, anti-Semitism raised its ugly head resulting in pogroms, such as occurred in Poland in the 1600s. Amsterdam in the Netherlands became one of their most stable sanctuaries.

The Muslim exodus from Spain, however, in 1492 after the defeat of Granada and by decree in 1499, had different consequences. Although the Muslims had lost their positions in Europe, the religion was still a significant power throughout the remainder of the globe. In the early 1500s the Ottoman Empire, one of three major Islamic powers,[42] occupied such lands as far east and north as Hungary, the Balkans, and Greece. Those Muslim communities along the North African coast of the Mediterranean may not have been considered part of the Ottoman Empire in 1492, but most historians would agree that they were part of that empire by 1517 when Egypt became officially aligned. Why some of the emigrating Muslims turned to piracy is speculative. Karen Armstrong suggests that fundamentalism in all three religions, Christians, Hebrews, Muslims, and perhaps others, gets a boost when its populace is under stress of one kind or another.

There is no doubt that at least some of the pirate nation leaders used literal interpretation of their particular holy book to justify actions such as piracy. Tripoli's ambassador, Sidi Haji Abdrahaman, in March, 1785, quoted the Koran in reply to Thomas Jefferson's query of

---

42 *Ibid-The other two Islamic empires were the Safavid in Iran and the Moghul in the Indian Subcontinent.*

why they had attacked a United States merchant ship who had done them no harm. (See Prologue 2 of this text).

If the fundamentalist response by the Muslims to their exile from Spain came much earlier and persisted longer than that of the Hebrews, which it appears to have done, then that likely constitutes one of the major differences between the two. The result is that some of these cultures who have resorted to violence and piracy have never been subdued by anyone.

Gardner W. Allen[43] in his classic work about the Barbary corsairs indicated that piracy along the Barbary Coast and in the Mediterranean has been present for centuries and stated that the culture was practiced by both Muslims and Christians alike. Many of the Christians joining the piracy ranks were captured sailors. Allen also confirmed that the Exodus of Muslims following the conquest of Granada in 1492 swelled the ranks of the corsairs along the Barbary Coast.

The most ruthless of the pirates, the brothers Barbarossa, appeared in Tunis in 1504, after moving from an eastern Mediterranean base where they could fulfill their own personal ambitions further away from their sultan's fleet. The elder brother, Horuk,[44] and his younger sibling, Khair-ed Din Barbarossa, were highly successful sailing their pirate vessels throughout the Mediterranean from their base in Tunis. They began to collect a significantly large fleet. What followed was years of turmoil including a retaking of the islands of Algiers[45] by a Spanish expedition led by Cardinal Ximenis. When Sheikh Salem called on his former protégé Horuk Barbarossa for help in evicting the Spanish from Algiers, Horuk responded by murdering the Sheikh and taking over his fleet in 1509.

Horuk continued to be a successful pirate until he was caught and killed by a pursuing Spanish galleon in 1518. The Spanish however failed to follow up on their success and ignored the corsair's base in Algiers, which Horuk had reclaimed. After his death Horuk was suc-

---

43 Allen Page 3. *Our Navy and the Barbary Corsairs*, Houghton, Mifflin & Co., Riverside Press, Boston. 1905.

44 also spelled Oruk

45 Wikipedia: The city name is derived from the Arabic name al-Jazā'ir, which translates as "The Islands", referring to the four islands which lay off the city's coast until becoming part of the mainland in 1525.

ceeded by his younger brother, Khair-ed Din, (original name Khidr) who was known around the Mediterranean as Redbeard, a nickname he inherited from his older brother, Baba [Horuk] Oruc.[46] Redbeard put Algiers under the protection of the Sultan of Constantinople (now called Istanbul). The Sultan rewarded the younger Barbarossa by making him governor general. He subsequently became commander of the Ottoman Navy and recaptured Tunis in 1534 which had been retaken by the Spanish. The very next year, 1535, Charles V of Spain (also called the Holy Roman Emperor) led an expedition of some 600 ships commanded by Admiral Andrea Doria, his Italian ally from Genoa, and put the port of Tunis and the city to siege. When Barbarossa came out to meet the Emperor in battle, thousands of Christian slaves closed the gates to the city behind him. He subsequently lost the battle and was forced to flee the city. The city was then sacked by the Spanish and some 30,000 people including women and children were massacred. In addition another 10,000 or so were forced into slavery. Khair-ed Din Barbarossa (Redbeard) never returned to the Barbary Coast but remained one of the great figures of the court at Constantinople until his death.[47] Tunis was held by the Spanish for about five years.

In 1541, Charles V led another expedition this time against Algiers. It was a disaster. Adverse weather made the invasion impossible, and the Spanish lost about 150 ships and all of the sailors who made it to shore were killed by the Arabs. The Holy Roman Emperor gathered his survivors and returned to Spain having led the most disastrous expedition ever recorded to that date. The Barbary States were now at their peak of power which lasted for thirty years until 1571.

In that year, 1571, Don Juan (some sources spell it Don John) of Austria led a coalition of several states including naval vessels from Venice, Spain, the Papal States, Genoa, Savoy, and Malta, to meet the growing threat of the Ottoman Empire. Calling themselves the Holy League, Juan's force consisted of 212 galleys six of which were large galleys called gallasses fitted with artillery. Sailing and rowing east from the port of Messina in Sicily, Don Juan's Holy League vessels

---

46 Encyclopedia Britannica
47 ibid.

were met by the Ottoman fleet. The Arabs, rowing and sailing west from Lepanto, Greece were commanded by Ali Pasha. Pasha's fleet was larger than the Christians, consisting of 286 galleys, 56 of which were small. The Arabs, however, were completely outgunned by the artillery of the Christians. The bottom line was that the Ottoman Navy was soundly defeated and the Christians beheaded their leader Ali Pasha, a demoralizing act. From then on the Ottoman Navy became a fleet of *"petty Pirates who continued to infest the Mediterranean until their extermination [from the Mediterranean] in the 19th century."*[48]

* * *

---

48 Allen, pages 5- 6. Riverside Press, Houghton, Mifflin and Co., Boston 1905. Our Navy and the Barbary Corsairs. Library of Congress. Available online at: Http://babel.hathitrust.org/cgi/pt?id=loc.ark:/13960/t3611fm4k;view=1up;seq=397

PROLOGUE 2

Setting the Stage- October 13, 1775-May 2, 1801

"Without a Respectable Navy – Alas America!" - Captain John Paul Jones of the Continental Navy

One source of information on the Barbary pirates was published in 2008, (copyright 2007) by author Brad Thor, who used an older article written by Gerard W. Gawalt, a specialist in the manuscript division of the Library of Congress, as a source for his novel titled *The Last Patriot.*[49]

The article Gawalt wrote is titled *America and the Barbary Pirates: An International Battle Against an Unconventional Foe.*[50] In the article Gawalt points out that creating a coalition to fight an international unconventional enemy, such as occurred in the Persian Gulf Wars of the last century, was nothing new for the United States since it first occurred well over 200 years ago. The United States, under the leadership of then President Thomas Jefferson (finally, after years of extortion), intended to put a stop to the activities of the Pirates of the Barbary Coast which included the North African states of Tunis, Tripoli, Morocco, and Algiers.

Capturing merchant ships and crews and holding them for ransom was a way of life for the Barbary Coast Pirates and provided the leaders of the above nation-states a source of wealth and naval power. For years a fearful and timid United States Congress and the

---

49 Simon & Schuster, Inc. New York, New York 2008.
50 Library of Congress (LOC), http://memory.loc.gov/ammem/collections/jefferson_papers/mtjprece.html

governments of other nations had avoided direct conflict with the Barbary Coast Pirates by paying tributes in cash and treasure. In fact the process of paying tribute was initially the policy of Great Britain.[51]

Because they were from a British Colony, the American vessels were protected by an extortion arrangement prior to the American Revolution. Even the Roman Catholic Church enabled the policy when one of its organizations, the French-based religious Order of Mathurins, provided ransom payments for those sailors captured by Barbary Coast pirates. The Vatican position was understandable for its humanitarian actions, but naïve in believing the inevitable results would help avoid violent conflict since the pirates were fundamentalist (today considered radicalized) Muslims. Although there were many in our country who advocated religious freedom, such as George Washington, Thomas Jefferson, and James Madison, no one else in a significant leadership position in the eighteenth and nineteenth centuries had yet appreciated fundamentalist Muslim reasoning or logic. It was not until West Point graduate Captain John Pershing dealt with the Moro Muslims [52] of the Southern Philippines during the Philippine American War, 1899-1902, that any of our more recent leaders or future leaders began to appreciate the practical knowledge and leadership of our founders.

When the American Revolution started, Great Britain's common enemy for years had been its neighbor across the English Channel, France. Putting into practice the phrase, "the enemy of my enemy is my friend," (a proverb most likely of Arabian origin) the French monarchy, (King Louis XVI) immediately became an ally of the revolutionary Americans, and American merchant ships came under the protection of the French Navy including its forays into the waters of the Barbary Coast.

"[Even though] The United States Navy recognizes 13 October 1775 as the date of its official establishment, when the Continental Congress

---

51 Ibid. LOC

52 Called Barbary Moors, from African homelands known as La Tierra de El Moros, the land of the Moros. In Spanish the word Moro became synonymous with Islam. Morocco is a derivative name.

passed a resolution creating the Continental Navy[53] [the Navy was not yet a reality, and when it became so it was short lived.]

"With the end of the American Revolutionary War, [what was left of] the Continental Navy was disbanded.[54] However, under President George Washington threats to American merchant shipping [nearly twenty years after the start of the American Revolution] by pirates in the Mediterranean led to the Naval Act of 1794, which created the U.S. Navy. The original six frigates[55] were authorized as part of the Act."[56]

The USS Constitution shown below and now well over 200 years old was one of the original six U.S. Navy frigates.

USS Constitution
Boston, Mass. (June 10, 2006) - USS Constitution, "Old Ironsides"
*-Photo credit U.S. Navy. [57]

---

53 Wikipedia: http://en.wikipedia.org/wiki/History_of_the_United_States_Navy
54 The ships of the Continental Navy and their fates are listed in Appendix A.
55 The frigates were the United States, the Constellation, the Constitution, the Chesapeake, the Congress, and the President.
56 Ibid (footnote Wikipedia above)
* The Constitution acquired the name because of her thick hull which caused enemy cannonballs to bounce away.
57 US Navy Photo: by U.S. Navy Journalist 1st Class Dave Kaylo, Public Domain.

After the Revolution in 1783 when the USA was fully established as an independent nation by the Treaty of Paris (with Great Britain and France), it had to defend its own merchant fleet but lacked the means to do so, since there was nothing left of the original Continental Navy. In fact it wasn't until the next year, 1784, that the first federal government maritime service was created called the Revenue-Marine. The Revenue-Marine was the forerunner of the U.S. Coast Guard. It was created at the request of U.S. Treasury Secretary Alexander Hamilton in order to enforce U.S. tariff regulations which were being challenged by rampant smuggling. Our newly formed nation was desperate for money and the tariffs on imports were an important source of funds.[58]

Ten sea going cutters[59] were originally ordered for the new service, but the mission of these 10 new vessels which were lightly armed, was strictly related to tariff enforcement and revenue collection.

Since it had neither the ways nor means to defend its own merchant fleet, especially overseas, the new United States Congress instructed Thomas Jefferson and John Adams, who were then acting as U.S. foreign ministers in France, to begin negotiations with the Barbary States to reach some sort of agreement to avoid further harassment of our merchant fleet. By early the next year, 1784, Congress had accumulated a purse of approximately $80,000 (close to $2 million in today's dollars) to be used as ransom money.

Negotiations were still ongoing when in July 1785 the Algerians captured two American ships and held 21 of their crew for ransom demanding nearly $60,000.

Foreign Minister (in France) Thomas Jefferson vigorously opposed paying any tribute to the pirates. He actually presented a proposal for a coalition of nations which included Great Britain, France and Portugal, Denmark, and Sweden as well as several of the Italian states. The coalition he proposed, Jefferson said, could compel the pirates to a *"perpetual peace."*[60] All of the nations with the exception

---

58 Wikipedia: http://en.wikipedia.org/wiki/Revenue_Marine
59 *Single masted sailing vessels or government vessels. Webster's dictionary.*
60 http://en.wikipedia.org/wiki/History_of_the_United_States_Navy

of Great Britain and France were in favor of Jefferson's proposal. The English and French, however, expressed *"apprehensions"* and therefore the proposal fell through.

Jefferson continued to oppose surrendering tribute or treasure to the pirates, but it wasn't until 1793 when by then Algiers had captured 11 more vessels that Congress begin to take him seriously.

Ransom payments and other tributes, continued to increase on an annual basis until *"In 1795 alone the United States was forced to pay nearly a million dollars in cash, naval stores, and a frigate to ransom 115 sailors from the Dey[61] of Algiers. Annual 'gifts' were settled by treaty on Algiers, Morocco, Tunis, and Tripoli."*[62]

But it wasn't just the pirates of the Barbary Coast with which the United States had to deal, it was also the French fleet. Although the French Revolution had early beginnings in 1789, (likely related to their observation of the success of the revolutionary Americans), by 1792 the French Revolution had taken on French nationwide support which toppled that nation's monarchy by September of that year.

One disastrous development between the new French government (which was at war with most of the rest of Europe) and the United States was the refusal by the Americans to pay further reimbursements to the French on the war debt accumulated by the Americans during the Revolutionary war.

The American refusal was based on the fact that the debt was owed to the former French monarchy (King Louis XVI) and not the new republican government. The new French government was also upset because of the Jay Treaty[63] which was a trade agreement between the U.S. and Great Britain. The Americans (essentially President George Washington) had already announced their neutral position regarding the hostilities between France and England. The quick French

---

61 Dey (Arabic: from Turkish Day) was the title given to the rulers of the Regency of Algiers (Algeria) and Tripoli under the Ottoman Empire from 1671 onwards. Wikipedia free dictionary.

62 http://memory.loc.gov/ammem/collections/jefferson_papers/mtjprece.html

63 Named after John Jay who was one of three representatives of the U.S. at the Treaty of Paris conference in 1783, which marked the end of the Revolutionary war. The other two representatives were Benjamin Franklin and John Adams.

response was to allow their former Navy, now acting as privateers, to interdict and seize American merchant ships.

Since all the Americans had as a federal maritime service was the Revenue-Marine with its 10 cutters, and since the six new frigates authorized in the Naval Act of 1794 were not yet built, there was little our fledgling nation could do about the harassment of either the pirates of the Barbary Coast or the French fleet. In addition the Naval Act of (January) 1794 contained a clause, inserted by dove-like members of Congress, that construction of the frigates would cease if a peaceful agreement could be reached with Algiers.

"In March 1796, as construction of the frigates slowly progressed, a peace accord was [indeed] announced between the United States and Algiers. In accordance with clause nine of the Naval Act of 1794, a clause that specifically directed that construction of the frigates be discontinued if peace was established, construction on all six ships was halted. After some debate and prompting by President Washington, Congress passed an act on 20 April 1796 allowing the construction and funding to continue only on the three ships nearest to completion: United States, Constellation, and Constitution."

[Although it started in 1796], *"by late 1798 (sic)[64] however, France [had seized 316 more [65]] American merchant vessels and the attempt at a diplomatic resolution had resulted in the XYZ Affair,[66] prompting Congress to approve funds for completion of the remaining three frigates: President, Congress, and Chesapeake."*[67]

---

64 (sic) Deconde, Alexander, The Quasi War, p-9. Scribner & Sons, NY 1966. Actually Secretary of State Timothy Pickering made the report to Congress on 17 June 1797.

65 http://americanconflicts.com/blog/quasi-war-1798-1800/

66 http://history.state.gov/milestones/1784-1800/xyz.The XYZ Affair was a political and diplomatic episode in 1797 and 1798, early in the administration of President John Adams, involving a confrontation between the United States and France that led to an undeclared naval war called the Quasi-War. The name derives from the substitution of the letters X, Y and Z for the names of French diplomats in documents released by the Adams administration.

67 http://en.wikipedia.org/wiki/Naval_Act_of_1794.

The XYZ Affair noted above and in the footnote to follow, was subsequently labeled by historians as a diplomatic failure because the U.S. diplomats took offense at the demands by the French diplomats who wanted a bribe before negotiations could take place. Although bribes were a common means of doing diplomatic business in Europe, the Americans were understandably offended by the suggestion.

As a result two out of three of the American diplomats, Charles Cotesworth Pinckney (who was denied recognition by the new French government) and John Marshall immediately left France without engaging in any negotiations. The diplomat who stayed was Elbridge Gerry, who felt he should try to deal with the senior French diplomat, French Foreign Minister Talleyrand, in order to avoid all-out war. After several months Gerry was ultimately successful in laying the groundwork for the end of diplomatic and (naval) military hostilities. In the meantime, however, the diplomatic failure resulted in an undeclared war which lasted for two years between 1798 and 1800. Called by some historians the Quasi-War, the diplomatic debacle also resulted in a firestorm of political rhetoric in the Congress of the United States.

"Popular opinion in the United States on relations with France was divided along largely political lines: Federalists [who favored a strong central government] took a hard line, favoring a defensive buildup but not necessarily advocating war, while "[Democratic-] Republicans expressed solidarity with the Republican ideals of the French revolutionaries and did not want to be seen as cooperating with the Federalist Adams administration. Jefferson looked at the Federalists as monarchists who were in bed with Britain and therefore hostile to American values."[68]

---

68 http://en.wikipedia.org/wiki/XYZ_Affair.

*American Elbridge Gerry, left, and France's
Charles Maurice de Talleyrand-Périgord, right.*

After reviewing the French Revolution history I think most scholars would agree that it is no wonder that rampant corruption was present in their diplomatic corps. France had just come out of a reign of terror that lasted from September 5, 1793 to July 28, 1794. Mass executions by the guillotine, ordered by anti-royalists against opponents of the revolution, plus inflation related to the paper money newly provided by the republican government created a reign of terror throughout France. Lawlessness throughout the new Republic didn't stabilize until May 18, 1804, when Napoleon Bonaparte finally brought a relative stability to France. During the reign of terror fear of being accused as an opponent of the revolution caused every man and woman to fend for themselves.

While diplomat Gerry continued his efforts in France, the U.S. Congress continued to pay tributes to the pirates and prepare for war with the French, who were also at war with most of the rest of Europe, including Great Britain. Although America's initial efforts included plans for a war on land, the actual fighting was confined to the oceans. The first U.S. ship to engage the French was the *Constellation*, which was the second[69] of the original six frigates to complete construction. Al-

---

69 *The first was the USS United States.*

though Congress had not declared war, the Naval Act of 1794 did authorize the American President to defend interdictions by the French privateers. The Act also appropriated additional funding to complete the construction of the new U.S. Navy.

At this point in this dramatic history it is worthwhile to review the commitments made by both France and the revolutionary Americans in the midst of the Revolutionary War.

The facts involved the *Treaty of Alliance,* which was an agreement negotiated by American diplomats Benjamin Franklin, Silas Deane, and Arthur Lee and signed on February 6, 1778. Both France and the U.S. agreed to a military alliance against Great Britain. The treaty required that neither party would agree to a separate peace agreement with Great Britain. It also stated that American independence would be a requirement of any future peace agreement. Specifically the Treaty of Alliance Article XI stated the following:

"And his Most Christian Majesty guarantees on his part to the United States, their liberty, sovereignty and independence, absolute and unlimited, as well as in matters of government as in commerce,–"[70]

In addition, article IX of the Treaty stated this: *"The contracting parties declare that being resolved to fulfil each on its own part the clauses and conditions of the present treaty of alliance, according to its own power and circumstances, there shall be no after claim of compensation on one side or the other, whatever may be the event of the war."*[71]

Considering the commitments the United States had made France, and after an abrogation of the Treaty of Alliance by the U.S. Congress in 1798, a review of the timeline of our relationships with France is appropriate. Later extensive Supreme Court and other jurisdictions ruled that the Congress has no authority to create (or ab-

---

70 Library of Congress: http://memory.loc.gov/cgi-bin/ampage?collId=llsl&fileName=008/llsl008.db&recNum=23

71 Info Please: Records of the United States Government, Record Group 11; National Archives http://www.ourdocuments.gov/doc.php?doc=4 Read more: Treaty of Alliance http://www.infoplease.com/t/hist/treaty-of-alliance/#ixzz3Sn8iqwfh

rogate?) treaties which are the sole propriety of the President of the United States[72]

American-French Timelines:

1782
After their defeat in Yorktown the British elected to negotiate peace terms with the United States. The U.S. Congress appointed three peace commissioners, John Adams, John Jay, and Henry Laurens.
Fully aware that they were violating their instructions to coordinate their negotiations with the French, the Americans signed articles of agreement with the British on November 30, 1782.
[French Foreign Minister] "Vergennes was not surprised, though it made it more difficult for him to defend the interests of his Spanish ally."[73]
Author's note: The French also violated the agreement 10 months later by signing the Treaty of Versailles with Great Britain and Spain on the same day that they signed the Treaty of Paris with Great Britain and the U.S. on September 3, 1783.[74]

1789
Both Washington and Jefferson stated publicly that the Treaty of Alliance with France should remain valid because there was no time limit specified in the original document. Many members of Congress disagreed because they saw an opportunity to get rid of the treaty when the French government reverted to a republic from the monarchy. The controversy grew in proportion when once again the French declared war on Great Britain and President Washington and the United States wanted to remain neutral.

---

72 U.S. Dept. of Justice Memorandum: http://www.justice.gov/olc/docs/memoabmtreaty11152001.pdf
73 Trentinian, Jacques de, http://www.xenophongroup.com/mcjoynt/alliance2.htm
74 Wikipedia:http://en.wikipedia.org/wiki/Timeline_of_the_French_Revolution1783

1793-1794
France sent a new minister, Edmond C. Genet, to the U.S. in April 1793. He encouraged the Americans to start privateer action against the British. When Genet allowed a French-sponsored warship, *Little Sarah*,[75] fitted out as a French privateer in Philadelphia to sail out of Philadelphia against direct presidential orders, Washington demanded that France recall the new minister. The French complied but Genet's replacement did not arrive until February 1794. Even then Genet elected to remain in the United States, probably because the reign of terror was still going on. Most Americans did not want another war with England, nor did they want disruption of the lucrative trade. The Genet *"episode embarrassed even the modest amount of Francophile support that remained in the US."*[76]

In November Minister John Jay negotiated a treaty which still bears his name, which consolidated a trade agreement with England but allowed the Brits to seize any French trade cargo aboard American ships. The French reaction was immediate. They broke relations with the U.S. and the French Navy began to harass United States ships in the Caribbean. The harassments continued and grew in numbers and intensity until 1800.

1797
President John Adams finally sent negotiators in November 1797 to attempt to resolve the problem, but which resulted in the XYZ affair previously mentioned and the Quasi-War which in reality had been started in 1794 but has been dated by historians as lasting from 1798 to 1800.

---

75 Princeton U Press Permalink: http://founders.archives.gov/documents/Jefferson/01-26-02-0629-0001

76 ibid.

1798

U.S. Congress unilaterally abrogated the Treaty of Alliance of 1778. France did not recognize the abrogation. (This was years before the Supreme Court decided that treaties were the sole propriety of the President of the United States).

1799

Saw the first U.S. successful engagement of the Quasi-War. The following facts are of interest:

"The United States Frigate Constellation was built under the direction of Colonel David Stodder at his naval shipyard on Harris Creek in Baltimore's Fells Point maritime community, according to a design by Joshua Humphreys and launched on 7 September 1797, just as the United States entered the Quasi-War with the revolutionary French Republic.

USS Constellation (left) in battle against the French Frigate L'Insurgente, Feb. 9, 1799. Image-U.S.Navy, Public Domain.[77]

---

77 *This file is a work of a sailor or employee of the U.S. Navy, taken or made as part of that person's official duties.*
The image is in the Public Domain.

- "The Naval Act of 1794 had specified 36-gun frigates; however, Constellation and her sister-ship Congress were re-rated to 38's because of their large dimensions, being 164 ft (50 m) in length and 41 ft (12 m) in width. The "ratings" by number of guns were meant only as an approximation, as Constellation could and did often carry up to 48 guns.
- "On 9 February 1799, under the command of Captain Thomas Truxtun, Constellation fought and captured the frigate L'Insurgente of 36 guns, the fastest ship in the French Navy; L'Insurgente was devastated by Constellation's first broadside with many dead and others deserting their guns. L'Insurgente tried to board and slowed to close but this allowed Constellation to shoot ahead and crossed her bows for a bow rake with another broadside. Constellation crossed to windward and L'Insurgente turned to follow with both crews now exchanging port broadsides instead of starboard. One of Constellation's 24 pounders smashed through the hull of L'Insurgente; unfortunately for L'Insurgente, her 12 pounders were not equal to the same task against Constellation's hull. Captain Barreaut had been shown one of Constellation's 24 pound cannon balls and understood that he was in a completely unequal contest with sails down and nothing comparable to reply with many already dead and wounded. He struck colors— the first major victory by an American designed and built warship."[78]

1779 (continued)
On December 14, 1799, George Washington died and Napoleon Bonaparte, the first significant leader with the title of First Consul in France since the revolution, declared a year of mourning. He also entered into negotiations regarding the Treaty of Alliance, which as mentioned previously was officially ended the next year.

While the Americans were engaged with the French Privateers in the late 1700s, the Barbary Coast Pirates were up to considerable mischief as early as 1784 with regards to the new independent nation of America. The American merchant ship first seized was the brigan-

---

78 Wikipedia: http://en.wikipedia.org/wiki/USS_Constellation_%281797%29

tine[79] *Betsy*. The event occurred on October 11, 1784 when Moroccan Pirates captured the American vessel and its crew. The Spanish government, long experienced in dealing with the Barbary Pirates, negotiated the freedom of the Americans and advised the new U.S. government to pay ransom and negotiate a treaty to prevent further attacks on their merchant fleet. Five months later:

"In March 1785, Thomas Jefferson and John Adams went to London to negotiate with Tripoli's envoy, Ambassador Sidi Haji Abdrahaman. When they enquired "concerning the ground of the pretensions to make war upon nations who had done them no injury", the ambassador replied:

It was written in their Koran, that all nations which had not acknowledged the Prophet were sinners, whom it was the right and duty of the faithful to plunder and enslave; and that every Mussulman[80] who was slain in this warfare was sure to go to paradise. He said, also, that the man who was the first to board a vessel had one slave over and above his share, and that when they sprang to the deck of an enemy's ship, every sailor held a dagger in each hand and a third in his mouth; which usually struck such terror into the foe that they cried out for quarter at once."[81]

The encounter with Ambassador Abdrahaman was probably Thomas Jefferson's first encounter with fundamentalist Muslim thinking, although it was not his first encounter with the Koran. Denise A. Spellberg, an Associate Professor of Middle Eastern Studies at the University of Texas, Austin, recently wrote a book titled *'Thomas Jefferson's Qur'an'* [82] in which she traced his first English copy of the holy book to be in his possession in 1765 when he was a law student at William and Mary. Jefferson apparently acquired the English translation of the Koran as a resource for his interest in Islamic law and subsequently the Islamic culture. Today most experts recognize that Islamic culture cannot be separated from the Koran, or from Sharia law.

As Dr. Spellberg (BA degree Smith, PhD Columbia) correctly points out, Thomas Jefferson specifically included the Muslim religion in his

---

79 A brigantine is a two masted sailing vessel with square rigging.
80 An ancient word for Muslim
81 http://en.wikipedia.org/wiki/First_Barbary_War
82 Spellberg, Denise, Alfred A. Knopf, a Division of Random House, NY, Toronto, 2013

vision for religious freedom in this country. However, that did not mean that the policy of appeasement for the Barbary Pirates by the United States or any other country was the proper course in dealing with the blatant aggression and unlawful actions of the fundamentalists. Jefferson, Washington, and James Madison, all of whom were believers in religious freedom and all of whom had a long-range vision for this country, were all basically opposed to the policy of paying tribute or treasure in extortion fees. But they were also pragmatic men who in their leadership functions had to consider the age-old question of which was more expensive, war or tribute.

Jefferson was technically the first Secretary of State, although in reality he was preceded by John Jay whose title was Secretary of Foreign Affairs. James Madison did not appear in the office until six other individuals had already served, but he came at a crucial time sworn in on May 2, 1801, just a few days before Yusuf Karamanli,[83] the Pasha of Tripoli, had sent his corsairs to cut down the flagstaff in front of the United States Consulate. The action occurred because then President Jefferson refused to knuckle under to demands for a $225,000 tribute. Cutting down the U.S. flag was considered an attack on our embassy and an act of war, a far cry from the U.S. response to the lethal Ben Ghazi attack in 2012.

Michael J. Crawford, writing for the Naval Historical Center, and who heads the Naval Historical Center's Early History Branch argues that *"the similarities between the Tripolitan War and the war on terrorism have little to do with the religion of the enemy, and everything to do with the problems of waging a campaign in a forbidding environment far from the United States' own borders."*[84]

The part of his statement concerning the religion of the enemy ignores the statement of a previous ambassador of Tripoli (Abdrahaman) given to Thomas Jefferson and John Adams. Otherwise Crawford's statements are valid including the fact that Congress could issue letters of mark and reprisal which were commissions granted

---

83 also spelled Yusef Q'aramanli

84 Crawford, Michael, Naval Historical Center, http://www.history.navy.mil/faqs/faq116-1.htm (web site was removed but restated @) http://www.history.navy.mil/research/archives/subject-collections/u-s-war-with-tripoli- and-war-on-terrorism.html

by the government to private individuals to take the property of a foreign state or enemy of the state.

Historian Crawford is also quite accurate in pointing out the problems of waging a campaign in a forbidding environment far from U.S. borders. But I would argue that the religion of the fundamentalist (radicalized) Muslim, especially his or her interpretation of the right to commit violent acts on infidels, has a lot more to do with the Tripolitan War and the war on terror than Crawford suggests. The primary motive in those days was money, and today it appears to be power and the expansion of fundamentalist Islam.

There was one other problem involving the British Royal Navy which had been ignored by the new independent government of the United States. Thomas Jefferson and his successors would have to deal with it. It was not only the Barbary Coast Pirates and the French Privateers that were causing problems for the fledging U.S. Navy; it was the policy of impressment by the British Navy to supplement their own crews.

Since Elizabethan times, manpower shortages in the British Navy were relieved by the practice of impressment. The British Navy used "press gangs" which roamed seaports both in Britain and in foreign locations to force any able-bodied man that they could kidnap into service. Even the Jay treaty, which was designed to encourage trade between the U.S. and Great Britain, failed to stop the Royal Navy from impressing American seamen into their service. While they were at war with France, British press gangs frequently boarded U.S. merchant vessels looking for French cargo.

American merchant ships were a common target for British impressment between 1793 and 1812.

More than 15 thousand American merchant sailors were impressed in order for the Brits to supplement their fleet during their war with France and Napoleon. By early 1812, the U.S. had had enough and declared war on Great Britain.[85]

* * *

---

85 Oregon PBS Web Site: http://www.pbs.org/opb/historydetectives/feature/british-navy-impressment/

PART I

CHAPTER ONE

March 4, 1801 Thomas Jefferson, a New Sheriff in Town

"Wars are not paid for in war time, the bill comes later." Benjamin Franklin

In Washington, D.C., Senate Wing, U.S. Capitol Building (under construction) on Wednesday March, 4, 1801, at approximately 10 minutes past 12 noon, after the Vice President, former New York Senator Aaron Burr, had been sworn in, Chief Justice John Marshall, a distant cousin of the president-elect and a member of the opposite (Federalist) political party, held out a copy of the Holy Bible and spoke to the recently elected President of the United States, "Raise your right hand and repeat after me."

It was a beautiful March day, mild for Washington with the temperature at 55°, although the streets were muddy from recent wet snow and rainfall. The President-elect and his entourage had to step carefully to avoid the mud on their walk to the new capital building. There were a number of firsts for the presidential inauguration. It was the first time that it was held in the District of Columbia, the first time a president-elect had walked to the ceremony (from a boarding house[86]), the first time the Marine band had played at an inauguration (and has ever since) and the first time a newspaper (the National Intelligencer) printed the inaugural address the very morning of the

---

86 Monticello, http://www.monticello.org/site/research-and-collections/first-inauguration the Conrad and McMunn boarding house at New Jersey Avenue and C Street

inauguration.[87] It was also the first and only time that a Vice President of the United States was sworn in who would later be called an assassin and charged with treason.

The President-elect was a tall slender man described by various acquaintances as "straight bodied and square shouldered," "bony", "6 feet 2 ½ inches tall [and] straight as a gun barrel," "very dignified in appearance," with a "mild and pleasant countenance."[88] He was said to have dressed as a common man although somewhat old-fashioned.

Thomas Jefferson

Eminently qualified to become the third president of the United States, the President-elect was a graduate of the College of William and Mary in 1764. He subsequently studied law at the college and was admitted to the Virginia bar in 1767 all the while managing his

---

87 Congressional web site, http://www.inaugural.senate.gov/swearing-in/event/thomas-jefferson-1801

88 Monticello, http://www.monticello.org/site/research-and-collections/physical-descriptions-jefferson

father's huge tobacco farms and estate. He was also the author of the Declaration of Independence and had previously served as a member of the Continental Congress replacing George Washington when that distinguished leader was called to lead the Continental Army. He subsequently held offices of Governor of Virginia, Minister to France, and Secretary of State under George Washington. In the election of 1796 he lost the Presidency of the United States by a mere three electoral votes to John Adams and by the procedures of the times automatically became Adams' Vice President.

President-elect Thomas Jefferson raised his right hand as directed by the Chief Justice and placed his left hand on the pro-offered Bible. Repeating after Chief Justice John Marshall's sentences as directed, Jefferson, in a sonorous voice said, "I, Thomas Jefferson,[89] do solemnly swear that I will faithfully execute the office of President of the United States, and will to the best of my ability, preserve, protect, and defend the Constitution of the United States…."

Jefferson's road to the presidency was a complicated one. In those days there was no provision for the Electoral College representatives from each state to vote separately for the president and vice president.

What happened on the previous election in 1796 was that there was no such thing as a running mate so the Federalist Party put up their two best candidates and their opponents, the Democratic-Republicans put up their two best. Jefferson lost to Adams, but since he had more electoral votes than Adams' "running mate" Thomas Pinckney, Jefferson was declared the Vice President according to the prevailing rules of the Electoral College at the time. Both Thomas Pinckney and Aaron Burr, the number two men on each party's ticket, were out of the race. Pinckney was a former governor of South Carolina, and Senator Aaron Burr was from New York. It was the first and only time that a member of the President's opposing party was elected as Vice President of the United States. The 12th amendment to the Constitution, ratified in 1804, corrected the problems of the previous two presidential elections by specifying that the Electoral College representatives vote separately for president and vice president and the candidate for vice president could

---

89 *Jefferson, like his new Secretary of State, James Madison, had no middle name.*

not be from the same state as the presidential candidate making the tie of any of the candidates unlikely. Ties were settled by the House of Representatives as before but each state could have only one vote, and rules for a quorum and majority were strict.

In the 1800 election when the electoral votes were counted, the incumbent and Federalist Party candidate, John Adams, was obviously defeated, but there was a tie between Jefferson and his companion party member, Aaron Burr, both of whom were the Democratic-Republican candidates for the presidency and supposedly the vice presidency respectively. Although Jefferson was recognized as the party leader by the Electoral College representatives, that carried little weight for the House of Representatives who had to settle any ties of the election. Federalist Party members obviously didn't want Jefferson to become president, so they backed the lesser of two evils in their opinion, Aaron Burr for the top job. After several days of voting after convening on February 9, there was still no resolution or decision. Even though the final tally varied of the first 35 ballots, the required majority for election, 9 votes out of 16 states, was not achieved. Finally on the 36th ballot on February 17, 1801, the tie was broken and Jefferson was the new president-elect. [90] Delaware's single representative, Federalist James A. Bayard, along with three other Federalists from South Carolina, Maryland, and Vermont cast blank ballots thus allowing Jefferson to gain a majority of 10 of the 16 states and thus the presidency.

Jefferson had been accompanied on his walk from the boarding house to the senate surrounded by members of the Virginia militia followed by a number of congressmen from his own party, the Democratic-Republicans. Jefferson had been a widower since 1782, when his wife, Martha (nee Wales Skelton) died some months after the birth of their fourth daughter. Jefferson was Martha's second husband, her first, Bathurst Skelton, having died after fathering one son. After nearly eleven years of marriage and four surviving daughters, Jefferson never remarried. There is, however, considerable evidence including rather recent DNA findings, that Jefferson, after Martha's death, had

---

90 Monticello, http://www.monticello.org/site/research-and-collections/first-inauguration

a sexual relationship with Sally Hemings, one of the slaves he had inherited from his wife's parents' estate and who was the illegitimate child of his father-in-law, John Wales. Sally was also the half-sister of Jefferson's wife, Martha. Some historians believe that Jefferson fathered as many as six of Sally Hemings' kids. One academic source offered the following:

"Recent DNA evidence presents a convincing case that Jefferson was indeed the biological father of Heming's children, and most historians now believe that Jefferson and Hemings had a long-term sexual relationship. Jefferson was ambivalent about slavery throughout his career. As a young politician, he argued for the prohibition of slavery in new American territories, yet he never freed his own slaves. How could a man responsible for writing the sacred words "We hold these truths to be self-evident, that all men are created equal" have been a slave owner? He never resolved his internal conflict on this issue."[91]

When he arrived at the Senate wing for his inauguration, it was so crowded that it was unlikely that all members of his entourage could get within the chamber, but they did manage to make room for three or four additional congressmen, two or three members of the Virginia militia, his best friend and choice for Secretary of State, James Madison, and the President-elect. Jefferson's inaugural address included two subjects worthy of note. The first was an apology for his lack of talent to run the country:

[After thanking supporters for their votes he essentially indicated I am here] "-to declare a sincere consciousness that the task is above my talents, and that I approach it with those anxious and awful presentiments which the greatness of the charge and the weakness of my powers so justly inspire.[92]

The second subject included phrases intended to heal the significant rift that had developed during the bitter Presidential campaign

---

91 U of Virginia, http://millercenter.org/academic/americanpresident/jefferson/essays/biography/1

92 http://www.loc.gov/exhibits/inaugural/exhibition.html#jefferson

between himself and the Federalists who dominated Congress, and with whom as a Republican president he had to work:

"-but every difference of opinion is not a difference of principle. We have called by different names brethren of the same principles. We are all Republicans. We are all Federalists."[93]

After his inaugural speech and completing the Oath of office and the obligatory handshaking, Jefferson put his arm around the shoulders of his best friend James Madison and said, "Walk with me back to the boarding house Jim, we will have a couple of beers and if you have time perhaps a bite to eat."

"I'd like that Your Excellency," replied Madison.

"You can 'can' that, James," returned the President sarcastically whispering in Madison's ear, "You know how I hate those formal titles. Washington didn't like them either although President Adams didn't seem to mind. Why don't you call me 'Mr. President' at least when we are in public? George seemed to prefer that. But when we're alone please call me Tom like you always have. How long have we been friends for God's sake?"

Jefferson and Madison first met in May 1776 when they were both serving in the Virginia legislature. Madison was eight years younger than Jefferson who was only 33 when he authored the initial Declaration of Independence.

Madison, looking around and seeing that they were still surrounded by Virginia militia, and with a grin on his face replied, "Yes, Mr. President."

That particular exchange set the precedent for properly addressing the President of the United States from then on.

During the approximately half-mile walk from the new Senate wing (now the Old Supreme Court Chamber) to the Conrad and McMunn boarding house at New Jersey Avenue and C Street, the new President and Madison were unable to converse due to the crowds lining the streets and demanding attention. Even at the boarding house it was nearly impossible for the Virginia militia troopers to maintain order surrounding the newly elected President of the United States who found it necessary to request a private dining area in order to

---

93 ibid

talk with his friend. There was one other person who accompanied the President and James Madison into the private dining area and that was a young Army officer, Lieutenant Meriwether Lewis. In those days there was no chief of the president's staff, but each of the presidents had a private secretary [94] and Lieutenant Lewis served in that capacity. The duty was approved by his commanding officers at the President's request. Lewis was no stranger to Jefferson, having grown up as the son of a neighboring farmer.

According to the Jefferson Monticello research collection[95] the new President knew who he wanted as his private secretary. Within days of his election he sent a letter to General James Wilkinson who at the time commanded the U.S. Army. In the same envelope to General Wilkinson, Jefferson sent another letter to his choice for the position, Meriwether Lewis, because he did not know where Lewis was at the time, and knew the general did know his whereabouts and would see that Lewis received it.

In the letter to General Wilkinson Jefferson listed the reasons for requesting the young lieutenant to serve as his secretary. Included in the list of reasons was Lewis's knowledge of the frontier and the military as well as Jefferson's personal acquaintance with the young officer. Two years later Meriwether Lewis, by then a captain, and his good friend Second Lieutenant William Clark would lead the famous Corps of Discovery Expedition (popularly called the Lewis and Clark Expedition) through the Louisiana Purchase territory to the West Coast of North America.

In the meantime though, Meriwether (his mother's family name) Lewis was privy to the conversations of the new President and his choice for Secretary of State, James Madison.

Although he was not a heavy drinker, Jefferson enjoyed a good beer, which was made at his estate at Monticello. Even today tourists can purchase tax-free bottles of beer, called Monticello Reserve Ale, at Monticello and at the brewery which has been reconstructed.

---

94 *For George Washington it was Tobias Lear V, and for John Adams it was William Smith Shaw. source:* http://wayback.archive.org/web/20081026204715/http://www.oldandsold.com/articles31n/white-house-history-11.shtml.

95 *http://www.monticello.org/site/research-and-collections/meriwether-lewis*

10   Never Subdued II

Proceeds go to support maintenance of the famous estate.[96] Jefferson actually supplied the Monticello manufactured ale to the Conrad and McMunn boarding house where he stayed in Washington.

Once settled in the private dining area requested by the new president, Jefferson and Madison were able to engage in some serious dialogue. One of the first problems to discuss was a growing crisis out of the Mediterranean. The U.S. Consul in Tripoli, James Cathcart, had recently informed President Adams that the Pasha (Muslim leader) of Tripoli was going to demand a new treaty. The United States had been paying tribute to all of the Barbary States to ensure free passage of our merchant vessels to trade in the Middle East. After explaining this information to Madison, President Jefferson said:

"I am thinking of telling him to jump in the lake, Jim. What do you think?"

"He will probably attack the first American vessel he sees. He might even declare war. Are we prepared for that?" Madison replied.

"I have dealt with people like Yusuf Karamanli,[97] before back in March of '75 when I was minister to France," Jefferson said. "Karamanli is just like Ambassador Sidi Haji Abdrahaman was then. He is a Muslim who uses passages in the Koran literally to justify his actions even if they are criminal. I know he will test us. We knuckled under to Abdrahaman's demands back then and have been paying tribute ever since. It's time it came to a stop.

"Jim," Jefferson continued, "I really need you as my Secretary of State. Have you come to a decision regarding my request? This situation with Tripoli is coming to a crisis, and I have no doubt that it will require military action to resolve. And yes, the answer to your question is indeed we are prepared for war if it comes to that. We have just commissioned three new frigates and Commodore Richard Dale tells me he can have them outfitted and ready to sail by early June. Out of necessity we will continue to pay tribute to the remainder of the Barbary States, even though we are behind on our payments, so I don't think they will jump into the conflict. Tripoli, however, is likely

---

96 http://www.starrhill.com/brews/brew_item/monticello-reserve-ale
97   Also spelled Qaramanli- http://www.monticello.org/site/research-and-collections/first-barbary-war

to be totally out of hand with their demands which we cannot afford in any case."

Jefferson was speaking with knowledge. Back in October, 1800, when he was still Vice-President, he was aware of a communication from the U.S. Consul in Tripoli, Cathcart, who had written to then Secretary of State, John Marshall. In that communication Cathcart had stated that Karamanli would declare war on the U.S. if he did not get an increase in tributes.[98] Just days later, the demand by Barbary Coast pirates arrived. They were insisting on an immediate payment of $225,000 (close to $3.9 million in today's value) plus an annual tribute of $25,000 (worth $431,000 today). The demand was made by Yusuf Karamanli, the Pasha of Tripoli, who was the most unreasonable of the Barbary Coast Muslim leaders.

"Yes, Mr. President," said Madison, fully aware of the presence of the President's personal secretary, Meriwether Lewis, and trusting that the young officer would pass the word of how to address the new President of the United States. "I have talked it over with Dolley and she will move with me and one or two servants to Washington so that I can assume the office of Secretary of State. And by the way, I fully agree with your decision to refuse Karamanli's demand for tribute. It is indeed time to let him know that although we are a new nation, we have the resolve to resist extortion like that."

"Thank goodness," said Jefferson. "It's a good decision on your part, will give you more experience, and hopefully, someday, will lead you to run for this very office. And speaking of that, I have another favor to ask of you, and perhaps also of Dolley."

"Anything we can do to help," replied Madison.

"Well, as you observed, President Adams has hosted a number of social events in the White House these last few years. He has had the advantage of having his wife Abigail to share that burden. I am going to ask my daughters Patsy and Polly [99] to help out when they are in

---

98 Wikipedia
99 Patsy and Polly were both Jefferson's married daughters, baptized Martha and Maria respectively and legally known by their husband's surnames as Martha Randolph and Maria Eppes. Source: U. of Virginia, Miller Center web page: http://millercenter.org/president/jefferson/essays/firstlady/martha

town, but there are going to be occasions when neither of them is available. Dare I ask Dolley?"

Two months later, the president did indeed ask Dolley Madison to act as hostess for various White House occasions. Dolley flourished in the role and became even more successful than Abigail Adams had been. She was so successful in establishing Jefferson's low key, common man approach to White House etiquette that she stirred up many political enemies. Politics being just as dirty, and perhaps even more so than it is today, resulted in widespread rumors that Dolley Madison was Jefferson's mistress. Both Jefferson and Madison were somewhat amused at the rumors, even when they resulted in a full-fledged sex scandal during Madison's bid for the presidency eight years later. In spite of the rumors Dolley Madison became First Lady of the United States in her own right after the election of her husband in 1808.

James Madison   **Dolley Madison**

* * *

CHAPTER TWO

May 10, 1801 العاهرة ابن من, an Arabic Oath

"We never pay anyone Dane-geld, no matter how trifling the cost; for the end of that game is oppression and shame, and the nation that plays it is lost!" -Rudyard Kipling from the poem *Dane-geld*

The Palace quarters of the Pasha [100] of Tripoli reverberated with the sound "Peda Sah" ("العاهرة ابن من"), an Arabic oath yelled by Yusuf Karamanli out loud as he held a synopsis of the original communication, which was sent to the American Consul James Cathcart by United States Secretary of State, James Madison. The letter clearly outlined the United States' position of refusal to pay the extortion demanded by the Pasha. It also informed Karamanli that the United States was sending a Navy squadron of warships to *"observe"*[101] the harbor, along with some pleas of hope that peace would be maintained.

The Arabic oath Pasha Karamanli yelled was equivalent to an English translation of "son of a bitch." Karamanli was fluent in both English and French and probably Spanish as well but liked to swear in his native Arabic.

Not one of the good guys, Yusuf, the youngest of three brothers, had killed his oldest sibling and exiled his next-in-line brother,

---
100 also spelled Basha
101 *Our Navy and the Barbary Pirates*, A. G. Weld, LOC, Internet archive, http://babel.hathitrust.org/cgi/pt?id=loc.ark:/13960/t3611fm4k;view=1up;seq=26

Hamet,[102] to gain the title of Pasha of Tripoli. He had been demanding an increase in annual tribute from the United States for the last year without much success. The U.S. was at least three years behind in payments to the Muslim leader. Having just received word of Thomas Jefferson's refusal to his demands, Yusuf was about to react with what could be (and was) interpreted as an act of war.

Four days later on May 14, 1801,[103] Karamanli watched from one of his castle parapets as a small group of his corsairs cut down the flagpole of the United States Consulate which was only a short distance from his palace. Attacking a U.S. Consulate or Embassy was, and still is, considered an act of war requiring some sort of response.

Our response in recent times has not been very warlike. As a matter of fact it was not so warlike in the spring of 1801 either, although Jefferson did respond by sending armed U.S. Navy frigates as a show of force to stand off Tripoli's harbor. Jefferson was hoping the appearance of armed United States vessels would at least give the illusion of a possible naval blockade even if no overt action was taken. The commander of the small Navy force, Commodore Richard Dale, was under presidential orders to avoid shots fired unless a United States ship was attacked. Even though Jefferson felt sure that the Pasha would test our resolve, he probably was a bit too cautious at first, although prudently so. Commodore Dale understood that he was not to start a war by himself.

Dale carried a letter from President Jefferson addressed to the Pasha of Tripoli, Karamanli, expressing the position of the United States. He also carried $30,000 in cash (probably in Spanish dollars) with instructions to give it to Cathcart, the American Consul in Tripoli, who was to give it to the Pasha if we were still at peace. The money was designated by Jefferson as a gift, but in reality was extortion money for the Pasha's personal use. The U.S. treasury did not have enough money to meet Karamanli's extortion demand.

So Dale, having been placed on a short leash by his commander-in-chief, was also very careful not to stir up any more trouble. In Gi-

---

[102] also spelled Ahmed

[103] Some sources, e.g. https://www.marinersmuseum.org/sites/micro/usnavy/06/06a.htm, indicate the action was actually on, May 10, 1801.

braltar, his first stop in the Mediterranean on July 1, 1801, Dale was informed that Karamanli had declared war on the United States.

The Pasha likely had preliminary knowledge of the United States' position even before Commodore Dale did. Secretary of State James Madison had written to the American Consul, James Leander Cathcart, on the day after the cabinet meeting outlining the new American policy. Whether the new policy was deliberately leaked from the Consulate or obtained by nefarious means is speculative. It's even possible that Karamanli did not have knowledge of the new policy when he ordered the attack on the Consulate's flagpole, and was just trying to further intimidate the United States into paying the demanded tribute. Whatever the circumstance, the symbolic declaration of war by Karamanli occurred in any case.

Dale was an experienced sailor who had been John Paul Jones's first lieutenant aboard the *USS Bonhomme Richard*, (originally a French merchant ship, the *Duc de Duras*), during the Continental Navy's famous engagement with the *Serapis* in 1779. He was also one of the six captains appointed in 1794 when the new U.S. Navy with its six new frigates (under construction) replaced the remnants of the Continental Navy.

Dale's orders, written by acting Secretary of the Navy, General Samuel Smith, who was filling in for his newly appointed brother, Robert, stated thus:

"But should you find on your arrival at Gibraltar, that all the Barbary powers have declared war against the United States, you will then distribute your force in such manner, as your judgment shall direct, so as best to protect our commerce and chastise their insolence by sinking, burning, or destroying their ships and vessels where ever you shall find them."[104]

After establishing his base of supply at Gibraltar in concordance with the governor of that city, the 45-year-old Dale proceeded to Algiers, carrying the United States' overdue tribute. Of course once he paid the tribute, he and his crew were welcome in Algiers. And now, nearly a month later his squadron was back at sea and was running short on drinking water. *"Dale's squadron consisted of the frigates President, 44 guns, [and which was the] flagship [commanded by] Capt.*

---

104 *Our Navy and the Barbary Corsairs*, A G Weld, p 92, LOC, Internet archive. http://babel.hathitrust.org/cgi/pt?id=loc.ark:/13960/t3611fm4k;view=1up;seq=26

James Barron; Philadelphia, 36 [guns], Capt. Samuel Barron; and Essex, 32 [guns], Capt. William Bainbridge, and the schooner Enterprise, 12 [guns and commanded by] Lieutenant Andrew Sterett."[105]

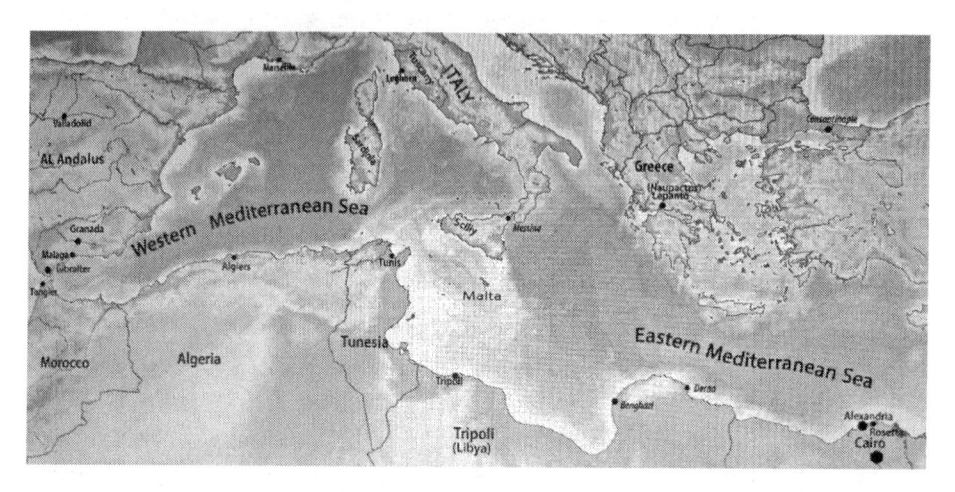

Barbary Coast map circa 1800 includes Morocco (Tangier), Algiers, Tunis and Tripoli. Cartography by Paul Hook, Mill City, Ore.

Dale dispatched one of the four vessels in his squadron, the USS Enterprise, to the British port on Malta to resupply his squadron's water. He then ordered Captain James Barron, who was the commander of Dale's flagship the USS President, and the rest of the squadron to head for Tripoli, where he intended to show the U.S. flag as a show of force. The other ships in his squadron besides his flagship were the frigates USS Philadelphia and USS Essex.

What would surprise (but probably should not have) Commodore Dale was the astute perception and subsequent actions of his young, age 23, junior officer Lieutenant Andrew Sterett, in command of the Enterprise. Sterett was born in 1778 in Baltimore, the son of ex-revolutionary war army Captain John Sterett. The elder Sterett in civilian life was a wealthy shipping magnate. Having grown up around merchant seamen and ships, the son, Andrew, had a keen interest in and a lot of knowledge about the sea and ships.

---

105 ibid. page 94.

May 10, 1801 من ابن العاهرة, an Arabic Oath

Because of his experience, he was commissioned by President Adams in 1798 as a U.S. naval officer with the rank of Lieutenant at the young age of 20. His first assignment was third lieutenant aboard the *USS Constellation* commanded by Captain Thomas Truxton. The *Constellation*, mentioned previously, was the first United States naval vessel to garner a significant victory during the "Quasi War" against the French warship, *L'Insurgente*, on Feb. 9, 1799. Andrew Sterett gained some notoriety in that action since he was responsible for the only American casualty.

What happened back then was a young American seaman abandoned his post in a panic during battle action with the French vessel. Lieutenant Sterett ran him through with his saber. There was such an uproar amongst the anti-Federalist politicians, who cited the incident as an example of the Navy's arrogance and brutality that some of them demanded punishment. The Navy brass saw it differently and actually promoted Sterett to the ship's first Lieutenant. *"A year later, Sterett was involved in a battle to a draw with the 54-gun French frigate, Vengeance. Soon afterward, he took command of the USS Enterprise."*[106]

As captain of the *Enterprise*, Lieutenant Sterett captured the French privateer *L'Amour de la Patrie*[107] on December 24, 1800. Having been aware of Sterett's previous accomplishments, Commodore Dale should not have been as surprised as he was by the young lieutenant's upcoming action on the way to Malta. According to one contributor to Wikipedia here is what happened on August 1, 1801:

"Soon after leaving the blockade, Enterprise came upon what appeared to be a Tripolitan cruiser sailing near her. Flying British colors as a ruse, the Enterprise approached the Tripolitan vessel and hailed her. The Tripolitan answered that she was seeking American vessels. At this the Enterprise struck the British colors, raised the American flag, and prepared for action.

"The Tripolitan vessel, Tripoli, and the Enterprise were quite evenly matched. Enterprise, with a complement of 90, was a 12-gun, 135-ton schooner built in 1799 that had seen action in the Quasi-War. In contrast,

---

[106] http://en.wikipedia.org/wiki/Andrew_Sterett#Resignation
[107] USS Sterett web site, http://destroyerhistory.org/goldplater/ns_sterett/

Tripoli, a lateen-rigged polacca[108] with two masts, was crewed by 80 men under Admiral Rais Mahomet Rous and armed with 14 guns. Although the Tripolitans held a slight advantage in firepower, Enterprise had to its advantage the larger crew and the element of surprise. The Americans were also significantly more experienced in gunnery action than the Tripolitans, who preferred to attack by boarding and taking over their opponents' ships.

"Shortly after Sterett had the American colors raised, he had his men open fire upon the Tripolitans at close range with muskets. In response, Tripoli returned fire with an ineffective broadside. The Americans returned fire with their own broadsides, which led Rous to break off the engagement and attempt to flee. Neither able to fight off the American vessel nor outrun her, the Tripolitans attempted to grapple Enterprise and board her. Once within musket range, Enterprise's marines opened fire on the Tripoli, foiling its boarding attempt, and forced Tripoli to try to break away once more. Enterprise continued the engagement, firing more broadsides into the Tripolitan and blasting a hole in her hull.

"Severely damaged, Tripoli struck her colors to indicate surrender. As Enterprise moved towards the vessel to accept its surrender, the Tripolitans hoisted their flag and fired upon Enterprise. The Tripolitans again attempted to board the American schooner, but were repelled [again] by Enterprise's broadsides and musketry. After another exchange of fire, the Tripolitans struck their colors a second time. Sterett once more ceased firing and moved closer to [the] Tripoli. In response, Rous again raised his colors and attempted to board Enterprise. Enterprise's accurate gunnery once more forced Tripoli to veer off. As the action continued, Rous perfidiously feigned a third surrender in an attempt to draw the American schooner within grappling range. This time, Sterett kept his distance, and ordered Enterprise's guns to be lowered to aim at the polacca's waterline, a tactic that threatened to sink the enemy ship. The next American broadsides struck their target, causing massive damage, dismasting her mizzen-mast, and reducing her to a sinking condition. With most of his

---

108 Lateen rigged refers to a triangular sail rigged at an angle near the top of the mast and the term polacca is a two or three masted vessel commonly used in the Mediterranean in those days.

crew dead or wounded, the injured Admiral Rous finally threw the Tripolitan flag into the sea to convince Sterett to end the action.

At the end of the action Tripoli was severely damaged; 30 of her crew were dead and another 30 were injured. The polacca's first lieutenant was among the casualties and Admiral Rous himself was injured in the fighting. In what amounted to a total American victory over the Tripolitans, Enterprise had suffered only superficial damage and no casualties. Sterett, whose orders did not give him the authority to retain prizes, let the polacca limp back to Tripoli. However, before setting her free, the Americans cut down Tripoli's masts and sufficiently disabled her so that she could barely make sail. Sterett then continued his journey to Malta and picked up the supplies for which he was sent before returning to the blockade.

After Enterprise left, Tripoli began its journey back to the port of Tripoli. On the way it ran into USS President and asked for assistance; Rous falsely claimed that his vessel was Tunisian and that it had been damaged in an engagement with a French 22-gun vessel. Dale suspected the vessel's true identity and merely provided Rous with a compass so he could find his way back to port. When he finally arrived at [the port of] Tripoli, Rous was severely chastised by Yusuf Karamanli, the Pasha (ruler) of Tripoli. Stripped of his command, he was paraded through the streets draped in sheep's entrails while seated backwards[109] on a jackass before suffering 500 bastinadoes".[110] [One source[111] says 'bastinadoes' means being beaten on the soles of one's feet].

Cindy Vallar,[112] writing about the *Barbary Corsairs* and using as a reference Joseph Wheelan's classic work[113] confirmed that Mahomet Rous received five hundred lashes which were distributed on his feet and backside.

The effects of the defeat and the treatment of Admiral Rous on the citizens of Tripoli and the recruitment of seamen for the corsair's

---

109 Being paraded through the streets while sitting backwards on a jackass was a common humiliating punishment for offenders in the Arabic world at that time.
110 http://en.wikipedia.org/wiki/AndrewSterett
111 http://www.earlyamerica.com/review/2002_winter_spring/terrorism.htm
112 http://www.cindyvallar.com/barbarycorsairs.html
113 *Jefferson's War: America's First War on Terror, 1801-1805.* Carroll & Graf 2003.

crews were demoralizing and devastating. They were reminded of it every time the American warships were seen patrolling just outside the harbor. In the United States when news of Enterprise's victory reached the public the reaction was just the opposite.

On October 3, 1801 while the *Enterprise* was in Gibraltar she was given orders to return to Baltimore with dispatches for the secretary of the Navy and the President. When the action reports were made public:

"The American government [Congress] gave a month's pay as a bonus to each of Enterprise's crew members, and honored Sterett by granting him a sword [Presented by the President himself] and calling for his promotion. Fanciful plays were written about the victorious Americans, and morale and enthusiasm about the war reached a high point."[114]

On November 17, 1801, after all of the hoopla was over, Steritt was ordered to discharge the crew and given leave after the ship's refurbishing. Nearly a year later in November 1802, she was back on station in the Mediterranean.

USS Enterprise *vs. Tripolitan Corsair Tripoli*, 1 August 1801. Lieutenant Andrew Sterett leaving USS Enterprise *to board the Tripoli after the corsair's surrender. Artwork by Orlando Lagman after Claudus, 1965. Courtesy of the Navy Art Collection, NH 54386-KN (Color).*

---

114 http://en.wikipedia.org/wiki/AndrewSterett

Commodore Dale, however, still feeling the "short leash" placed on him by President Jefferson and lacking the number of ships and armor to be effective against the aggressive corsairs, took a passive approach. He established an observation post near the entry to Tripoli's harbor and sent one of his vessels to escort any American merchant vessel that appeared in his vision to wherever its destination was intended. He maintained this policy for several months, which given the resources available to him to cover a 1200 mile coastline, proved in the end to be for the most part not very fruitful, as we shall see.

CHAPTER THREE

Feb. 6, 1802 Tribute or War? Was Kipling Right? *

"They know they cannot meet us with force any more than they could France, Spain or England. Their system is a war of little expense to them, which must put the great nations to a greater expense than the presents which would buy it off." - Thomas Jefferson referring to the Barbary Corsairs

After his inauguration President Jefferson had pleaded with members of Congress and actually addressed Congress on the need to provide wider latitude for the executive office in dealing with the Barbary Pirates. Finally, on February 6, 1802 Congress passed an *"act for the protection of commerce and the seamen of the United States against the Tripolitan cruisers".*[115]

When Jefferson realized that the passivity of his Navy squadron was not accomplishing the results he intended, which was to win a war declared on us by Tripoli and assure that we would no longer have to pay tribute, he called a meeting of his cabinet. It was Friday, April 9, 1802. Gathered in a conference room in the relatively new White House were Treasury Secretary Albert Gallatin, Secretary of State James Madison, Secretary of War Henry Dearborn, Attorney General Levi Lincoln and Secretary of the Navy Robert Smith. Seated behind President Jefferson was his personal secretary Lieutenant Meriwether Lewis, notebook at the ready.

---

115 Tucker, Spencer C., Editor, The Encyclopedia of the Wars of the Early American Republic, ABC-CLIO, Santa Barbara, 2014, p 911-912.

* See epigram page 13

The first White House (etching)
Library of Congress-CW Janson

"Gentlemen I have called this meeting for one specific purpose. The most recent communications from our Consuls in the Barbary Coast indicate that hostilities have not abated and our Navy has not been particularly effective in stopping pirate activities, even though pirate boardings of American merchant vessels have apparently temporarily ceased, at least as far as we know. Because of the time lapse in receiving reports we really don't know what's happening.

"In my hand are copies of a circular that Secretary Smith sent to all naval commanders in February. Take a moment to peruse the information and refresh your memories," said the President, as he handed out the circulars.

CIRCULAR TO NAVAL COMMANDERS, 18 FEBRUARY 1802

INSTRUCTIONS

To the Commanders of armed vessels belonging to the United States:
   Given at the city of Washington, in the district of Columbia, this 18th day of February, in the year of our Lord, one thousand eight hundred and two, and in the 26th year of our Independence.

WHEREAS it is declared by the act entitled "An <u>act for the protection of the commerce and seamen of the United States</u>, against the Tripolitan cruisers", That it shall be lawful fully to equip, officer, man, and employ such of the armed vessels of the United States, as may be judged requisite by the President of the United States, for protecting effectually the commerce and seamen thereof, on the Atlantic ocean, the Mediterranean and adjoining seas: and also, that it shall be lawful for the President of the United States to instruct the commanders of the respective public vessels, to subdue, seize, and make prize, of all vessels, goods, and effects, belonging to the Bey of Tripoli, or to his subjects.

THEREFORE, And in pursuance of the said statute, you are hereby authorized and directed to subdue, seize, and make prize, of all vessels, goods, and effects, belonging to the Bey of Tripoli, or to his subjects, and to bring or send the same into port, to be proceeded against and distributed according to law.

By command of the President of the United States of America.
TH: JEFFERSON
President of the United States of America.[116]

After giving his cabinet members a minute or two to refresh their memories, President Jefferson continued:

"Secretary Smith do you have a comment?"

"Yes, sir I do. Commodore Dale should have received that circular three or four weeks ago. The reports I am getting from him and copies of reports sent over to me by Secretary Madison from the other consulates are conspicuous in the low number of enemy confrontations reported by the Commodore or any of his squadron's ship captains. Things could have changed in the last three or four weeks but I was hoping to receive another report before talking to you about it. I believe the Commodore is on his way home since his crew enlistments are about to expire and I also know that they have had significant numbers of ill sailors for one reason or another. Another problem that the commanders are reporting is

---

116 http://founders.archives.gov/documents/Jefferson/01-36-02-0394

that the heavy frigates are very difficult to manage when they are in the shallow waters near the shores of the Barbary Coast, especially Tripoli. We will likely get the word from the horse's mouth in about two to three weeks."

"Thank you Secretary Smith. Considering the travel time of anywhere from 3 to 5 weeks for communications and since I believe time is of the essence in controlling the pirates I would like to hear any comments or recommendations from the rest of you. Let's start with you, Secretary Dearborn."

"I don't understand it sir. Commodore Dale has an excellent record. For those of you who don't know, when he was a midshipman he was captured during the Revolutionary War by the British and spent several months in a British prison under the most brutal of conditions. After he escaped, was recaptured and escaped again, he wound up on the *Bonhomme Richard* when John Paul Jones commanded it during his battle with the *Serapis*, back in '79. He has well over 20 years of unblemished service, not to mention a couple of years in the merchant fleet. Perhaps he is ready to retire. He certainly has paid his dues."

"How about you, Attorney General Lincoln?" asked the President.

"I only served for a few weeks when our militia besieged Boston after Lexington and Concord. If you don't mind Mr. President, I will leave those kinds of comments up to the military experts."

"Thank you Mr. Lincoln. Secretary Madison?"

"I agree with Secretary Smith and Secretary Dearborn, Mr. President. With Commodore Dale returning and likely in need of a significant break or rest, we should probably replace him with somebody who can put the fear of God into these pirates. In addition, if the rumors I hear are correct, the Navy is already addressing the problem of operating in shallow waters. Is that not true?"

"I am not so sure that God wants fear of Him inserted into anybody, Jim. And yes the rumors you hear are true; we are currently in the process of constructing a number of shallow draft vessels that can operate in the waters off the Barbary Coast. However, we do need someone who will demonstrate the resolve of the United States in these matters.

"I have one more question," continued President Jefferson. "Do you, any of one of you think that continuing to pay tribute to the Barbary Pirates should be an option on the table in negotiations?"

Jefferson was surprised by the response. All of the cabinet members murmured agreement that it should be an option. There was not one single dissenting vote.[117] Two of the cabinet members did qualify their assents. Both Madison and Smith voiced their objections to paying tribute but qualified them by allowing that it might be necessary to renew "presents" (bribes or tributes) for the Pashas on occasion.[118]

"Okay, thanks everyone. Secretary Smith please stay for a minute. The rest of you are free to go."

President Jefferson then gave orders to Navy Secretary Smith to let him know when Commodore Dale arrived. He was told not to wait to find a suitable replacement, and to get the new squadron underway to the Mediterranean as soon as possible. The new squadron was to be put in charge of a senior commander until Dale's replacement was available, hopefully with additional assets in the form of warships and gunboats with shallow drafts.

There were undoubtedly other supplementary discussions, especially between President Jefferson and his good friend James Madison, because the next day Madison wrote to the American Consul, James Leander Cathcart. Madison's message to Cathcart was that he should not be "tied down to [a policy of] refusal of presents"[119] (tributes) in negotiations with the Muslim leaders. In other words, Secretary of State Madison was letting his consuls know that the option of paying tribute was still on the table for any negotiations with the Barbary Corsairs. (A year later when negotiations with Tripoli were in

---

117 http://www.monticello.org/site/research-and-collections/first-barbary-war
118 Lambert, Frank, The Barbary Wars, p 138, Hill & Wang, NY, 2005.
119 Volubrjotr, http://politicalvelcraft.org/2013/05/27/memorial-day-1801-first-war-with-the-united-states-by-islam-remembering-those-who-were-enslaved-killed/

the tank, Cathcart, the consul, would be listed as *persona non grata* in the Barbary Coast governments of Tripoli, Tunis, and Algiers).

Commodore Dale returned to the United States in April, 1802, and resigned from the Navy. His replacement Commodore Richard Morris arrived off the coast of Gibraltar in late May 1802.

In Dale's defense, historians would later confirm that the frigates in his squadron were too heavy to operate in the shallow waters off the Barbary Coast effectively, and that his instructions from the secretary of the Navy and the President were not clear initially.[120]

Others were more critical. Naval historian, William M. Fowler Jr., writing for the website, Military.com, states that Commodore Dale deserved a good deal of the blame for the failure of his squadron to subdue the pirates.[121] Fowler also quoted the American Consul in Tunis at that time, William Eaton, who was writing to his fellow consul in Tripoli, James Cathcart, about Commodore Dale's squadron: *"What have they done but dance and wench?"*[122]

Ordered by the Secretary of the Navy to replace Commodore Dale, Richard Morris astonishingly was accompanied by his wife and one male child aboard his flagship. Although it was not an uncommon practice in those days for the ship captain to bring his wife along on a voyage, it did require approval of higher ranking authority and many crewmembers shared a superstitious belief that it was unlucky.

Morris' flagship, the *USS Chesapeake*, a frigate, arrived in the waters off Gibraltar on May 25, 1802. When the other ships in his squadron (some traveling separately or later assigned) arrived, Morris would have an additional six frigates and a sloop to add to the ships already in the Mediterranean. The total number of warships in his squadron at full strength would number ten, at least for a short time. They included the frigates:

---

120 Hollis, Iran, The Frigate Constitution, pages 74-76. Houghton, Mifflin, Riverside Press, Cambridge, 1900 (google books). Free reading on line. C.

121 http://www.military.com/NewContent/0,13190, NH_0705_Crucible-P1,00.html

122 Source: William Eaton to James Cathcart 4 August 1802, Area Files of the Naval Records Collection, 1775-1910. National Archives Microfilm M 625.

1. *USS Adams* commanded by Hugh Campbell, arrived in Gibraltar July 22, 1802.
2. *USS Boston* commanded by Daniel McNeill. After dropping off the American minister Robert R. Livingston (to negotiate the purchase of New Orleans) in France during the winter of 1801, she arrived in the Mediterranean sometime before May 16, 1802 (even before Morris arrived). She returned to the U.S. with battle damage in October 1802.[123]
3. *USS Chesapeake*, the squadron flagship, commanded by Richard Morris, arrived in Gibraltar May 25, 1802.
4. *USS Constellation* commanded by Alexander Murray, also arrived in May, 1802.
5. *USS John Adams* commanded by John Rodgers left Norfolk on October 22, 1802. Unable to locate the squadron commander upon arrival, the *John Adams* wound up escorting American vessels throughout the Mediterranean. She finally caught up with Commodore Morris on January 5, 1803 on the island of Malta.
6. *USS New York* commanded by James Barron, joined Morris's squadron at Malta probably early February 1803.

The squadron also included the ships:

7. The *USS Enterprise*, the 12 gun schooner still commanded by Andrew Sterett.
8. A new addition, a sloop of war, the *USS George Washington* commanded by John Shaw.
   The *Washington* made just a couple of trips to deliver tribute to the Pasha of Algiers and other Barbary Pirates. Her activity in the Mediterranean was limited and she was sold in Philadelphia in the fall of 1802.

And finally, the two frigates from the first squadron (still on station near Tripoli):

9. The *USS Essex* commanded by William Bainbridge, returned to

---

[123] USS Boston: http://www.woodenmodelboat.com/model/woodpro/all/USS_boston.htm

the Washington Navy Yard for repairs in the summer of 1802. She did not return to the Mediterranean until August 1804, with Samuel Barron's brother James in command.
10. The *USS Philadelphia* commanded by Samuel Barron. The ship left Gibraltar for the United States in April 1802, and did not return to the Mediterranean until August 24, 1803 with William Bainbridge in command.

When the *USS Adams* (not to be confused with the *USS John Adams*) arrived in Gibraltar on July 22, 1802 carrying orders for Commodore Morris, the Commodore ordered her captain, Hugh Campbell, to block the *Meshuda*, a Tripolitan Corsair, from sailing out of the harbor[124] *"lest she escape and prey on American shipping."*[125] The *Adams* was not relieved of that duty until April 8, 1803. After a short trip to the Italian Tuscany Coast (see chapter 4) she then joined the rest of Morris's squadron off the shores of Tripoli in the blockade of that port.

The sister ship *USS John Adams*, after she caught up with the squadron commander on the island of Malta on January 5, 1803, was given orders to join the blockade in Tripoli which she did for several weeks.

Commodore Richard Morris had replaced Commodore Truxton[126] (Secretary of the Navy Smith's first choice) commanding the *USS Chesapeake* when the latter was relieved of command after an argument with the secretary of the Navy. Four days out of Hampton Roads (Norfolk) on the way to Gibraltar, the *Chesapeake*, now under Captain [127] Morris's command, ran into foul weather sustaining considerable damage to its

---

124 The Meshuda was originally a US Merchant vessel, the Betsy, which the Tripolitans captured in 1796

125 Wikipedia, http://en.wikipedia.org/wiki/USS_Adams_(1799)

126 Truxton was the captain of the USS Constellation, which defeated the French frigate L'Insurgente in the Quasi-War.

127 The title of Commodore was deleted in the 1950s in favor of an actual rank, rear Admiral (lower half). Before that a rear admiral in the Navy had two stars. After the rank of Commodore was deleted a one star admiral's rank was assigned to the senior captains who commanded squadrons. (Some sources say there were no Commodore's in the U.S. Navy after the 1950s, but when the author was at sea, we used Commodore as an honorific title in the 1960s for the squadron commander, who was still just a senior captain).

masts. Morris used the damage to the *Chesapeake* as an excuse to stay in Gibraltar for several months, even though the repairs took just weeks. When he finally did leave Gibraltar he took his time cruising all the Mediterranean vacation spots and did not arrive in Tripoli until June 7, 1803.[128]

In the meantime, Morris sent Captain Alexander Murray commanding the *USS Constellation* to Tunis with the annual tribute (read extortion) paid by the United States and gifts for the Bey (also called the Sultan, Dey, Pasha, Basha or King and sometimes called Emperor). The Bey was pleased that he finally received the late payment on May 28, 1802,[129] but he made a further demand of Murray of an armed corvette or brig.[130] Murray consulted with the American Consul in Tunis, William Eaton, who was outraged at the demand.

Eaton was also in the midst of a plot for Hamet Karamanli, Yusuf's older brother, to retake his rightful position as the Pasha of Tripoli, probably the first warranted regime change by the U.S. To support the plot, since Hamet was in exile in Tunis, Eaton had sent a dispatch to the United States Department of State asking for $23,000. Due to the long interval of communications between his boss, Secretary of State James Madison, and the Consulate, the negotiations were stalled. Captain Murray made it plain to Consul Eaton that he wanted nothing to do with the plot involving Hamet Karamanli.

Three weeks after Captain Murray and the *USS Constellation's* appearance in Tunis on June 17, 1802, the Muslim leader of Morocco, Mohamed IV, of the Alauite Dynasty,[131] declared war on the United States. Having gotten wind of the payment to the Bey of Tunis, he was upset because he hadn't received his delayed tribute too.

Nine days after that, on June 26, the *USS Franklin*, a small eight gun brig and the second ship to honor Benjamin Franklin's name, was captured by corsairs from Tripoli and brought into Algiers as a prize. The American Consul in Algiers, Richard O'Brien, tried to free the five cap-

---

128 Barrseitz (blogger) http://barbarywars.wordpress.com/timeline/
129 ibid.
130 Small warships, smaller than a sloop or schooner, with 8 to 12 guns.
131 The dynasty had been present since 1631.-Wikipedia

tured Americans of the crew by offering ransom, but they had already been transported to Tripoli and paraded through the streets in chains.

The bottom line was even though the squadron commander, Richard Valentine Morris, was apparently not as engaged as he should have been; the commanders in his squadron appeared to be doing their jobs.

There were other indications that the Tripoli blockade was not working. A letter written by Captain Andrew Morris, (not to be confused with Commodore Richard Morris) who was commander of the *Franklin* and who was captured with that vessel is quoted below. The letter was written to the American Consul William Eaton of Tunis and is available at the U.S. Naval Institute, Naval History and Heritage Command:[132]

"Tripoli, July 21, 1802

William Eaton, Esq.,
Tunis.
DEAR SIR:
I expect ere this Mr. O'Brien has informed you of my capture, but as I had not an opportunity during the Corsair's tarry at Algiers to inform him of particulars, I take this early opportunity to mention that I sailed with the Brig Franklin, belonging to Messrs. Summert & Brown of Philadelphia, from Marseilles with an assorted Cargoe [sic] for the West India market, on the 8th ultimo, and on the night of the 17th then off Cape Gallos was boarded by one of the Tripoline Galliottes, mounting four guns that sailed from this place about the 20th of May. I shall pass over the ocurrances [sic] of that night as you are well acquainted with the conduct of the Barbarians towards the unfortunate that falls into their hands ... They proceeded with the prize to Algiers where we arrived on the 20th and as I conjectured by the representations of consul O'Brien they were obliged to make a hasty departure on the 27th following, without accomplishing their intentions which was to sell the Brig & ca[rgo] ... what with contrary winds and calms we did not reach the port of Bizerte in your neighborhood, until the 7th instant w[h]ere after a tarry of five days we departed leaving the Brig there and arrived at this place the 19th instant ...

---
132 http://www.navalhistory.org/2012/07/23/richard-dale-strikes-barbary-pilots

The most provoking circumstance was off this port, when we arrived within about twelve miles the Corsair with our flag reversed began to salute the town, and so continued at intervals until we anchor'd, which was more than five hours, and all this in view of a Swedish and American Frigate, who never made the smallest effort to obstruct our progress, at all events they had it in their power to run the pirate on shore before he could get within shot of the forts. I do not wish to attach any blame to any man but this transaction was too public to remain a secret and as an American excites my indignation....

It was the too sanguine assurances that I had from several quarters of the impossibility of their cruisers [sic] to get out that led me to sea without Convoy or Arms, fatal experience has convinced me to the contrary but I hope it will prevent any more falling into their hands and excite our Vessels of war to more vigilance.

With respect, etc.
ANDREW MORRIS

Commodore Richard Morris, sailing his flagship to various Mediterranean vacation spots, was apparently unaware of this incident involving the corsair's capture of an American vessel and its crew for some time. One naval historian, David Foster Long,[133] called Morris *"the embodiment of insolence"* since he whiled away his time on a Mediterranean cruise with his wife and child, and did not reach his assigned mission in Tripoli until more than a year after he had sailed.

Commodore Richard Morris must have learned of the *Franklin's* capture along with its master, Andrew Morris, sometime in August, 1802, about two months after the incident occurred. We say this because another source[134] indicates Commodore Morris reviewed the plan to restore Hamet Karamanli as the Pasha of Tripoli when he was in Malta in the month of August 1802. Chances are he met with William Eaton and Hamet himself at that time, because he rejected Eaton's plan as being too risky and a drain on his resources. He was also said to have informed Hamet that he would bring his squadron to

---
133 Long, David Foster, Gold Braid and Foreign Diplomatic Relations, page 28, US Naval Press, 1988-
134 http://barbarywars.wordpress.com/timeline

Tripoli, *"perhaps in June."*[135] We also know that Morris was still in Malta five months later on January 5, 1803, when John Rodgers, the captain of the *USS John Adams*, caught up with him on that date, and he had not yet been to either Tunis or Tripoli.

Eaton was already contemplating requesting his own recall because he felt that he could no longer deal with the Muslim leader in Tunis. On November 9, 1802, Eaton sent another dispatch to the Department of State, requesting $23,000 to cover expenses in connection with the Hamet plot. On December 20, Eaton, citing his frustrations with the Navy and Commodore Morris's rejection of helping with the Hamet plot to replace Yusuf Karamanli, actually made his formal recall request to Secretary of State Madison.[136]

Eaton had also borrowed 34,000 Spanish dollars from a local lender, Hadji Unis Ben Unis, in January 1803, to pay ransom on the Bey's hostage from Sardinia, Countess Maria Anne Porcile.[137] Ben Unis was the chief commercial agent of the Tunisian government. The kidnapped 12 or 13 year-old countess was being held for ransom because she had been promised as an additional wife for the harem of the Tunisian prime minister. This debt would prove to be significant in what happened later.

Upon receiving the communication near the end of January 1803, Madison requested a meeting with the President, who had already ordered a reinforced Navy squadron to the Mediterranean on January 17. By the time the meeting was possible it was Tuesday, February 1, and any decisions made concerning Consul William Eaton, the Consulate in Tunis, the Hamet plot, or Commodore Morris, would be irrelevant. They wouldn't matter because of a series of dramatic events that would cause the Bey of Tunis to threaten the U.S. with war, and imprison Commodore Morris, Captain John Rodgers of the *USS John Adams,* and James Cathcart and hold them for ransom while their frigates were anchored in the bay. The same series of events could not happen with today's modern communications, but with the delay of four to six weeks that occurred in the

---
135 ibid
136 ibid.
137 ibid

early 1800s the events surely could and did happen. Here's what occurred:

- On January 17, 1803, the *USS Enterprise* still under the command of Andrew Sterett captured a foreign brig, the *Paulina* out of Algiers, headed toward Tunis. When the Bey of Tunis heard about it, he called in William Eaton and raised holy hell claiming that at least part of the cargo aboard the *Paulina* was his. He then threatened the U.S. with war.[138]
- Tunisian Consul Eaton, not having heard from the State Department, wrote to his counterpart in Tripoli, James Cathcart, on January 22, 1803, requesting help paying off his debts due to the Hamet plot, and the ransom of Countess Porcile. Cathcart, knowing he was no longer welcome in Tripoli and probably fearing for his life if word of Eaton's plot to replace Yusuf Karamanli with his brother Hamet leaked out, headed for Malta where he knew Commodore Morris was anchored.

Commodore Morris, now having knowledge of the Tunisian ruler's threat of war from Cathcart, sent Lieutenant Andrew Sterett[139] and the *Enterprise* to Tunis on January 31. Apparently not too concerned, Morris left Malta with his squadron which included himself and Cathcart aboard the *USS Chesapeake*. Besides Morris on the *Chesapeake,* the squadron also included Captain John Rodgers on the *USS John Adams*, and Captain James Barron on the *USS New York*. Barron had sailed from the Washington Navy Yard in November 1802 and had joined Morris's squadron on Malta sometime in January or early February 1803.

Morris headed for Gibraltar but stormy weather forced him to change course and he arrived with his ships in Tunis on February 22.[140] Another source,[141] John Rodgers' biographer Paullin, says Morris returned to Malta before heading for Tunis. Paullin also says Morris was

---

138 ibid.
139 *Some sources spell it Sterrett.*
140 *London, Joshua, Victory in Tripoli, John Wiley & Sons, Jan 7, 2011, Hoboken New Jersey.*
141 *Paullin, Chas. O. Commodore John Rodgers, a Biography p-102. Arthur Clark Co. 1910, Cleveland*

not only accompanied by the *New York* and the *John Adams* but also the captured vessel, the *Paulina* whose ownership was under dispute.

American Council William Eaton, feeling a little more confidence at the site of three American frigates and the *Enterprise* in the bay of Tunis, goes with Commodore Morris to see the Bey. Morris, after several days of negotiations, including some private discussions with Eaton and Tripoli Consul James Cathcart, agreed to pay the balance of Eaton's debt if Eaton can come up with the rest. Some days later Eaton sold his personal yacht, *Gloria*, for 12,000 Spanish dollars.

On March 4, 1803, Morris prepared his squadron for departure. The Bey, Hamud[142] Bassa bin Ali, saw the preparation and promptly placed Morris, Rodgers, and Cathcart under arrest[143] and demanded they pay off Eaton's debts. Because they did not have enough cash he held them for ransom.

Rodger's biographer Charles Paullin has a little different version of events:

"At first Morris insisted that the cause of the prize [the captured ship, Paulina] should be tried at Gibraltar, but on the Bey's threatening war he agreed that the question of the ownership of the cargo might be decided at Tunis. Having obtained one concession, the bey made a fresh demand. Finally the commodore lost his patience, and abruptly closed the contention. Without taking formal leave of the bey, he and his aides made arrangements to return to the fleet. While they were on their way to their boat at the wharf, they were overtaken by one of the Bey's agents, who arrested Morris and refused to let him leave the city until he had paid a debt incurred by our consul to Tunis, William Eaton, in behalf of the United States and in prosecution of a plan to set upon the throne of Tripoli the brother of the reigning pasha."[144]

---

142 Also spelled Hammoud

143 One source attributes the arrest to Morris's failure to offer a customary departing gunnery salute. Fremont-Barnes, Gregory, The Wars of the Barbary Pirates, p-43, Osprey Publishing, Oxford, 2006.

144 Paullin, Chas. O. Commodore John Rodgers, a Biography p-103-4. Arthur Clark Co. 1910, Cleveland

Hamud Bassa the Bey of Tunis- photo credit Wikipedia

On March 10, 1803, Eaton coughs up the 12,000 Spanish dollars he got from selling his yacht and also borrowed some cash from the French Consul.[145] The Bey accepts the cash and a promise from Commodore Morris that he would pay the balance and tells the Americans to get out of Tunis with both of their diplomats and to not come back. Morris and the squadron leave Tunis with both Eaton and Cathcart aboard and head for Gibraltar with an intended to stop in Algiers.

Captain John Rodgers' biographer once again has a slightly different version:

"Finally Morris agreed to pay and the bey agreed to accept twenty-two thousand dollars, about two thirds of the whole claim; and the commodore was permitted to return to his ship. Cathcart and Rodgers remained a few days longer on shore to complete the settlement of the difficulty. As Eaton was at swords points with the bey he also embarked, and Morris appointed Dr. George Davis of the navy to act as consul. This disgraceful episode came to an end on March tenth with the sailing of the squadron for Algiers. Morris always blamed Eaton with enticing him

---

145 http://founders.archives.gov/documents/Madison/02-05-02-0174

on shore and thus causing the indignity that he suffered, but it must be said that he has not proved his charges against the consul.

"On March nineteenth, the fleet arrived at Algiers, and on the next day the American consul, Richard O'Brien, visited the flagship and poured into the commodore's ear a tale of woe respecting the refractory ruler to whose court he was accredited. The Dey had a grievance against President Jefferson, who had sent him thirty thousand dollars in money instead of naval stores to that value, which had been expected. The disappointed ruler refused either to accept the money or to permit it to be returned to the donor. He now further exhibited his displeasure by declining to receive Cathcart, who had been appointed to succeed O'Brien as consul. Admonished by his experiences ashore at Tunis, Morris did not leave his ship. After a brief stay he sailed for Gibraltar, where he arrived on March twenty-third."[146]

While in Gibraltar, William Eaton transfers to the *USS Perseverance*, and later sails for Boston.[147] The Naval officers blamed Eaton for the whole mess. Eaton, in an "at sea" letter to Secretary of State James Madison dated March 22, 1803, blamed Cathcart, (whom he had previously mentored), and Tunisian Prime Minister *Yusuf Sahib-al-Taba*,[148] who he had enlisted to help with the Hamet Karamanli plot. (See the Epilogue for a synopsis of the fascinating life of James Leander Cathcart, former sailor, corsair captive and slave, minister for Tripoli, and American diplomat).

* * *

---

146 Paullin, Chas. O. Commodore John Rodgers, a Biography p-104-05. Arthur Clark Co. 1910, Cleveland
147 http://barbarywars.wordpress.com/timeline.
148 http://founders.archives.gov/documents/Madison/02-04-02-0533

CHAPTER FOUR

May 2, 1803 Our Country Right or Wrong

"Our Country! In her intercourse with foreign nations may she always be in the right; but right or wrong, our country!" Lieutenant Stephen Decatur, USN

Robert R. Livingston had been sent to France in 1801 to negotiate the purchase of New Orleans because the Spanish had revoked a U.S. – Spanish treaty that permitted U.S. merchants to store goods in the port city of New Orleans. These goods were awaiting transport up the Mississippi to settlers in both the Ohio and Tennessee River valleys. After Napoleon came to power, Spain allied itself with France, causing the British to react by cutting Spanish access to New Orleans and other ports using its powerful Navy.

The Spanish had signed a secret agreement with France, called the Treaty of San Ildefonso, which allowed the return of the Louisiana territory to France. Signed in 1800, the Treaty gave Spain's Charles IV's son-in-law, the Duke of Parma, power over Tuscany, a former Italian Papal state and center of cultural and artistic enlightenment, as payment for returning the Louisiana Territory to French control. Some fascinating facts are:
- Charles IV of Spain was a cousin of King Louis XVI of France.
- The Duke of Parma, (born in 1751), Charles IV's son-in-law, was Ferdinand, a descendant of Isabella and Ferdinand V (born in

1451), and the grandson of Isabella of Spain, originally Isabella Farnese (born 1692).
- The Duchy of Parma was originally created for Pierre Luigi,[149] who was the son of Pope Paul III. One of various popes to have fathered children before his election, Pope Paul III had four illegitimate offspring. One of his mistresses, Silvia Ruffini, was the mother of Pierre Luigi.[150]
- The Duchy passed to the Bourbon family through some of Isabella's and Ferdinand's descendants, the Farnese family. The Duke of Parma, Ferdinand, (the one born in 1751) at the time of the transfer back to France was in control of Tuscany after the Treaty of San Ildefonso.

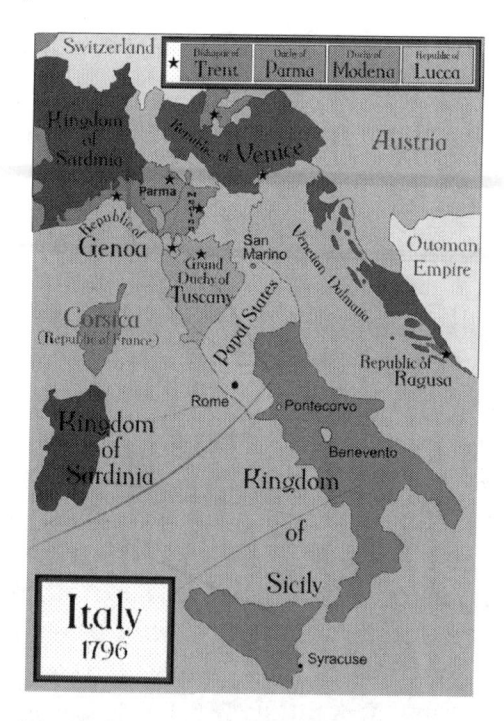

**Grand Duchy of Tuscany and the Duchy of Parma above.
Photo credit Wikipedia**

---

149 *The Louisiana Purchase: A Historical and Geographical Encyclopedia* edited by Rodriguez, Junius P., Santa Barbara, July 2002.
150 Wikipedia, http://en.wikipedia.org/wiki/Duchy_of_Parma

The revocation of the U.S. – Spanish agreement concerning New Orleans was brought about after the Treaty of San Ildefonso. Although most historians now deny any Napoleonic influence on the revocation of the agreement, which allowed American merchants to store cargo in New Orleans, the U.S. was fearful of French domination over the Mississippi River and New Orleans. That concern was most likely the reason President Jefferson sent future President James Monroe to Paris in April, 1803 to help Robert Livingston negotiate the purchase of New Orleans. The negotiations had been going on for over two years.

When Monroe arrived in Paris, Livingston had some startling news. French officials were offering the whole Louisiana territory for sale including the port of New Orleans. The offer included some 828,000 square miles for the remarkable price of $15 million which amounted to somewhere between three and five cents an acre (depending on what authority you read).

Negotiations were quickly concluded and the purchase completed on May 2, 1803, doubling the size of the United States. Some say Napoleon offered the territory because he had just suffered a defeat in Haiti during a slave revolt and was about to take on the British Navy. Napoleon himself had this to say:

"This accession of territory affirms forever the power of the United States, and I have given England a maritime rival who sooner or later will humble her pride."[151]

That precognitive statement, along with the fact that Napoleon was stressed for funds to carry on his wars with Great Britain and other European nations, as well as his recent defeat in Haiti, were the likely reasons for the offer. Although Napoleon had promised Spain that he would keep the Louisiana territory, there was nothing Spain could do about him breaking his promise by selling it to the United States.

After leaving Tunis and Algiers, Commodore Morris spent more time in the familiar port of Gibraltar provisioning his ships. On April 6, Morris, who originally had his flag aboard the *Chesapeake,* shifted it to the *USS New York.* Morris's old flagship, the *USS Chesapeake,* had been

---

[151] *The Louisiana Purchase: A Historical and Geographical Encyclopedia* edited by Rodriguez, Junius P., Santa Barbara, July 2002 http://www.mahalo.com/louisiana-purchase/

plagued by issues such as a rotted mast and bowsprit, so she headed home for repairs. Laid up for repairs at the Washington Navy Yard in June 1803, the *Chesapeake* remained idle for nearly four years.[152]

Rank hath its privileges, so the Commodore not only transferred his flag to the *New York* but brought along with him the *Chesapeake's* First Lieutenant, Isaac Chauncey, and transferred the *New York's* commanding officer, James Barron to the *Chesapeake*. Besides her new captain, James Barron, the *Chesapeake*, heading home, carried aboard Lieutenant Andrew Sterett,[153] the hero of Tripoli, who had just relinquished command of the *Enterprise* to Isaac Hull.

The transfer must have been a shock to Captain Barron. He had commanded the *New York* since it's re-commissioning in 1802 after the Quasi-War. He now had to transfer the running of his ship to his own former First Lieutenant, Isaac Chauncey, who had served with him aboard the *USS President*. That was when Barron was the commanding officer of the flagship for Commodore Dale.[154] Now Chauncey would be the acting captain of the *USS New York*, the new flagship for Commodore Morris.

All of the changes instituted by Commodore Morris also affected the schooner the *USS Enterprise*. After the change of command, *Enterprise* was now under the command of Lieutenant Isaac Hull, who then joined Commodore Morris's flotilla, led by his new flagship the *USS New York*, along with the *John Adams*. The sister ship to the *John Adams*, the *Adams*, relieved of guarding the *Meshuda*, also had orders from Morris to lead a merchant convoy to Leghorn (Livorno, Italy) and would rejoin the squadron after depositing Cathcart in Leghorn. Cathcart was an American Consul who worked for the Secretary of State, and knowing he was no longer welcome in the north African

---

152 Hickman, http://militaryhistory.about.com/od/shipprofiles/p/War-Of-1812-Uss-Chesapeake.htm

153 *Register of Officer Personnel United States Navy and Marine Corps and Ship's Data 1801-1807*. http://www.history.navy.mil/library/online/PERSONNEL%20AND%20SHIP%20DATA%201801-1807.pdf

154 US Wars.com, http://www.mywarof1812.com/leaders/chauncey-isaac/

Barbary states had requested transport to Leghorn where there was an American consulate headed by Thomas Appleton.

Just a day or two out of Gibraltar on the way back to Malta there was an accident aboard Morris's new flagship involving gunpowder and a fire which resulted in 19 casualties (14 of which were deaths)[155] and considerable damage to the ship.[156] The flagship arrived in Malta in damaged condition on May 1 and did not rejoin the blockade of Tripoli for nearly three weeks when repairs were complete.

As previously noted, the sister ship to the *USS Adams*, the *USS John Adams*, commanded by John Rodgers, caught up with squadron commander Morris on the island of Malta January 5, 1803. In Malta she was given orders to join the blockade in Tripoli which she did for three or four weeks. The *John Adams* accompanied Morris into Tunis on February 22, along with the *USS New York,* and the *Chesapeake*. After the diplomatic disaster in Tunis, all three ships and their masters were kicked out of the Barbary State in March by Hamud Bassa the Bey of Tunis. They then headed to Gibraltar (via Algiers) to reprovision along with the rest of the squadron.

After the *New York's* accident, Rodgers was given new orders on May 3, 1803, by Commodore Morris to cruise the Mediterranean in the *USS John Adams* independently. Shortly thereafter she got into a gun battle and captured the very ship, the 28 gun *Meshuda*, (now flying a Moroccan flag) that her sister ship, the *Adams*, had been guarding in Gibraltar. After she was joined by the *USS Enterprise* and the now repaired *USS New York,* (sans the Commodore's wife who was expecting a new baby) *"[the USS] John Adams engaged a flotilla of enemy gunboats off Tripoli on 22 May [1803] sending them scurrying back into the harbor to safety."*[157]

Just five days later, on May 27, 1803, the squadron encountered a small Tripolitan fleet consisting of one large ship and nine gunboats headed for Tripoli. Morris ordered three of his ships, the two *Adams*

---

155 Paullin, Chas. O. *Commodore John Rodgers, a Biography* page 105. Arthur Clark Co. 1910, Cleveland

156 *Naval Institute Proceedings*, Volume 41, page 14, original: University of Virginia. 1915.

157 Rubbings, USS John Adams, http://www.findagrave.com/cgi-bin/fg.cgi?page=vcsr&GSvcid=274533

and the *Enterprise* to interdict the enemy by placing themselves between the gunboats and the harbor. Once they were in position the wind died and they were exposed to Tripoli's shore batteries. After several hours a mild breeze allowed the Americans to escape unscathed.[158] Ten days later Morris went ashore to negotiate with Yusuf Karamanli.

Not surprisingly negotiations broke down when Yusuf demanded $200,000 (Spanish) and Morris offered just $15,000.[159] On June 18,[160] with negotiations still stalled, Morris returned to the island of Malta, leaving three of his ships, the two *Adams* frigates and the 12 gun *Enterprise* to continue the harbor blockade.[161] On June 22, Captain Rodgers on the *USS John Adams,* and Lieutenant Isaac Hull, who had replaced Andrew Steritt as commanding officer of the *USS Enterprise*, re-engaged the nine gunboat flotilla and Tripoli's largest cruiser, a 22 gun polacre (a polacre is a nautical term, meaning a three masted sailing vessel).

The sister ship, the *USS Adams*, remained outside of the harbor covering the two attacking ships' sterns while Captain Rodgers maneuvered his heavier vessel into the shallow waters of Tripoli, right alongside the enemy cruiser. Lieutenant Hull, after chasing one of the smaller gunboats, maneuvered his 12-gun schooner *Enterprise* closer to shore to cover enemy shore batteries and the rest of the smaller gunboats beginning to align up for action. Subsequently a 45 minute artillery battle resulted in the enemy's cruiser striking its colors. At the same time they were lowering their flag a final broadside from their own guns apparently released a spark into a powder keg or magazine aboard the enemy vessel triggering a tremendous explosion. According to Rodgers' own action report recorded by *Victory in Tripoli* author Joshua London,[162] the blast de-masted the enemy cruiser's main

---

158 *Almanac of American Military History, Vol. 1,* edited by Spencer Tucker p 440, ABC-CLIO, 2012.
159 http://barbarywars.wordpress. timeline com/
160 Another source (see next footnote) states he departed Tripoli on June 10.
161 *Naval Institute Proceedings,* Volume 41, p-14, original: University of Virginia. 1915.
162 London, Joshua, *Victory in Tripoli*, pages 128-129.John Wiley & Sons, Jan 7, 2011, Hoboken New Jersey.

and mizzen masts which rose 150 to 160 feet in the air. It also blew up bulkheads and deck along with sails and rigging and all parts associated.

Enemy sailors previously had abandoned ship before the colors were struck and swam to shore fleeing American artillery. They had just returned by boat when the explosion occurred. All of them were killed.

Captain Rodgers, who estimated the number of the enemy crew to be about 200, thought most of them were killed in the explosion as well as their captain. Author London described it as the single most significant action taken by the Mediterranean Squadron up to that point.[163]

Commodore Morris, in Malta when he received word of the victory, decided that such a significant message had been sent from the United States to Yusuf Karamanli that he ordered cessation of the Tripoli blockade. John Rodgers' biographer offers his opinion:

"Soon after this event Rodgers received orders to raise the blockade and proceed to Malta, which he did, arriving in port on June twenty-eighth. Commodore Morris had now decided to abandon his operations against Tripoli and to return to Gibraltar with his fleet by way of Messina, Naples, and Leghorn. To say the least, this movement was injudicious. Morris defended it on the ground that his heavy ships could accomplish nothing more at Tripoli, that there was a possibility of obtaining some light draft vessels at Messina or Naples, that the fleet was needed in the straits to oppose Morocco, that it was dangerous to separate his ships, and that the "Adams" must be sent home. The commodore was evidently confused by a multiplicity of objects. He was basing his actions too much upon probabilities. The war with Tripoli was an actuality, and his ships could have continued the blockade with advantage."[164]

Whatever action he did had little consequence because President Jefferson, having gotten word of the fiasco at Tunis, had already ordered the secretary of the Navy to recall the Commodore. The recall

---

163 ibid page 129.
164 Paullin, Chas. O. Commodore John Rodgers, a Biography p-110-11. Arthur Clark Co. 1910, Cleveland

was dated June 21, 1803, but Morris did not receive it until August 21.[165] The recall did not mince words:

"*You will consider yourself suspended in the command of the squadron on Mediterranean station and of the frigate New York.*"[166]

Morris would later be subject to a court of inquiry and summarily dismissed from the service. Here is the sequence of events:

President Jefferson disgusted at the lack of positive results from Commodore Morris and the resultant expelling of James Leander Cathcart and William Eaton from the Barbary Coast consulates did not wait to correct the situation. Communications being what they were in the 1800s, in June the President ordered Morris's recall right after he heard of the Tunisian diplomatic disaster.

After Morris dumped the expelled diplomats in Gibraltar in March 1803, and William Eaton had departed for Boston, Cathcart boarded the *Adams* and was dropped off in Leghorn.

Leghorn was the English name of an Italian port called Livorno on the northwest coast of Italy in the province of Tuscany. Leghorn (Livorno) is about 100 miles east of the French port of Marseille on the Ligurian Sea portion of the Mediterranean, and was a common rendezvous point for both military and commercial Mediterranean shipping in the 1800s. (See map on page 16). Cathcart would stay there until July 1803 when he was picked up by Morris's squadron. By then, Secretary of State James Madison had reshuffled his assets in the Mediterranean:

"*There had also been a complete change in negotiators. Cathcart was no longer welcome in Tripoli, Tunis or Algiers; Consul William Eaton had left Tunis on orders from the bey and returned to America; and Tobias Lear had arrived as Consul General in Algiers in November 1803 to replace Richard O'Brien, who had long sought to leave the post. Lear was also to take over negotiations with the pasha in Tripoli with instructions based on Cathcart's revised guidance, allowing present [tribute] on treaty signature, periodic tribute and ransom for captives if necessary.*"[167]

When Cathcart, Morris, Eaton, and Rodgers were kicked out of Tunis they had to leave some American representation behind. The only per-

---

165 London, Joshua, Victory in Tripoli, John Wiley & Sons, Jan 7, 2011, Hoboken, New Jersey p- 129.
166 Ibid.
167 http://www.monticello.org/site/research-and-collections/first-barbary-war

son acceptable to the pasha or bey of Tunis was the squadron surgeon, Dr. George Davis, who would act as the American consul until a suitable replacement could be found. Davis had been laying the groundwork for new negotiations ever since and that was the reason Cathcart was on board the *Adams* on July 11, 1803:

"On July eleventh, the whole fleet together with the prize 'Meshouda' sailed for Messina [Sicily], where it arrived three days later. Here Morris tried to obtain the loan of some gunboats, and was referred to Sir John Acton, the chief minister of the King of the Two Sicilies, residing at Naples, to which port the fleet next proceeded. Sir John conditionally promised Morris ten gunboats and two bomb ketches for use against Tripoli in the following spring. The fleet left Naples on August third and ten days later arrived at Leghorn, where the ships were separated. The 'Enterprise' was sent to Malta for dispatches, the 'Adams' to Tunis with Consul Cathcart, and the 'John Adams' to Gibraltar with a convoy. Rodgers left Leghorn with five merchantmen under his protection on the twenty-fourth of August, and, after calling at Barcelona and Alicant, arrived at Malaga on September eleventh. Here he found the commodore who had recently come from Leghorn with the 'New York,' and also Lieutenant Richard Somers in the schooner 'Nautilus' lately from America. Somers brought dispatches from the government, which contained the surprising intelligence that Morris was suspended from his command and Rodgers was appointed to succeed him. 'We have been for some time much disappointed with the conduct of Captain Morris,' Secretary Smith wrote to the new commander-in-chief. 'He has not done anything which he ought to have done and despairing of his doing anything and also as a mark of our disapprobation; it has been determined to suspend him. We, besides, can obtain from him no information what he is proposing to do. We have generally to rely upon others with respect to his movements.'"[168]

When Lieutenant Richard Somers arrived in Gibraltar on July 28, 1803 as the new commander of the *Nautilus* he carried with him not only the recall orders of Commodore Morris, but the appointment orders of the new temporary Commodore of the Mediterranean fleet of the U.S. Navy, John Rodgers. Not finding either the squadron com-

---

168 Paullin, Chas. O. Commodore John Rodgers, a Biography, p-111. Arthur Clark Co. 1910, Cleveland

mander or his new flagship the *USS New York*, or the *USS John Adams* with Captain John Rodgers in Gibraltar, he did a quick re-provisioning of his ship and left in search of the recipients of the new orders he carried. He was told in Gibraltar by the harbor master that Commodore Morris was most likely in Malta but that he should stop at every port along the way. Luckily enough he left his anchorage in Gibraltar on July 31 and found Commodore Morris three weeks later in Leghorn.

Lieutenant Somers had received the new orders for the commodore and for Captain Rodgers directly from the secretary of the Navy since he was part of the new squadron commanded by Commodore Preble. Somers' ship was the first ship of that squadron to leave the United States on June 30, 1803. As expected the *Nautilus* was also the first ship of that squadron to arrive in the Mediterranean which she did on July 28. Not privy to the wording of the orders, Somers was only aware of the fact that there was going to be a change of command, but was also told by Secretary of the Navy Smith to keep his mouth shut about that until after the orders were delivered to both men involved. Somers did his duty, finally found Morris in Leghorn after three weeks of searching and was told by Commodore Morris who knew he carried orders for Captain Rodgers, that he was to keep his station with the flagship, and that he was expecting to meet Captain Rodgers after his mission escorting merchantmen was complete.

Now aware of his relief of squadron command and with orders home, Morris took his ships and headed for Gibraltar. His stop in Malaga was where he and Somers found Rodgers.

Thus when his lookouts aboard the *Nautilus* reported the presence of the *John Adams* Somers first had his signal man hoist a series of flags[169] requesting a meeting. He then launched the captain's skiff and approached the heavy frigate.

Standing in the bow of the skiff, megaphone in hand, Somers saluted the *John Adams'* stern mounted ensign, then turned and addressed the officer of the deck, "Commanding officer of the United States' warship *Nautilus* requests permission to board." The officer of

---

169 *The signals were from Captain James Barron's 'Barron Signal Book' which replaced the 'Truxton Signal Book' in 1802. earlyradiohistory.us/1963hw01.htm*

the deck, who had been forewarned by his own commanding officer to grant the permission, replied "Permission granted."

Captain Rodgers, a stickler for naval tradition, had not only forewarned his officer of the deck when he saw the signal flags and the approaching skiff from the *Nautilus*, but provided side boys,[170] who saluted the new arrival when he stepped on deck from the rope ladder, and offered hands to steady the new arrival. Captain Rodgers was also on hand to welcome the Lieutenant, shake hands after salutes were exchanged, and give the traditional "welcome aboard." All of these traditions were of course European and primarily British in origin, but quickly retained by the Americans whose Navy was established and trained by emigrant veterans of other navies like Britain's or veterans of some other country's navy or merchant fleet.

"Thank you Captain Rodgers. I am Lieutenant Richard Somers, and I have dispatches for you from the Secretary of the Navy," said Lieutenant Somers patting a leather valise that hung from his shoulder.

"I am delighted Lieutenant," replied Captain Rodgers, "And I've seen you before. Weren't you with John Barry on the *United States* during the Quasi-War"? Rodgers was thinking to himself, *'nobody with a nose like that could possibly be misidentified.'*

"Yes sir, I was."

"I thought so. Please follow me to my cabin, Lieutenant, and we will see what you have in that pouch." Rodgers was also curious that there had been no communication from the squadron's flagship which he noted had recently moored in the harbor. He raised the question to Lieutenant Somers.

"I see Commodore Morris' flagship tied up over there."

"Yes sir. He received some dispatches as well."

---

170 Side boys are Naval Officers of lesser rank, representing a naval custom originating when dignitaries boarding ship from a smaller boat needed assistance to get on board. Today the custom is strictly honorary. The higher the rank the more side boys are present and the custom is used both for boarding and debarking.

Captain John Rodgers
Wikipedia

Lt. Richard Somers
http://remembertheintrepid.
blogspot.com

Just before they entered the captain's cabin one of the lookouts reported a new set of signals from the flagship. Captain Rodgers, familiar with the newly issued *Barron's Book of Signals*, turned to read them. The Commodore was requesting a meeting of all squadron Captains aboard his flagship.

After reading his new orders Captain Rodgers looked up at Lieutenant Somers. "Did you know about this Lieutenant?"

"I am not privy to your orders Captain. All I was told by the Secretary of the Navy was that there was going to be a change of command."

"Indeed. Well I guess all of the ship captains will know more when we meet with the Commodore in a couple of hours. I'll walk you back to your skiff," said Rodgers dismissively.

"On September fourteenth, Rodgers and Morris [and Somers] anchored at Gibraltar, where they found Commodore Edward Preble who had recently come from America with a new squadron, bringing orders for *all the vessels of the old squadron, with the exception of the 'Enterprise,' to return home. Morris sailed for Washington with the 'Adams' on September twenty-fifth. Rodgers would have soon followed him with the 'New York' and 'John Adams' had not a cause arisen for delaying his departure."*[171]

The "cause" author Paullin is referring to in the above quotation was the recent actions of the Moroccan ruler or emperor who was actively menacing merchant shipping of the United States. Just a month earlier one of the Moroccan ships, the *Mirboka*, captured an American vessel with its crew and was subsequently captured itself by the *USS Philadelphia* under the command of William Bainbridge. The *Philadelphia*, one of the heavy frigates of the very first squadron under Commodore Dale, had just returned to the Mediterranean on August 24, 1803, after a 17 month hiatus. Rodgers, now with his own Commodore's flag, was actually senior to the newly arrived Commodore Edward Preble, but the two of them consulted about the situation in Morocco.[172]

Recognizing that his orders to return to the United States were still valid, Rodgers told Preble that he (Preble) should take the lead in confronting the Moroccan leader and offered to take on the confrontation with the *New York* and the *John Adams* to bolster Preble's squadron as a show of force. Morocco on a map of today is the country immediately south of Spain on the North African coast and its principle port is Tangiers which is a bit west and south of Gibraltar. On September 17, 1803 the two Commodores took their vessels to Tangiers in hopes of communicating with the emperor, Mulay Suleiman.[173] Not finding him there the Commodores left several of their vessels to blockade the port of Tangiers and one or two other Moroccan ports, possibly Sale and Marrakesh. Commodore Rodgers then took the *New York* and cruised along the west coast of Morocco (Atlantic side) and Commodore Preble returned to Gibraltar.[174]

Not having success in locating the emperor, both Commodores returned to Tangiers the first week in October, aligned their fleet in

---

171 Paullin, Chas. O. Commodore John Rodgers, a Biography p-111. Arthur Clark Co. 1910, Cleveland
   172 ibid. page 112
   173 also spelled Slimane
   174 ibid.

battle formation, and kept their crews at battle stations including sleeping hours. The only breaks permitted were for visits to the head (toilet) and for chow. Emperor Suleiman showed up on October 6, took one look at the impressive American forces and decided to negotiate a peace settlement. He did this in spite of having an army of some 20,000 soldiers in the port and shore batteries of artillery amounting to 105 cannons. In addition, the emperor sent gifts of cattle, sheep, and fowl to the American fleet indicating his willingness to negotiate.

The negotiations then proceeded and according to Charles Paullin:

"He [Suleiman] readily agreed to give up the prisoners and property that had been captured by his ships, and to reaffirm the treaty of 1786 which his father had made with the United States. On their part the commodores agreed to surrender the 'Meshouda' and 'Mirboka.' Within less than a month, by a proper show of force, Preble and Rodgers had obtained an honorable treaty with Morocco without the payment of a cent for tribute or presents. James Simpson, the American consul at Tangier, and Tobias Lear, who had been recently appointed consul-general to Algiers, assisted them in the negotiations."[175]

Commodore Preble's diary entries of October 6 and October 13 were succinct and to the point:

"October 6th-the Emperor of Morocco, with 25,000 Troops arrived [in] Tangier.

"October 13th-Peace re-established with the Emperor of Morocco and the Treaty of 1786 Ratified and confirmed."[176]

* * *

After the peaceful settlement with Morocco, Commodore Rodgers in the *New York* and Captain Hugh Campbell in the *John Adams* headed back to the United States. Campbell, a previous master of the USS *Adams*, had taken over command of the *John Adams* when Rodgers replaced Morris and went to the *New York*. Commodore Morris

---

175 ibid page 113.
176 *The American Historical Record Volume 1, P-54-55, (Preble's Diary) edited by Benson John Lossing, Chase and Town Publishers, 1872*

had taken over as captain of the *Adams* for his return to the U.S. and had preceded Rodgers and Campbell home.[177]

On October 31, 1803, Captain William Bainbridge commanding the *USS Philadelphia* ran his ship aground about 5 miles east of Tripoli while chasing a Tripolitan cruiser. The event would turn out to be a disaster for the United States because despite his efforts he could not free the vessel and it was easily captured by Tripoli's corsairs. Bainbridge and 306 of his officers and men were made slaves of the pasha of Tripoli. That was the worst part of the disaster but it wasn't the last. The vessel itself was refloated by its captors and once repaired could have become a part of the pirate fleet.

**Stranding and capture of USS Philadelphia, 31 October 1803
Sketch by William Bainbridge Hoff.
It depicts Philadelphia under attack by gunboats off Tripoli, after she ran aground on uncharted rocks while chasing a small enemy vessel. - U.S. Naval History & Heritage Command Photograph.**

---

177 Clare; Israel Smith, *Naval History of the United States*, vol.12, page 79, Union Book Co. 1899. Digitized by University of California, 2013

Arriving on this scene six weeks later was a young Navy officer, Lieutenant Stephen Decatur Jr., the son of a merchant seaman and former Revolutionary War veteran and officer of the Continental Navy. Decatur had served as a midshipman on the frigate *USS United States* under Commodore Barry, the Navy's most senior officer, and was a Quasi-War veteran as well as a veteran of Commodore Dale's first Mediterranean squadron. He also served as First Lieutenant for the *USS New York* under James Barron's command.

Most recently when he was back in the United States, Decatur had taken command of and recruited the crew of the *USS Argus* which was part of Preble's new squadron. When he arrived in the Mediterranean with the 18 gun vessel, he exchanged command of the vessels with Isaac Hull the most recent commander of the E*nterprise*. Then:

"On December 23, 1803, Enterprise and [the frigate] Constitution confronted the Tripolitan ketch Mastico sailing under Turkish colors, armed with only two guns and sailing without passports on her way to Constantinople [now called Istanbul] from Tripoli. On board were a small number of Tripolitan soldiers. After a brief engagement Decatur and his crew captured the ship, killing or wounding the few men defending the vessel. After its capture the small ship was taken to Mastico, condemned by Commodore Preble [whose flagship was the Constitution] as a legitimate prize of war, and given a new name, Intrepid."[178]

The *Intrepid* and its future commanders would become immortal symbols for the US Navy, as you will see.

Edward Preble's biographer, Christopher McKee, points out that there were three outstanding senior United States naval officers in the first part of the 19th century. The first of these was Thomas Truxton who dominated the aggressiveness and professionalism of the U.S. Navy during the Quasi-War with France. The second one was Commodore John Rodgers, described previously, and the third was Edward Preble. McKee also states that there were three reasons that Preble became the stronger figure of the three:[179]

---

178 Wikipedia, http://en.wikipedia.org/wiki/Stephen_Decatur
179 McKee, Christopher; *Edward Preble a Naval Biography, 1761-1807*, Naval Institute Press 2014, Preface.

1. His intellect, which allowed him to understand the military, commercial and diplomatic responsibilities of the American squadron and integrate them with American policy.
2. He had the character and personality to act on his analysis and translate it into effective action.
3. He was lucky.

The reasoning and planning by Preble and his staff that would mitigate the disaster of the capture of the *Philadelphia*, I believe, confirms author McKee's suppositions. And he and Lieutenant Decatur, who led the attack to mitigate the *Philadelphia's* loss, were lucky indeed.

Lieutenant Stephan Decatur   **Commodore Edward Preble**

It was not until November 24 when Preble first heard of the capture of the *Philadelphia* from the master of the British frigate *Amazon*[180]

---

180 The American Historical Record Volume 1, P-55, (Preble's Diary) edited by Benson John Lossing, Chase and Town Publishers, 1872.

that he realized how much of a disaster it really was. Yusuf Karamanli, the Pasha of Tripoli was now in possession of one of the world's best warships, not to mention the state-of-the-art naval artillery for the time. If he were to deploy these assets against the Americans it might be possible for the pasha to cause real trouble. There was only one American ship in the region that could match the power of the *Philadelphia* when it was repaired, and that was Preble's own flagship the *Constitution*. Something had to be done but Preble needed more information.

On November 27, Preble anchored the *Constitution* off Malta and sent in a boat which retrieved a message that had arrived from Captain William Bainbridge of the captured ship *Philadelphia* detailing the ship's loss. The message had probably arrived in Malta via Dr. George Davis. He was the Morris' Squadron surgeon, who was left as acting Consul in Tripoli when Morris and the diplomats became persona non grata in the Barbary Coast city. Therefore one may conclude that most likely Davis was the one who obtained a letter from Bainbridge and entrusted it to the unnamed Danish Consul.

Mark Lardas, author of the best detailed description of the attack[181] that would mitigate the capture of the *Philadelphia*, indicates that the Bainbridge communications to Preble were smuggled out of Tripoli by the Danish Consul.

Preble immediately dispatched the *USS Vixen* to Gibraltar with copies of the reports and his own assessment. The messages were to be forwarded to the secretary of the Navy. On December 12, 1803, Preble and the *Constitution* were in Syracuse, Sicily, when the *Vixen* returned having been unable to reach Gibraltar due to bad weather. Four days later, the weather looking a little better, Preble sent Lieutenant Somers and the *Nautilus* with the dispatches to Gibraltar. He then took the *Enterprise* with Lieutenant Decatur now commanding and headed for Tripoli intending to scout the area for current infor-

---

181 Lardas, Mark, *Decater's Bold and Daring Act, The Philadelphia in Tripoli 1804*, Osprey Publishing LTD, Oxford, UK, 2011.

mation. That was when they encountered and captured the *Mastico* on December 23.

The day after Christmas the weather turned foul again so the Commodore on the Constitution and Decatur on the *Enterprise* escorting their prize, the *Mastico*, abandoned further patrol of the Barbary Coast and headed for Syracuse on the southeast coast of Sicily. Preble declared the captured vessel a legitimate prize of war and renamed it the *Intrepid*.

Preble's diary entry of January 12, 1804 indicated that he sailed for Malta aboard the *Vixen* on "squadron business." Preble had chosen Syracuse, (also called Saragosa) Sicily, over Malta as his operating base, likely because the British Navy was thoroughly ensconced in Malta and he wanted to avoid any further conflicts. He was aware no doubt that Stephen Decatur had fought a duel with a British naval officer previously in Malta and had been sent home to the U.S. because of it. Decatur was never punished for that episode since dueling was felt to be an honorable way to solve problems during the 18th and 19th centuries.

Preble's diary entry for January 14, 1804: *"Arrived at Malta, saluted the Garrison, was received with politeness and attention by the [English] Navy and Army."*[182]

Preble's squadron business in Malta no doubt had some routine things to accomplish, but his real mission involved the end stages of planning a raid on Tripoli to solve the problem of the captured frigate *Philadelphia*. Preble had realized early on that because of the condition of the captured *Philadelphia*, a recapture and recovery by sailing her out of the harbor under the guns of the enemy would be extremely risky and likely to fail. The only reasonable course of action was to destroy the vessel and the best method to do that was to burn her. Preble had first suggested that solution in a letter to the secretary of the Navy in December 1803,[183] but he was not the only one to come to that conclusion. The captured master of the *Philadelphia*, William Bainbridge, also thought that would be a proper solution as did

---

182 *The American Historical Record Volume 1, P-55, (Preble's Diary) edited by Benson John Lossing, Chase and Town Publishers, 1872*

183 Lardas, Mark, *Decater's Bold and Daring Act, The Philadelphia in Tripoli 1804*, p-23, Osprey Publishing LTD, Oxford, UK, 2011.

a number of Preble's junior officers including Stephen Decatur, who was chosen to lead the raid and had presented a plan to do just that. Lieutenant Charles Stewart, Captain of the *USS Siren*, (the original ship was spelled *Syren;* Preble's diary spelled it *Siren*) who was actually senior to Decatur, had also presented a similar plan.[184]

The Siren was a two masted brig with 16 guns mounted as carronades which were slides which would absorb and control the recoil better than carriages. She had a crew of 160 officers and men and a draft of twelve and one half feet. Her job under the command of Lieutenant Stewart during the raid was to cover Decatur's retreat after his party had set fire to the *Philadelphia*. Decatur would sail with his raiding party in the captured Tripolitan ship *Mastico* now renamed *Intrepid*. His crew would dress like Mediterranean merchant sailors of the time.

Preble's diary indicated that the Intrepid and the Siren *"sailed for Tripoli to burn the Philadelphia" on* February 6, 1804. His next diary entry wasn't until February 19: *"Siren and Intrepid have arrived, having executed my orders."* That short sentence and the only diary entry for the date belies the anxiety that Preble must have felt during the intervening 16 days of waiting for the raiding party to return. They were at least a week overdue when they finally came back. For a detailed and fascinating account of the raid, the problems encountered, including a storm that delayed the final attack, spoiled food that put further stress on the attackers, the heroics of the individuals involved, and the ultimate success, I refer the reader to naval historian Mark Lardas' exceptional work *Decatur's Bold and Daring Act, The Philadelphia in Tripoli 1804* noted above and in the footnotes.

Lardas attributes the success of the raid to four major factors:[185]
- Lieutenant Decatur's decision to not await the rendezvous with Lieutenant Stewart in the *Siren* which may have becalmed both vessels.
- The presence of a Maltese speaking native, Salvatori Catalano, who completely fooled the pasha's corsairs guarding

---

184 ibid. page 26.
185 ibid. page 64

the captured vessel and allowed the Intrepid to tie up to the target.
- Commodore Preble's plan which allowed no action except the burning of the *Philadelphia* (just in case his junior officers thought they might be able to salvage the frigate).
- The speed with which the raid was executed, no doubt due to the planning and practice put in ahead of time.

As a result of the successful raid, Lieutenant Decatur became a national hero and all of the men involved benefited from the success. A number of new naval heroes were recognized, but the one who benefited most was Stephen Decatur. Preble recommended him for promotion and Congress agreed, promoting him to full Captain, even bypassing some of his senior fellow lieutenants and the rank of Master Commandant.[186]

**Burning of the USS Philadelphia,
Edward Moran-Naval History and Heritage Command:
Public Domain photo #KN-10849 (color). Edward Moran**

---

186 Unlike today's naval commissioned officer ranks which range from O 1 (Ensign) to O 11 (five-star admiral), in the early 1800s' commissioned officers ranked from passed midshipman (which was one step above midshipman cadet), to Lieutenant (ranging from fourth through first Lieutenant) to Master Commandant, Captain, and Commodore.

CHAPTER FIVE

May 26, 1804 The Easy Way to Make General

"It is a settled policy of America, that as peace is better than war, war is better than tribute. The United States, while they wish for war with no nation, will buy peace with none." James Madison

There was a lot happening in the spring and summer of 1804. William Eaton, the former consul in Tunis had not given up on his plot to replace Yusuf Karamanli with his brother Hamet. Supported by Secretary of State James Madison and President Jefferson, Eaton, a former non-commissioned officer in the Continental Army, had previously been commissioned as a captain in the Legion of the United States.[187] He had also, at the recommendation of the Secretary of State, recently been commissioned as a naval agent. He departed the United States on May 26, 1804, aboard the *USS President* under the command of Samuel Barron.

Eaton intended to raise an army along with Yusuf Karamanli's brother, Hamet, to invade Tripoli, capture Derna, a major seaport, depose Yusuf, and replace him with Hamet. But first he had to find Hamet. It was likely the first mission by the United States to attempt to force a regime change of a foreign government.

Sam Barron was the older brother of Captain James Barron who had been the original commanding officer of the *USS President* when

---

187 *A post-Revolutionary war Pittsburgh militia which became a part of the U.S. Army. See later text.*

Commodore Dale used it as a flagship of the first Mediterranean squadron. Eaton was to report directly to the new Commodore, Samuel Barron, who would replace Commodore Preble.[188]

In addition to these changes involving the Mediterranean squadron, Lewis and Clark started out on their expedition of discovery in late May 1804. And in June squadron surgeon George Davis was expelled from Tunis by the Bey, who was rattling his saber to show support of his Muslim colleague in Tripoli who was still at odds with the U.S. Navy.[189]

Commodore Preble's diary entry of August 3, 1804 was short and to the point: *"attacked the town [Tripoli] and harbor and captured three gunboats. Lieutenant Decatur was killed."*[190] The Decatur that was killed was not Stephen, but his younger brother, James, who commanded one of the gunboats in the attack. James was about to take possession of an enemy gunboat which had surrendered when the captain of the enemy vessel pulled a pistol and shot Decatur in the head. The ammunition was unusual in that the pistol that the enemy captain used fired two lead balls wired together. The center of the wire struck Decatur in the forehead, whipping the lead balls around his head one of each striking the temple on each side and killing Decatur instantly.[191] The treacherous enemy assassin then escaped, by means unknown.

Not yet aware that President Jefferson and Secretary of the Navy Smith had decided to send yet another Navy squadron to bolster the attacks on the Barbary Coast Pirates, Preble continued his attacks on Tripoli throughout August and early September 1804. On August 7 Preble's diary indicated that he attacked the batteries, and some 115 cannon, behind the walls of the city:

"Attacked the batteries. Lost Lieut. Caldwell, one midshipman, (Mr. Dorsey) and several men."[192]

The diary editor's footnote indicated that the second attack on Tripoli started at 2:30 in the afternoon and an hour later a red-hot cannonball from the city's artillery penetrated the hull of gunboat

---

188 www.barbarywars.wordpress. timeline com/
189 ibid.
190 Preble's diary August 3, 1804.
191 ibid. second column editor's footnote number two page 56.
192 Ibid, Aug. 7, 1804.

number nine, triggering an explosion from the ship's magazine, destroying the vessel and with it Lieutenant James Caldwell, Midshipman John Dorsey, and eight of her crew.

The next day Preble's diary indicated that the *USS John Adams,* now under the command of Captain Isaac Chauncey and fully provisioned with stores, returned from the United States. Aboard the *John Adams* was William Eaton who had transferred from the *USS President.*

Now aware that he was about to be relieved by Commodore Sam Barron, and that the stormy season was fast approaching, Preble increased his assault on the Tripolitan stronghold. Yusuf Karamanli was no doubt feeling the pressure because on August 10 when Preble sent negotiators under a white flag to attempt to exchange prisoners, Karamanli offered to accept $500 per hostage to end the war.[193] Preble rejected the offer and on August 28 he attacked Tripoli with his whole squadron. In the following days he continued the assault on Tripoli with gunboats and cannon from his frigates. Then on September 4, Preble sent in the *Intrepid* now rigged as a fire ship or floating mine with magazines full of gunpowder. In command of the raid was Lieutenant Richard Somers, captain of the *Nautilus,* he of the prominent nose and with a heart full of courage.

Somers was assisted by Lieutenant Henry Wadsworth of the *USS Constitution* and a young ardent sailor by the name of Joseph Israel who snuck aboard the *Intrepid* as a non-recruited volunteer. Israel was born in 1786 near Annapolis Maryland. He ran away from home and joined the Navy at age 15 on January 15, 1801. He served on the frigate Maryland under John Rodgers, transferred to the *Chesapeake* and subsequently the *New York* in the first two expeditions against Tripoli in 1801-02. Israel transferred to the *USS Constitution* in October 1803 and served on that ship as a midshipman until 1804. On August 20, 1804, Israel was given a field promotion to lieutenant and put in command of the prize ship *Intrepid.* He volunteered for the mission along

---

193 www.barbarywars.wordpress. timeline com. *For the captured crew of the Philadelphia that would amount to $153,500 alone, worth just shy of $1 million in today's economy.*

with Lieutenant Somers and Lieutenant Wadsworth but was refused permission by Commodore Preble. He went anyway.[194]

The *Intrepid* was loaded with 100 barrels of gunpowder, pieces of scrap iron to act as shrapnel and various containers of shot and shell. The officers were supposed to direct the *Intrepid* with a lashed down rudder toward an appropriate enemy target, light a fuse, and then escape with their crew by boat. Shortly after entering Tripoli's harbor after dark on September 4, 1804, the *Intrepid* disintegrated in a massive explosion. Although the editor of Preble's diary indicated that Lieutenant (some say Master Commandant) Somers, Lieutenant Wadsworth, and Lieutenant Joseph Israel were never heard from again, other sources [195] indicate that the remains of the officers and some ten of the crew washed up on Tripoli's shore the following morning. Dead bodies sometimes speak volumes.

The Richard Somers family website, *Remember the Intrepid,* (see footnote below) says there are currently eight of the crew buried in a mass grave beneath Green Square in Tripoli, where followers of Libya's modern dictator Muammar Gadhafi once gathered. Another five of the crew are buried nearby in a small cemetery beneath a grove of olive trees. Efforts by the Somers family and the United States Congress to recover the remains and return them to the U.S. are still currently under way to this day (as of spring 2015).[196]

A week after the disaster, an ill Commodore Samuel Barron arrived off Tripoli and relieved Commodore Preble of command of the Mediterranean squadron. In November the fifth presidential election of the United States was held pitting incumbent Democratic-Republican President Thomas Jefferson against Federalist Charles Cotesworth Pinckney. Jefferson easily defeated Pinckney in the first presidential election conducted following the ratification of the Twelfth Amendment to the United States Constitution. The 12th amendment required the Electoral College to vote separately for the president and vice president. Jefferson had dropped Vice President Aaron Burr as a running mate in favor of George Clinton who easily won the office

---

194 *Remember the Intrepid,* http://www.richardsomers.org/TheIntrepid13.pdf
195 Colimore, Edward, *Philadelphia Inquirer,* Oct 25, 2011
196 ibid.

and served under both Jefferson and James Madison as the nation's fourth vice president.

* * *

In a letter dated March 20, 1805, to Secretary of State James Madison from the American Consul in Leghorn, Thomas Appleton, the status of Commodore Samuel Barron's health was noted thus:

"In a letter which I received a few days since from a friend at Malta in date of the 25th of February it appears that Commodore Barron was then in a very dangerous state of health. Yesterday I was informed by a gentleman who left Palermo on the 9th instant, that the Captain of the British sloop of war the Termigant assured him that about three weeks previous he spoke to two Tripoline corsairs of six guns and fifty men each, cruising in search of Americans between Corsica and Sardinia. Upon this advice [and] arriving at Malta, Commodore Barron immediately dispatched a number of brigs and schooners in pursuit of them: there can then be no doubt, either that they have been overtaken, or returned to Tripoli; as vessels are continually arriving here from all directions and we have no other intelligence of them. I am nevertheless apprehensive that an American vessel called the Alfred has fallen into their hands, as she sailed from Malta for Messina about the same time the Tripolines were seen off Corsica, and in four weeks she had not reached her destination. I have thought it, sir, incumbent upon me to give you this early information in the possibility that the circumstance of two enemies' vessels being out should have reached America, and that of our Squadron being in pursuit of them might be unknown. I have judged it equally necessary to advise you of the state of health of Commodore Barron, which is regarded as desperate; for it is even probable, that he may be ignorant of the danger of his own situation."[197]

Commodore Barron's liver disease was so incapacitating that it affected his management abilities as squadron commander. The fact that he lived another five years or so makes me believe it was

---

197 National Archives, Founders On line http://founders.archives.gov/documents/Madison/02-09-02-0159

most likely an infectious rather than a malignant liver disease and most likely hepatitis A, caused by a virus which in those days was not uncommon in contaminated food. Sailors were at a particularly high risk for exposure. At any rate there was no doubt that at times he was not only physically but also mentally incapacitated and unable to make rational decisions. As a result the Barbary War for the most part became stagnant over the spring and early summer of 1805 and left three people vying for the Commodore's ear in an effort to having some influence on the squadron. These included second-in- command John Rodgers, General Consul Tobias Lear, whose opinions had largely been ignored by Commodore Preble and who now had a chance for more of a say in diplomacy, and Samuel Barron's younger brother James, Sam's closest confidant who had returned to the Mediterranean as commanding officer of the *USS Essex*.

Joshua London in his 2011 book *Victory in Tripoli*[198] indicated that Commodore Samuel Barron issued secret orders on September 13, 1804, to Isaac Hull who was captain of the *USS Argus* (having exchanged ship commands with Stephen Decatur as previously noted). According to London, Barron issued these orders in the presence of William Eaton and instructed recently promoted Master Commandant Isaac Hull to assist Eaton in any way he could in the plan to replace Yusuf Karamanli with his brother Hamet. Hull and Eaton apparently rewrote the oral orders for the official record after the fact. There was no doubt however that Eaton had the support of Secretary of State James Madison and therefore also (supposedly) of General Consul Tobias Lear. Master Commandant Hull followed the orders precisely.

---

198 *John Wiley & Sons, Jan 7, 2011 (acquired by Turner Publishing Co. Nashville)*

***Master Commandant Isaac Hull, 1804. Photo credit:
Naval History and Heritage Command, Washington, DC***

William Eaton and Isaac Hull spent some time trying to perfect the plan involving Hamet Karamanli. Eaton had run away from home and enlisted in the Army at the age of 16. During the American Revolution he had risen to the rank of sergeant. He later accepted a commission as a captain in the Legion* of the United States.[199] During one of their

---

199 Heitman, Francis Bernard, *Historical Register and Dictionary of the United States Army, 1890*. P-139. Internet Source, http://books.google.com/books?id=m1zEG 4ySqlsC&pg=RA5PA1864&dq=legion+of+the+us&hl=en&sa=X&ei=2QRQVPH_KcWVy ATptIDoBw&ved=0CD0Q6AEwBQ#v=onepage&q=legion%20of%20the%20us&f=false

*The Legion was created at the recommendation of Secretary of War Henry Knox. Congress then agreed to augment and fund the new militia which was designated to defend the Indian frontier and eventually became part of the U.S. Army. The initial Legion was created in Pittsburgh.

conversations Eaton had raised the question of his rank to Master Commandant Isaac Hull:

"You know Captain Hull, I was only a captain in the Legion. How is that going to sit with the mercenaries and Marines I'll have to lead if we go through with the desert march of some 500 miles on the way to Derna?"[200]

Hull, being of quick wit, replied, "What was that General Eaton?"

"Are you serious?"

"I am. In the first place a lot of those mercenaries will be Arabs and Moros, and they respect rank. Second, Lieutenant O'Bannon of the Marines I'm sure knows you are a war veteran although he is probably ignorant of your rank. Do you happen to have a Legion uniform with you?"

"I do."

"Get the coat for me. I have an extra set of epaulets which are not unlike the army's. I'll get our sail maker to attach them for you."

And that, my friends, is likely how Naval Agent William Eaton became a general.

General William Eaton in 1807, photo credit Wikipedia

---

200 *also spelled Derne*

Israel Smith Clare in his 1899 book *Library of Universal History* said this:

"*Learning that Hamet Caramelli, [sic] after having passed a wandering life for some years, had taken refuge among the Mamelukes of Egypt, Mr. Eaton at once commenced operations. Commodore [Samuel] Barron having been directed to cooperate with and assist Mr. Eaton in his projective movement as far as he might deem it discrete-immediately after he assumed command in the Mediterranean, he dispatched the Argus, Captain Hull, with Mr. Eaton to Alexandria, where they arrived on the twenty sixth of November. It [the Argus] was to await the issue of this scheme of Mr. Eaton, and, if practicable cooperate with the land force thus raised, and a joint attack on Tripoli, that active naval operations against that city had been suspended till the summer of 1805.*"[201]

According to author Israel Smith Clare,[202] three days later on November 29, 1804, Marine Lieutenant O'Bannon along with midshipmen Eli Danielson (a son-in-law of William Eaton's),[203] and George Mann set out for Rosetta and thence to Cairo. Eaton's personal journal differs slightly:

"*[November] 28th Embarked [aboard the Argus] for Grand Cairo by [way of] Rosetta. Lieut. Blake of the Navy, Lieut. O'Bannon of the Marines, Midshipmen Mann and Danielson, Mr. Farquhar and Seid Selim, Ali, a drogoman, (sic)[204] and six servants.*"[205]

In order to even begin to implement the Hamet Karamanli plot, Eaton first had to find the elusive Muslim. He was not without help in

---

201 Clare, Israel Smith, Library of Universal History: Containing a Record of the Human Race etc. Library of the University of Chicago Durrett Collection 1899 page 99.

202 ibid. P-99.

203 The Life of the Late Gen. William Eaton Principally Collected from his Correspondence and Other Manuscripts. The New York Public Library 287176, Ebenezer Miriam and Company, 1813, p-278. Other sources indicate Danielson was a stepson or nephew. Author Richard Zacks (The Pirate Coast) reports Danielson as a beloved stepson who was killed in a duel Aug. 5. 1808.

204 The correct spelling is dragoman which means translator, interpreter, or guide.

205 The Life of the Late Gen. William Eaton Principally Collected from his Correspondence and Other Manuscripts. The New York Public Library 287176, Ebenezer Miriam and Company, 1813, p-274. Available online: http://books.google.com/books?id=4alDAAAAYAAJ&printsec=frontcover&source=gbs_ge_summary_r&cad=0#v=onepage&q&f=false

doing just that. On December 1, 1804 the *Argus* entered the mouth of the Nile at about 1 p.m. and an hour and a half later was met by an English barge with the dragoman from the English Consulate at Rosetta about three miles from the city. In the barge was a Doctor Frencesco Mendrici, who was the chief physician to the Bey of Tunis, and who would later prove to be a good friend of Eaton's.

At about 3 p.m. the barge with Eaton now on board was met at a landing by a Major Misset who was a British resident of Cairo and had taken refuge outside of the city to avoid the violence between the Turks of the Ottoman Empire and another Muslim faction, the Mamelukes who were rebelling against the government.[206] It was also rumored that Hamet Karamanli was fighting along with the Mamelukes against the Ottoman Government. That could prove to be a problem in getting him out of Egypt to resume his rightful role of Pasha of Tripoli. It's interesting to note that different factions of the Muslim religion were warring with each other even more than 200 years ago as so many of them still are today.

Major Misset conducted General Eaton and his party to the British Consular's residence where they stayed the night but were unable to continue to Cairo because a Skiak, who was a religious chief of some sort had seized all of their boats. The next day, December 3, 1804, Eaton and his party were able to hire a boat called a *marche* [207] and then spent the rest of the day loading provisions. The next day they departed for Cairo. Captain Vincengo, [208] who was Major Misset's secretary, and Dr. Mendrici went along but Navy Lieutenant Blake returned to Alexandria and the *Argus*. Eaton noted in his journal that his party now had 18 able-bodied men, but he was including the four servants accompanying Dr. Mendrici and Captain Vincengo.[209]

The descriptions that Eaton wrote in his journal of his journey to Cairo aboard the *marche* is graphic in its detail of descriptions of wild bands of Arabs who raided villages along the shores of the Nile and

---

206 ibid. page 274 -5.
207 From the French word meaning to walk or move. Eaton himself described it as 'a species of schooner peculiar to the river of about 40 tons. ibid page 278.
208 Also spelled Vincents in Eaton's journal.
209 ibid. page 275.

stole camels, buffalo, and cattle. There were other mounted marauders of the desert including approximately 500 Albanians who had deserted the Viceroy's army. They had plundered the very village that was robbed a day later by the wild bands of Arabs mentioned above. It was no wonder that the populace of Egypt was praying for the return of English rule which had at least some semblance of law and order. As Eaton wrote:

"I make this digression to show the deplorable situation of the inhabitants of Egypt. Their prayer for the return of the English is universal and humanity prays with them."[210]

On the morning of December 8, 1804, Eaton's entourage entered the outskirts of Cairo at approximately 9 a.m. He noted they were followed by crowds of people curious as to their appearance, but felt sure they had passed as foreign dignitaries representative of the Army and Navy of the United States. Since the crowds kept *"that respectful distance peculiar to the people of the East toward strangers of distinction."*[211]

On Dec. 9, 1804, according to Eaton's Journal, he had been invited to an appointment with the Viceroy of Egypt who controlled egress from the country. He also had gained knowledge of Hamet Karamanli's whereabouts through Hamet's former Secretary of State and two of his ex-governors. These disillusioned Hamet ex-officials, who served Hamet before his exile by his brother, confirmed that Hamet was indeed fighting with the Mamelukes against the government.

Accompanied by Dr. Mendrici and Captain Vincengo, Eaton arrived at the palace in ceremonial splendor. Six Arabian horses and several torchbearers led the parade from the British house. From Eaton's Journal is the following:

"The streets for the distance of a mile and a half were margined with spectators, curious to see men who had come from the New World. Guards, grooms and servants were stationed to receive us at the gate of the Citadel. The 'courbose' [presumably a courtyard or parade ground] was paraded with troops regularly drawn up. The flights of stairs which led to the grand saloon were flanked with young men

---
210 ibid. page 279.
211 ibid.

superbly armed and in rich Turkish uniform. The hall was large and splendid; and the court which attended the Viceroy surpassed everything I have seen of the kind. His Highness, with a dignified air of affability, rose from a sofa of embroidered purple and damask cushions; and, taking me by the hand, seated me next to himself and the gentleman in company on the right and left."[212]

During the rest of the evening Eaton demonstrated his experience and diplomatic skills. After the usual social chatter the Viceroy dismissed his court leaving only himself and his interpreter to discuss business which no doubt the Viceroy had in mind. The Viceroy opened the discussions with a leading statement implying that such an entourage from the United States must have more in mind than curiosity. Eaton, determined to be forthright and honest with the Viceroy, made a candid explanation of his business speaking in French which was promptly translated into Turkish. He carefully explained the events with Tripoli including the negotiations of peace and the violations of the process by Yusuf Karamanli. He then compared the war of the Barbary Coast Pirates to other provinces of the Ottoman Empire, stressing the honorable conduct of the rest of the Ottoman Empire with regards to its relationship with the United States. Eaton stated the similarity of religions between Islam and the United States noting that each worshiped one God, and that both cultures exercised humanity for their members and forbid the shedding of unnecessary blood. Eaton then declared:

"We sought in his province a legitimate sovereignty of Tripoli; [referring to Hamet] who had been treacherously driven from his government and country; and in whose good faith we could place reliance and whom we intended to restore to his throne; and in so doing, stamp conviction in the world that we do not unsheathe the sword for conquest nor for spoil, but to vindicate our rights; and that we were ready to seize any honorable means to prevent the further effusions of blood."[213]

He also related to the Viceroy the fact that the United States was aware of the collateral damage caused by the war and that it often fell on the innocent victims of Yusuf's avarice rather than the aggressor himself. In the end Eaton had convinced the Viceroy of the United States' good intentions. The Ottoman official and royalty not only

---
212 ibid. page 281.
213 ibid. page 282

agreed to the U.S. intentions and resolution, but stated that he knew Hamet and with his influence was sure he could find him. He initially noted that if Hamet was involved with the Mamelukes that there might be some difficulty allowing him out of Egypt. Eaton handled that problem perfectly.

"I replied [said Eaton] that an object of distress could not be an object of resentment to an exalted mind; and it was more like God to pardon than to punish a repenting enemy."[214]

The Viceroy nodded his assent. Not only that, he sent couriers in search of Hamet and provided a letter of amnesty for Hamet serving with the Mamelukes and giving him permission to leave the country. Over the next few weeks there were multiple episodes of doubt concerning the effectiveness of the Viceroy's documents of amnesty and passports of egress and safe conduct from Egypt. One of the things that caused the most trouble was a rumor started by the French Consul in Alexandria, a Mr. Drouette,[215] who insinuated that the Americans were really British spies whose actual intentions were to aid the Mamelukes in their rebellion against the Turkish government. Again and again Eaton and his entourage were forced to either pay bribes or diplomatically convince the Turkish authorities, primarily the generals and governors of the area, that they were legitimate. Eaton even communicated his difficulties with the Viceroy. The Viceroy promptly fined one of the governors who was giving Eaton difficulty several thousand piasters[216] for not honoring the documents he had personally signed. Eaton was finally able to meet up with Hamet Karamanli on Sunday, March 3, 1805.

Hamet had come to the conclusion sometime before to march by land through the Libyan Desert to Derna and Ben Ghazi.[217] He did this for three main reasons and Eaton concurred. The first of these was the party consisted of approximately 500 men, 100 of who were Christians recruited on the spot, and not all of them could board the *Argus* for transport. Secondly, if Hamet took a ship and separated himself from his Arab army they would likely lose patience and confidence

---

214 ibid. page 283
215 ibid. page 286
216 ibid. page 292
217 also spelled Benghazi

and abandon the cause. And finally, by marching through the desert they could likely avoid Turkish checkpoints and thus reduce the hazard of arrest which they had already experienced to some extent, the problems being solved by diplomacy and bribes.

Therefore the plan was to rendezvous with Isaac Hull in the *Argus* whose crew would supply them with arms and ammunition including two artillery field pieces. Eaton, being the experienced diplomat that he was, negotiated a treaty with Hamet outlining in detail what was expected of both parties. He intuitively understood the second of the 10 Commandments of Muslim diplomacy (see Chapter 11). The treaty, labeled Convention, is reproduced from Eaton's Journal:

CONVENTION[218]

Between the United States of America, and His Highness, Hamet Caramanly,[219] Bashaw of Tripoli.

God is Infinite

ARTICLE I. There shall be a firm and perpetual peace, and free intercourse between the government of the United States of America and His Highness Hamet Caramanly, Bashaw, the legitimate sovereign of the kingdom of Tripoli, and between the citizens of one, and the subjects of the other.

ARTICLE II. The government of the United States shall use their utmost exertions, so far as comports with their own honor, and interest, their subsisting treaties, and the acknowledged law of all nations, to reestablish the said Hamet Bashaw, in the possession of his sovereignty of Tripoli, against the pretensions of Joseph Bashaw, who obtained said

---

218 ibid. page 297-300 also available on line from Yale's Law school library: Originals Huntington Library Microfilm, San Marino, CA. http://avalon.law.yale.edu/19th_century/bar1805c.asp

219 There are several different ways to spell Karamanli and the recorder of the treaty chose a different one of them.

sovereignty by treason, and who now holds it by usurpation. And who is engaged in actual war against the United states.

ARTICLE III. The United States shall, as circumstances may require in addition to the operations they are carrying on by sea, furnished to Hamet Bashaw, on loan, supplies of cash, ammunition and provisions; and, if necessity require, debarkations of troops also, to aid and give effect to the operations of said Hamet Bashaw, by land, against the common enemy.

ARTICLE IV. In consideration of which friendly offices, once rendered effectual, His Highness, Hamet Caramanly, Bashaw, engages on his part, to release to the Commander-in-Chief of the forces of the United States in the Mediterranean without ransom all American prisoners who are, or may hereafter be, in the hands of the usurper, Joseph Bashaw.

ARTICLE V. In order to indemnify the estate and all expense they have or shall incur in carrying into execution their engagements expressed in the second and third article[s] of this convention the said Hamet Bashaw transfers, and consigns, to the United States the tribute stipulated by the last treaties, of his Majesty the King of Denmark, his Majesty the King of Sweden, and the Batavian Republic, as the condition of peace with the Regency of Tripoli, until such time as said expense shall be reimbursed.

ARTICLE VI. In order to carry into full effect the stipulation expressed in the previous article, said Hamet Bashaw, pledges his faith and honor, faithfully to observe, and fulfill the treaties now existing between the Regency of Tripoli and their Majesties the Kings of Denmark and Sweden, and the Batavian Republic.

ARTICLE VII. In consideration of the friendly dispositions of his Majesty the King the two Sicilies towards the American squadrons, his Highness Hamet Bashaw, invites his said Sicilian Majesty to review their ancient friendship: and proffers him a peace on the footing that to be definitively concluded with the United States of America, in the fullest extension of its privileges, according to the tenor of this convention.

ARTICLE VIII. The better to give effect to the operations to be carried on by land, in the prosecution of the plan, and the attainment of the object pointed out by this convention, William Eaton, a citizen of the United

States, now in Egypt, shall be recognized as General and Commander-in-Chief of the land forces, which are, or may be, called into service against the common enemy, and his said Highness, Hamet Bashaw, engages that his own Subjects shall respect, and obey him as such.

ARTICLE IX. His Highness, said Hamet Bashaw, grants full amnesty, and perpetual oblivion towards the conduct of all such of his subjects as may have been seduced by the Usurper, to abandon his cause, and who are disposed, to return to their proper allegiance.

ARTICLE X. In the case of future war between the contracting parties, captives on each side should be treated as prisoners of war, and not as slaves, and shall be entitled to reciprocal and equal exchange, man for man, and grade for grade, and in no case shall ransom the demanded prisoners of war, nor tribute required as the condition of peace, neither on the one part nor the other. All prisoners on both sides shall be given up at the conclusion of peace.

ARTICLE XI. The American Consular Flag in Tripoli should forever be a sacred asylum to all persons who shall desire to take refuge under it, except for the crimes of treason and murder.

ARTICLE XII. In the case of faithful observance and fulfillment on the part of his Highness, said Hamet Bashaw, of the agreements and obligations herein, the said Commander-in-Chief of the American forces in the Mediterranean, engages to leave said Hamet Bashaw, in the peaceable possession of the city and Regency of Tripoli, without dismantling its batteries.

ARTICLE XIII. Any article suitable to be introduced in a definitive treaty of peace between the contracting parties, which may not be compromised in this convention, shall be reciprocally on the footing of the treaties subsisting with the most favored nations.

ARTICLE XIV. This convention shall be submitted to the President of the United States for his ratification: in the meantime there shall be no suspense in its operations.

Done at Alexandria in Egypt, February 23, 1805, and signed by said Hamet Bashaw, for himself and successors, and by William Eaton, on the part of the United States.

[Signature of] WILLIAM EATON
[Signature in Arabic and Seal of] Hamet Bashaw

In the presence of [Some days later]

P. N. O'Bannon, Lieut. of Marines
Dr. Francisco Mendrici.
Pascal Paoli Peck.[220]

Eaton then added an additional article labeled secret (in case friends of Yusuf saw it) which encouraged Hamet to use his utmost abilities to turn over Yusuf and his admiral, Maurad Raiz,[221] alias Peter Lisle, to be held as hostages by the United States to assure the stipulations of the above treaty. This secret article was also signed by both Eaton and Hamet, and witnessed by the same trio of individuals as the original convention. It's interesting to note that the alias of Maurad Raiz or Reiz was:

"[A] renegade Scot named Peter Lisle. Lisle had been a sailor on the similarly named Betsey[222] when the Moroccans captured it in 1785. When the United States ransomed the crew of the Betsey, Lisle stayed behind and converted to Islam, taking the name Murad [or Maurad] Reis [or Raiz].

Lisle traveled to Tripoli, and by virtue of his nautical skills and marriage to the Bashaw's daughter, he rose to command of the Tripolitan navy."[223]

Now well into the new year 1805, Eaton had put up with several setbacks. On March 2 the Pasha's provisions aboard a Nile boat were seized by Turkish authorities and everyone, with the exception of the American officers, was prohibited from leaving the boat. Several of

---

220 *Peck was another Navy midshipman besides Danielson.*
221 *Also spelled Reiz but spelled Daiz in Yale's version.*
222 *ibid. As opposed to the Betsy (with one e) which was captured in 1796.*
223 *King, Maj. David M. Master's Thesis, US Army Command and General Staff College, FT. Leavenworth, 1994*

his servants who had already left with some baggage were arrested and put in prison. When Turkish guards and patrols advanced on the Pasha's camp they were stopped by the fiddle playing Marine,[224] Lieutenant Presley O'Bannon. The whole affair had been instituted by the Turkish supervisor of revenue who had not yet been bribed.[225] Eaton indicated in his journal that the day was spent in arranging to bribe the Turkish supervisor with the help of the British Consul, Mr. Briggs.

Just prior to that episode, several days' delay occurred because of apparent embezzlement or mismanagement of Eaton's expedition funds by Richard Farquhar. Eaton promptly fired Farquhar and assumed the responsibility himself. There were several other glitches involving the settling of accounts owed but finally on March 8, 1805, the expedition got underway. It included nine Americans: Lieutenant Presley O'Bannon, USMC, Passed[226] Midshipman Pascal Peck, Cadet Midshipman George Washington Mann, and six Marine privates. Eaton sent his son-in-law, (or nephew, or stepson depending on which authority you read) Midshipman Danielson, back aboard the *Argus*.[227]

Eaton's journal indicated that the expedition included 25 artillery men commanded by French Lieutenants: Connant and Roco (or Rocco or Roc) and Selim Comb, previously mentioned as Eaton's interpreter but who also acted as his bodyguard. Author Richard Zacks, using the microfilm of Eaton's papers from the Huntington Library, San Marino, California, indicated that French Consular records named a person called Roc, who had aided two criminals in escaping from the French Consulate in Alexandria, circa March 1, 1805.[228]

Also included in the expedition were 38 Greek soldiers and about 90 Arab mercenaries recruited by the Pasha himself. In addition there

---

224 Zacks, Richard, *The Pirate Coast*, book's dust cover, Hyperion, New York, 2005.

225 *The Life of the Late Gen. William Eaton Principally Collected from his Correspondence and Other Manuscripts.* The New York Public Library 287176, Ebenezer Miriam and Company, 1813 page 301.

226 *There were two midshipman ranks. A passed midshipman was one step above a cadet midshipman and was considered a commissioned officer.*

227 Zacks, Richard, *The Pirate Coast* page 167

228 ibid. page 171

was some Arab cavalry under the orders of two Arab Sheiks, al Taiib and Mahamat. The caravan consisted of 107 camels, (Sheik al Taiib was supposed to supply 190 camels)[229] some of which were cavalry, and a few jackasses, and about 400 personnel in the expedition plus the usual camp followers including some wives and prostitutes. They marched about 15 miles the first day.

* * *

---

229 ibid. page 173.

CHAPTER SIX

April 16, 1805

"Changing one's mind is more often a sign of prudence than of ignorance." - Spanish Proverb

The March through the Libyan Desert was filled with much adventure which included mutiny, rebellions, desertions, thievery, political intrigue, and avarice. The facts are described in detail not only by Eaton's journal and papers but by competent authors such as Richard Zacks,[230] so we will not repeat them here. Suffice it to say that the diplomatic skills of William Eaton, the military attitude and confidence of Lieutenant Presley O'Bannon, the leadership ability of the Pasha in exile, Hamet Karamanli, and the resolve of all of these people were sufficient to put down the rebellions and mutinies, solve the other problems, and arrive at their destination, Bomba. There they met up with the *Argus* and Captain Hull on April 16, and the next day with the *USS Hornet* under the command of Lieutenant Samuel Evans. At the point of exhaustion after a desert march of some 400 miles (Eaton estimated 600) and with their supplies dwindled to almost nothing, the reinforcements showed up just in time.

Later, Midshipman Pascal Peck reflecting on his journey through the Libyan Desert had this to say in a letter dated from Malta, July 4, 1805:

"When I think on our situation in the Desert, where no other christian ever sat his foot, and consider what thieves the Arabs are, who would

---

230 Zacks, Richard, *The Pirate Coast*

shoot a man for the buttons on his coat, and their religious prejudices, which would have been sufficient to warrant our deaths, as christians and enemies to their religion, I frequently wonder how it was possible for us to succeed in reaching Bomba. Certainly it was one of the most extraordinary expeditions ever sat on foot. We were very frequently 24 hours without water, and once 47 hours without a drop. Our horses were sometimes three days without, and for the last 20 days had nothing to eat except what they picked out of the sand. The country was a melancholy desert throughout, and for the space of 450 miles we saw neither house nor tree, nor hardly anything green, and, except in one place, not a trace of a human being."[231]

On April 23, 1805 Eaton and his caravan broke camp and marched about 10 miles over rocky and mountainous terrain for Derna, their target for the start of the rebellion to depose Yusuf Karamanli. The next day they marched an additional 15 miles, by which time they were just five hours away from Derna. Still having trouble with the mutinous Arabs on the 24th and 25th, Eaton continued to approach closer to Derna and finally on the 26th from a point of high ground he was able to spot the *USS Nautilus* under the command of Lieutenant Dent. The *Nautilus* was one of the three gun boats that would help with artillery support from the sea during the land assault on Derna. The next day the other two vessels, the *Argus* and the *Hornet* also appeared at about five in the morning.

What happened next is best explained by the report from Master Commandant Isaac Hull to the squadron commander, Commodore Samuel Barron:[232]

---

231 Navy Department Library: http://www.history.navy.mil/library/online/barbary_derna.htm

232 Naval History & Heritage Command:http://www.history.navy.mil/library/online/barbary_derna.htm

"UNITED STATES BRIG Argus
DERNE 28th April 1805

"Sir, I have the honor to inform you, that at 9 O'clock in the morning of the 27th being about 10 Miles to the Eastward of the Town of Derne, with the Hornet in Company, we discovered the Nautilus at Anchor very close to the shore, which led us to suppose that Captain Dent had fallen in with Mr. Eaton's Army, as he had been sent in shore for that purpose the day before. We made all sail for the Nautilus, and at 3 past 10 spoke [to] her, and was informed by Capt. Dent that he had had communication with Mr. Eaton the night before, and that he wished to have the field Pieces landed as soon as possible, and that Mr. Eaton intended to make an attack upon Derne as soon as he could get possession of them, being then about two and a half miles from the Town, and the Enemy having sent him a challenge, hoisted out our boat to send the field pieces on shore with such supplies as Mr. Eaton was in want of, but on approaching the shore we found that it was impossible to land the guns without hauling them up an almost perpendicular rock twenty feet above the boat. But with the perseverance of the officer and men sent on this service, they affected the landing [of] one of them, by hauling them up the steep rock. Mr. Eaton, finding that we should loose time in landing the other, sent it off again informing me that he should march for the town as soon as he could possibly mount the field piece that he had on shore. [I] gave Lieutenant Evans orders to stand close in shore, and cover the Army while they were preparing to march, in case the enemy should come out against them, as they had already made their appearance in large numbers outside of the town, gave orders for the necessary preparations to be made for the attack by sea upon the town and batteries, and stood down very close to the town. - At 2 P. M. Mr. Eaton began the attack by land, at [the] same time the Hornet [commanded by] Lieut. Evans anchored with springs on his cables, within one hundred yards of the battery of eight guns, and commenced a heavy fire upon it.

"The Nautilus took her station to the Eastward of the Hornet, at ½ a miles distance from shore, and opened upon the town & battery. The Argus anchored without, and a little to the Eastward of the Nautilus, and began firing on the town and battery - The fort kept up a heavy fire for about an hour, after which the shot [was] flying so thick about them, they abandoned it, and run into the town and gardens back - The guns of the vessels were turned on the beach, and kept a heavy fire upon the enemy to clear the way for the few brave Christians Mr. Eaton had with him, to enter the fort as they were gaining ground very fast though a heavy fire of musquetry[sic] was constantly kept upon them from behind the houses and old walls near the shore. At about a half past 3 we had the satisfaction to see Lieut. O'Bannon, and Mr. Mann, Midshipman of the Argus, with a few brave fellows with them, enter the fort, had down the enemy's flag, and planted] the American Ensign on the walls of the battery, and on turning the guns of the battery upon the town, they found that the enemy had left them in great haste, as they were found primed and loaded at their hand. -

"Whilst our men were turning the guns of the battery upon the town, Hamet Bashaw had taken possession of the back part of it, which brought the enemy between two fires, which soon silenced them, and about four in the afternoon we had complete possession of the town and fort, sent all our boats on shore, for the purpose of carrying ammunition to the fort, and to bring off the wounded men, as soon as possible, that they might be dressed. – Mr. Eaton gave the necessary orders at the fort, and went into the town to see everything quiet, and to make arrangements for the town's being well guarded during the night. At a half past five, he returned on board to get his wound dressed, having received a musquet [sic] ball through his left wrist. "On collecting our men we found one killed and thirteen wounded a list of which I have the honor to send you.

[Signed] "ISAAC HULL"

"Killed:
John Wilton, a Marine

Wounded:
William Eaton, Esq.
David Thomas, a Marine

Bernard O'Brian [also a Marine][233]
George Emanual (Greek)
Spedo Levedo
Bernardo Jamace
Nicolo George
Capt. Lucca
Names unknown 3
Angelo Fermoso Maltee
John Wilton, a Marine"

    Isaac Hull dispatched his report to the Commodore via the *USS Hornet* to Malta, along with Eaton's description of the victory as well. The *Hornet* ran into high winds which limited their progress and they returned to Derna's port the next day. The delay apparently gave Eaton a chance to elaborate on his first report. Author Zacks suggests that perhaps Eaton was either into the sauce or was affected by his wound when he wrote the additional letter to Commodore Samuel Barron because Eaton tended to criticize the Commodore's hints that limits should be placed on the American support of Hamet Karamanli. He even predicted quite accurately that Yusuf would propose peace in order to rid himself of his brother as a rival.[234] Eaton of course knew that Yusuf and his army from Tripoli were on the way and that a confrontation was likely.

    What he didn't know was that his diplomatic rival, Consul General Tobias Lear, in collusion with the very ill Samuel Barron, had conspired to discourage Eaton from carrying out his mission. Sam Barron actually told Eaton that the Navy would no longer supply Hamet with any essentials and informed him that Lear was already headed for Tripoli to engage in peace negotiations.[235]

    One source[236] indicates that the first elements of Yusuf's army led by Hassan Aga, appeared outside the city of Derna the day after Eaton's attack of April 27. Actual contact with Eaton's defenders didn't

---

233 Zacks, Richard, *The Pirate Coast* page 234.
234 ibid. page 235.
235 ibid. page 246.
236 http://barbarywars.wordpress.com/timeline/

occur until May 12, according to Eaton's journal or on May 13, according to another source.[237]

On May 18, 1805, more of Yusuf's forces appeared and gave battle to Eaton's defenders. Over the next few days skirmishes took a gradual toll on Eaton's forces so that by May 29th Eaton felt they were in a desperate position. Although Eaton was unaware of it, Sam Barron had resigned as Commodore of the Mediterranean Fleet on May 22, 1805, and turned over the command to John Rodgers. On May 29, Lear sent his ultimatum to Yusuf, and by June 4 it was all over with the American flag raised over the consulate in Tripoli.

The battle for Derna was a decisive victory by "General" Eaton and undoubtedly put enough pressure on Yusuf Karamanli that he agreed to a peace ultimatum issued by General Consul Tobias Lear. However, Eaton had been left out of the agreement process and always felt it was an unethical settlement since it left Yusuf in charge as the Pasha of Tripoli and ignored the promises that had been made to Hamet. The controversy exists to this day as you will see.

Eaton gave several reasons why continuing his military campaign to completion and restoring Hamet to the throne of Tripoli would have resulted in a more successful and peaceful situation.[238]

1. The decisive victory that Eaton could have achieved would have persuaded the other Barbary States to moderate their demands on the United States.
2. At just a fraction of the $60,000 paid to Yusuf in the peace settlement arranged by Tobias Lear, Eaton could have easily paid for the expenses necessary to march his army to Tripoli.
3. He could have easily captured Tripoli with the assistance of Navy bombardments, reinforcement by the Marines, and established a government more friendly to the United States.
4. The United States could actually have saved money because Hamet had promised to reimburse the U.S. for expenses incurred.
5. Eaton felt that the peace treaty Lear had negotiated ac-

---

237 barbarywars.wordpress.com/timeline.
238 King, Maj. David M. Master's Thesis, US Army Command and General Staff College, FT. Leavenworth, 1994, chap 6.

tually compromised America's reputation and honor and showed our country to be unreliable allies with no resolve for victory.

Major David King in his Masters' thesis gave these reasons why allowing Eaton to complete his mission to restore Hamet as the Pasha of Tripoli was unlikely to succeed:[239]

1. Captain Rodgers, as second-in-command, succeeded the command of the Mediterranean Squadron when Commodore Samuel Barron became deathly ill. If Eaton were allowed to continue his campaign to restore Hamet, Rodgers would have been forced to detach several vessels and supply ships to support the campaign. This would have had to happen in the face of a continuing threat from the Bey of Tunis who was threatening to seize American ships blockading Tripoli. Thus bad things were likely to happen either to Eaton's campaign or to the blockade of Tripoli.
2. Rodgers would have to still face the shore batteries in Tripoli that Preble had faced the previous fall, and Yusuf had added two or three batteries to the north and western parts of the town. In addition, Tripoli's artillerymen had been practicing with the help of a renegade captured crewman from the *USS Philadelphia* and were using heated shot, which had the potential for significant damage (starting fires) with any kind of direct hit.
3. The question remained whether or not Eaton could overcome the hazards of an additional forced march another 750 miles or so to Tripoli. Granted that some of Rodger's ships could carry most of the troops, but Hamet would have had to leave behind about three-fourths of his army, the camels, and artillery. Eaton had to suppress at least six mutinies on his first forced march. It was unlikely he could put up with another six or more on an even longer march.
4. Any glitches in an amphibious landing on a hostile shore, should it be elected, were certain to spell disaster.

---

239 ibid.

5. And finally, considering the time it took him to get from Alexandria to Derna he would run out of time on the longer march to Tripoli before the fall bad weather for naval operations was upon them.

The controversy of Tobias Lear's negotiated peace versus Eaton's desire to restore Hamet to Tripoli's throne still exists, and caused a rift between President Jefferson, Eaton, and the U.S. Senate which passed a resolution condemning Lear's peace treaty. I believe the whole situation is best summed up by Major King's thesis in his Abstract:[240]

"In 1801, Yusef Caramanli, ruler of Tripoli, declared war on the United States. Yusef expected the United States to agree to pay tribute in exchange for protection from Tripolitan corsairs. Instead, President Thomas Jefferson sent the Navy [and] four years later the war continued. When a former consul to Tunis named William Eaton proposed using Yusef's brother Hamet in a campaign against Tripoli, Jefferson agreed to let him try. Eaton sought out Hamet in the Egyptian desert and assembled a mixed army of U.S. Marines, mercenaries, and Arabs. Eaton and his army then marched 500 miles across [a] North African [Desert] to the Tripolitan town of Derne. With assistance from the Navy, Eaton captured Derne in America's first joint and combined military operation since the Revolutionary War.

Alarmed by the fall of Derne, Yusef quickly agreed to a peace settlement in which the U.S. paid Yusef $60,000. Eaton protested that if the U.S. negotiator had not agreed to such shameful terms, Eaton could have captured Tripoli and enforced a more favorable peace. An examination of the evidence shows that Eaton's chances of success were poor and that the U.S. negotiator was correct in ending the war."

In the aftermath, the casualty cost for the battle of Derna to Eaton's forces was a total of 14 dead and several wounded which extended beyond the casualties first reported by Isaac Hull. Of the American Marines, two were KIA[241] and two additional WIA. Eaton himself sustained a wound to his left wrist which left him with a permanent disability in the use of his left arm and hand. Both Eaton and Lieutenant O'Bannon returned to the states as national heroes. O'Bannon and

---
240 *ibid. King, Abstract p-iii.*
241 *KIA =killed in action, WIA =wounded in action.*

his Marines were immortalized in the Marine hymn and Lieutenant O'Bannon himself was given a sword by Hamet in a design similar to that of the Mameluke's scimitar. Later the state of Virginia awarded O'Bannon another sword of similar design which Marine officers to this day carry as part of their dress uniforms.[242]

After all the hoopla surrounding Eaton's and the U.S. Marines' achievement in the Tripoli port of Derna, the controversy in Congress concerning the peace agreement exploded, led by the majority party Federalists. One of the first things discovered was a secret article in the peace treaty that allowed Yusuf Karamanli to detain his brother Hamet and his family as virtual prisoners for a period of two and a half years. Tobias Lear was the one responsible for the secret article. He was the same individual, once personal secretary to President George Washington, who had embezzled funds from Washington.[243] He also had stolen and suppressed Washington's papers, including his diary and at least six important letters that might have changed the perception of history about Washington and Jefferson.[244] Author Zacks notes that this failed businessman was a proven liar who was protected by Jefferson and had headed the extremely sensitive peace negotiations with Tripoli.

After Congress had condemned Tobias Lear's peace agreement with Tripoli, the next episode that would lead Eaton to national prominence would be at Aaron Burr's trial for treason.

* * *

---

[242] Hickman, Kennedy, First Barbary War, Battle of Derne, Internet source, http://militaryhistory.about.com/od/battleswars1800s/p/derne.htm
[243] Zacks, Richard, The Pirate Coast page 217.
[244] ibid. page 218

CHAPTER SEVEN

February 19, 1807

"More men are guilty of treason through weakness than any studied design to betray." François de la Rochefoucauld[245]

The truth of the epigraph quoted above does not apply in this case to Aaron Burr, the former vice president who was arrested for treason in the state of Alabama on February 19, 1807. In fact the opposite of the epigraph meaning is more likely the case for Mr. Burr. Let me give you some background.

When the presidential election of 1800 was held there was a tie between Aaron Burr and Thomas Jefferson. In a book review for the February 13, 2000 *New York Times*, Jean Edward Smith, a professor of political science at John Marshall University, citing either author Thomas Fleming or Roger G. Kennedy, stated that Burr did nothing to encourage his supporters nor did he seek the Presidency. However, multiple sources would disagree.[246]

Whether or not Professor Smith is correct, Jefferson didn't believe it and never quite forgave Aaron Burr for trying to win the top spot when the election was transferred to the House of Representatives to break the tie. As a result, when Burr became involved in a duel with former Secretary of the Treasury Alexander Hamilton, and wound up

---

245 http://thinkexist.com/search/searchquotation.asp?search=treason
246 A) Smithsonian.com;
B) http://history1800s.about.com/od/leaders/a/electionof1800.htm;
C) historynow.com

killing him, it was the perfect excuse to drop Burr from the presidential ticket. Here is how the animosity between the two dueling prominent politicians came about.

First of all, it was no secret among the pundits of Washington D.C. at that time that Aaron Burr was no longer in favor in the Democratic Republican party as a repeat vice presidential nominee. So Burr, knowing that he was going to lose his job as VP, elected to run for governor of New York. This so exasperated Alexander Hamilton, a staunch Federalist that he felt he could not hold back public criticism of Aaron Burr. One of the main points that irritated Hamilton was that his father-in-law, Phillip Schuyler, had lost his Senate seat to Aaron Burr back in 1791. Another point was that Hamilton thought that Burr was an unethical and dangerous politician. Burr was also a longtime political enemy of Hamilton's. Hamilton had publicly opposed Burr during the House of Representatives' multiple votes to break the Electoral College's tie vote for President of the United States when Aaron Burr and Thomas Jefferson were initially tied in the election of 1800.

Hamilton had also voiced his opposition to Burr in the New York gubernatorial race of 1804 and was likely responsible for Burr's loss in that election to Morgan Lewis who was also a Democratic Republican. Burr was running as an independent for the New York governor's job. It is interesting to note that Burr was a theological graduate of the College of New Jersey, where Burr's father, the Reverend Aaron Burr, had been president, and which later became Princeton University. Burr also studied law and although one source [247] claimed he practiced in New York with Alexander Hamilton in 1883, that claim could not be documented. If true, perhaps such close an association would give both men the chance to evaluate each other's politics and ethics. Hamilton was a long time Federalist who believed in big government while Burr was a Democratic Republican, much more conservative. He opposed big government and was an advocate for states' rights. The animosity between the two was years in the making and long-standing.

---

247 http://www.ushistory.org/valleyforge/served/burr.html

David O. Stewart, author of *American Emperor: Aaron Burr's challenge to Jefferson's America*, writing for the *Constitution Daily*,[248] noted that in the decade prior to the duel Hamilton had repeatedly disparaged Burr calling him unprincipled and in effect a little Caesar. But the words he issued just before the 1804 duel and which Hamilton would not retract included the word despicable, which in those days implied personal perversions. Stewart noted that twice before Hamilton had previously withdrawn insulting words that referred to Burr's character. This time there was no retraction so Burr issued the challenge. Stewart also noted that both men had been involved with duels before although Hamilton had never fired a shot directly at his opponent. Burr on the other hand had fought a duel in which both he and his opponent luckily missed each other but the honor was satisfied by the shots fired.

To be fair, several sources including Stewart indicate that Burr never said anything in public to disparage or insult Hamilton in spite of all the verbal attacks the former Secretary of the Treasury had made. Most historians feel that Hamilton was respected by Burr even though the former Secretary was his political opposite. He challenged Hamilton to a duel to defend his own honor.

There is a wealth of descriptions of the Aaron Burr/Alexander Hamilton duel that occurred on July 11, 1804. Descriptions of the event by the seconds of both men varied of course as to who had fired first so that detail is still in dispute although most historians think that Hamilton fired the first shot. They also say that is likely because the smooth bore dueling pistols had hair triggers which Hamilton, with less firearms experience, could easily have caused him to accidentally release his first shot. Anyway all observers agreed that only two shots were fired. Hamilton's shot missed his target and Burr's struck Hamilton in the right upper quadrant of his abdomen, apparently ricocheted off one of his lower right ribs and embedded itself in the upper lumbar or lower thoracic spine. The bullet also likely penetrated both liver and

---

248 http://blog.constitutioncenter.org/2014/07/when-political-arguments-were-murderous/.

lung, causing massive hemorrhage and probably a pneumothorax, causing the right lung to collapse.

From the attending physician's description there was undoubtedly nerve damage in the spinal cord affecting both of Hamilton's lower extremities since he lost all feeling below the waist. That would likely place the vertebral penetration at the T10 level where the spinal cord controls sensation below the umbilicus (belly button). It was a mortal wound and Hamilton knew it and told the attending physician that it was such. He died shortly thereafter. Speculation still exists as to whether or not Hamilton intended to miss his first shot as he stated he might do.

As author Stewart indicates, both men lost in the fight; Hamilton his life, and Burr his future.

Burr-Hamilton Duel- Photo credit: Wikipedia

Now just over two and a half years later on February 19, 1807, Burr having been acquitted of two charges of murder because of the duel, one charge filed in New Jersey (the duel was fought at Weehawken, New Jersey), and one in New York, was now faced with another criminal charge; that of treason. Here's how that came about:

General James Wilkinson and Aaron Burr had fought in the Revolutionary War together in the Québec campaign of 1775-76. The two had corresponded over the years by way of a cipher invented by Wilkinson. During a series of ciphered conversations that occurred after Burr lost his job as vice president, there is evidence of a conspiracy suggested by the coded letters.[249] From Eaton's papers compiled by a friend, Charles Prentiss, and published in 1813 two years after Eaton's death, is this quote:

"At the next session of Congress, 1806-7, Gen. Eaton returned to the seat of government, principally for the purpose of adjusting his accounts. The conspiracy of Aaron Burr [by then a public scandal] had excited great attention and considerable alarm throughout the union. Wilkinson, [who was then the Commanding General of the US Army] who, from the best testimony appears to have originally been concerned [i.e. involved] with Aaron Burr, but had found it safe and prudent to deny the connection, and become an outrageous patriot, had arrested several persons in the territory of Orleans, denying them the privilege of habeas corpus,[250] and had ordered them transported by water to the District of Columbia."[251]

According to the Eaton Journal, Wilkinson's prisoners arrived in the District of Columbia in January 1807. It also indicated that President Jefferson had been made aware of Burr's treachery several months before by Eaton, but had not entirely accepted it as truth since he was still at odds with Eaton about the Tripoli settlement. When Jefferson also heard of the plot from the Army's Commanding Officer, he instructed Justice Marshall, through the District Attorney of the District of Columbia, to transfer the prisoners arrested by Wilkinson from the hands of the military to civil authorities. Marshall, the die-hard Federalist, followed the letter of the law. Since there were no charges filed, he insisted that the testimony or deposition of William

---

249 Lindner, Doug, the Treason Trial of Aaron Burr, University of Missouri at Kansas City, 2001. Available online: http://law2.umkc.edu/faculty/projects/ftrials/burr/burraccount.html

250 Habeas corpus is a legal term meaning the right to appear before a judge or the right to obtain a writ against illegal detention or imprisonment.-Random House Webster's College dictionary

251 The Life of the Late Gen. William Eaton Principally Collected from his Correspondence and Other Manuscripts. The New York Public Library 287176, Ebenezer Miriam and Company. Page 396. Also available on the internet: http://books.google.com/books?id=4aIDAAAAYAAJ&pg=PR1&dq=how+did+wm+eaton+get+to+Cairo+in+1804%3F&source=gbs_selected_pages&cad=2#v=onepage&q=how%20did%20wm%20eaton%20get%20to%20Cairo%20in%201804%3F&f=false

Eaton was needed and demanded that such be taken forthwith. That testimony taken from Eaton's Journal is presented below:

"Early last winter, [1805] Col. Aaron Burr, late Vice President of the United States, signified to me, at this place [Washington, D.C.] under the authority of the general government, he was organizing a secret expedition against the Spanish provinces on our southwestern borders; which expedition he was to lead and in which he was authorized to invite me to take the command of a division. I had never before been made personally acquainted with Col. Burr; and, having for many years been employed in foreign service, knew little about the estimation this gentleman now held in the opinion of his countrymen and his government: the rank and confidence by which he had so recently been distinguished, left me no right to suspect his patriotism. I knew him [as] a soldier. In case of war against the Spanish nation, which from the tenor of the President's message to both houses of Congress seemed probable, I should have thought it my duty to obey such an honorable call of my country; and in that impression, I did agree to embark in the expedition. I had frequent interviews with Col. Burr in this city,- and for considerable time his object seemed to be to instruct me by maps, and other information, in the feasibility of penetrating to Mexico,-always carrying forward the idea that the measure was authorized by the government. At length, sometime in February, he began by degrees to unveil himself. He reproached the government for want of character, want of gratitude, and want of justice"[252]

Eaton went on to describe how Burr tried to elicit his (Eaton's) sympathy by referring to the resentment he must have felt after having experienced the government's duplicity in settling for a less than honorable peace treaty with Tripoli, and the delay in reimbursing Eaton for his debts encountered in the adventure with Tripoli, and the rescue of Countess Maria Anne Porcile, the teenager held hostage for the Tunisian prime minister's harem in 1803. At this point Eaton began to suspect that the expedition may not have been authorized by the U.S. government after all. He needed more information though,

---

252 ibid. pages 396-7.

to confirm his suspicions, and the more they talked the more Burr opened up.

In his deposition Eaton outlined what Burr had proposed. According to Eaton's testimony, Burr wanted to revolutionize the western territories and establish a monarchy for which he (Burr) would be the sovereign. He wanted New Orleans to be his capital and planned to organize a force on the Mississippi and extend the conquest to Mexico. Eaton pointed out a number of problems to Burr that might impede his ambitions. First of all there was a general feeling of affection toward the current government and secondly a lack of funds available for what he wanted to accomplish.

In addition, Eaton pointed out the resistance Burr was likely to meet in the presence of the U.S. Army on the frontier as well as difficulty if Miranda *"was able to Republicanize Mexico."*[253] Francisco de Miranda was a Venezuelan who traveled across the United States and Mexico as well as Europe to gain support for the independence of his native country and other Spanish colonies in the Western Hemisphere, which of course included Mexico. Miranda had dined at the White House in 1805[254] as a guest of President Jefferson's.

Eaton further testified on Burr's response to Eaton's objections. The testimony probably would not be allowed or permitted in todays' courts if the defense objected on the grounds of hearsay. Here is what Burr is believed to have said:

- He (Burr) had personal contacts in the territories of Kentucky, Louisiana and Tennessee who had unlimited resources for funds.
- He assured Eaton that the U.S. Army would act with him and that it could be reinforced by as many as 10,000 or 12,000 men from the above territories.
- He said he had powerful agents in the Spanish colonies.
- He stated *"We must hang Miranda."*

---

253 ibid. page 398

254 Internet source: a href="http://law.jrank.org/pages/2423/William-S-Smith-Samuel-G-Ogden-Trials-1806.html">*William S. Smith and Samuel G. Ogden Trials: 1806 - Miranda Dines At The White House, Rebel Vessel Sails From New York, President's Role At Issue*</a>

Burr then proposed to give Eaton second-in-command of his army. When Eaton inquired who was to be in first command, Burr had answered General Wilkinson, who was not only the highest ranking officer in the United States Army, but governor of the Northern Louisiana territory.

From Eaton's Journal:

"I asked Mr. Burr if he knew General Wilkinson. He answered yes: and [then] echoed the question. I said I know him well. 'What do you know of him?' said Mr. Burr. I know, I replied, that General Wilkinson will act as Lieutenant to no man in existence. 'You are in error,' said Mr. Burr, 'Wilkinson will act as Lieutenant to me.'"[255]

From the tenor of that conversation and others during the next couple of months it became clear to Eaton that there was indeed a conspiracy involving not only the previous Vice President of the United States but the Commanding Officer of the U.S. Army. One conversation in particular convinced Eaton that Burr not only was plotting to commit treason in the West but to actually overthrow the government of the United States itself:

"He said if he could get control over the Marine Corps, and secure the naval commanders, Truxton, Preble, Decatur and others, he would turn Congress neck and heels out-of-doors; assassinate the President; seize on the Treasury and the Navy; and declare himself the protector of an energetic government."[256]

Eaton now found himself in a dilemma. Burr for all intents and purposes had deposited the defeat of the plot into Eaton's hands, yet there was nothing in writing and as far as Eaton knew. Burr had not disclosed his plans to anyone else that would support Eaton's testimony on the subject. The only others who Eaton thought knew about the plot were General Wilkinson, Burr's son-in-law Joseph Allston, and Ephraim Kibbe, a former captain of Rangers in the Army. Kibbe was

---

255 ibid. page 398.
256 ibid. page 399.

also a Louisiana politician with influence. He would later become the first governor of the Louisiana Territory.

After much thought on the subject Eaton took it to the President. Jefferson however, was not as alarmed as maybe he should have been and declared to Eaton that he had too much confidence in the people and government of the territories in question to show any apprehension or alarm. At that point Eaton felt his silence was the better part of valor but took the precaution of giving the information to selected members of Congress. The yogurt did not hit the fan so to speak until Eaton broke his silence and began speaking publicly of the plot in October, 1806, and General Wilkinson apparently became aware that certain members of Congress were in possession of knowledge of the plot. Wilkinson then did what all conspirators do to protect their own interests. He turned on his partner in crime.

Wilkinson then started arresting some fall guys in the plot. That action brings us back to the reason for William Eaton's deposition and testimony, which then became a matter of public record and sworn in public court in Washington, D.C. on January 6, 1807. The inevitable result of Eaton's testimony was the trial for treason of Aaron Burr that occurred in the spring of 1807. It is arguably the most famous treason trial ever held. It included five of the most famous personalities of the day, President Thomas Jefferson, ex-Vice President Aaron Burr, Chief Justice of the United States John Marshall, Chief of Staff of the U.S. Army James Wilkinson, and the most recent hero of Tripoli, former State Department Consular, Naval agent and Army "General," William Eaton.

On Trial for Treason
Aaron Burr, 3rd Vice President of the United States
Photo Credit- Library of Congress

Chief Justice John Marshall The Presiding Judge

President Thomas Jefferson Advisor to the Prosecution

General James Wilkinson Unindicted Conspirator

Although William Eaton's testimony in deposition certainly gave prosecutors reason to indict General James Wilkinson in the plot, a grand jury voted 9 to 7 not to do so.[257] Wilkinson, a key

---

257 Linder, Doug, The Treason Trial of Aaron Burr, http://law2.umkc.edu/faculty/projects/ftrials/burr/burrtrial.html

grand jury witness against Burr, never actually testified in the trial, probably because early on the prosecutors knew his testimony would be impeached, and although the defense lawyers viciously attacked his grand jury testimony they could not issue a subpoena to Wilkinson after Justice Marshall ruled on August 31, that further witness testimony was to be excluded as requested by their own motion.

Marshall based his decision on the fact that the Constitution required a strict definition of treason[258] in that the accused had to be shown that he actually had levied war in the precise terms of the indictment, and the witnesses so far in the trial had not been able to establish proof of that.

President Jefferson, who really wanted Burr to be convicted, had also previously been subpoenaed to provide letters of communication with Wilkinson including the translation of the ciphered communications with Burr which Wilkinson himself had translated. Jefferson never did honor the subpoena, and now with Marshall's ruling he could not testify himself. Editor Hobson[259] indicated that Marshall's ruling effectively ended Aaron Burr's trial although it lasted another six weeks.

If the reader is interested in some fascinating testimony available online in which Eaton is cross-examined by Aaron Burr himself I refer you to *The Treason Trial of Aaron Burr* by Doug Linder, the manuscript of which is also available online. (See the footnote below).

Another key figure in the trial was Harman Blennerhassett, a not so famous but wealthy landowner whose plantation was on an island near Marietta, Ohio. Aaron Burr first met the gentleman in 1805 while exploring the Ohio River and was invited to dinner. Thereafter the two became friends and Blennerhassett wound up building boats and recruiting troops for Burr's expedition to Mexico. A key point in the trial was whether or not Burr was present on Blennerhassett's Island at any

---

258 Hobson, Charles, The Aaron Burr Treason Trial, available online; p-7
259 ibid.

time during the build-up of troops and supplies for the intended war.

Justice Marshall himself had this to say about that point:

"That this indictment, having charged the prisoner with levying war on Blennerhassett's Island, and containing no other overt act, cannot be supported by proof that war was levied at that place by other persons in the absence of the prisoner, even admitting those persons to be connected with him in one common treasonable conspiracy. 2dly. That admitting such an indictment could be supported by such evidence, the previous conviction of some person, who committed the act which is said to amount to levying war, is indispensable to the conviction of a person who advised or procured that act."[260]

So inevitably the die was cast. Aaron Burr was acquitted of the charge of treason and subsequently of a charge of preparing and providing a means for a military expedition against Spain. The end result was that Burr would never be an influential politician or citizen again. See the Epilogue for details of his ultimate fate.

* * *

---

[260] Linder, Doug, *The Treason Trial of Aaron Burr*, (Marshall's Opinion) http://law2.umkc.edu/faculty/projects/ftrials/burr/burrtrial.html

PART II

CHAPTER EIGHT

June 22, 1807

"I contend that the strongest of all governments is that which is most free."-William Henry Harrison

While the Burr trial was still under way and trade agreements and other areas of cooperation with the British were working to some extent, the problem of impressment of American sailors by the British Navy was still an active issue in 1807. On June 22 of that year the British warship *Leopard* attacked the American frigate *Chesapeake* off the coast of Norfolk, Virginia, in an attempt to recover three American merchant sailors who had escaped British impressment service and sought refuge aboard the frigate. The Americans; William Ware, Daniel Martin, and John Strachan were accompanied by a British deserter, Jenkins Ratford, who gave a false name upon enlistment in the American Navy.[261]

The four men, after escape from the British, had made their way to Portsmouth, Virginia, in order to enlist in the United States Navy where the *Chesapeake* was preparing to sail to the Mediterranean. In Portsmouth they were observed by British officers who recognized them and reported their enlistment in the U.S. Navy to their own British fleet commander stationed in Halifax, Nova Scotia. The result was a British demand for return of the sailors. When James Barron, the commodore of a new Mediterranean Squadron onboard his flag-

---

[261] Letter from Commodore James Barron to Vice Admiral Berkeley, commander of the British North American Station at Halifax, Mariner's Museum. Internet Source: http://www.marinersmuseum.org/sites/micro/usnavy/08/08b.htm

ship, the *USS Chesapeake*, found out that three of the *Chesapeake's* new sailors were actually escaped impressed Americans he refused to return them. Barron was not aware that Ratford was a British deserter since he had used a false name.

When British Vice Admiral George Cranfield Berkeley was made aware of Barron's refusal he ordered all ships of his fleet if they saw the *Chesapeake* on the high seas, to stop her and recover the deserters. Thus the attack by the *Leopard*, which was lying in wait and commanded by Captain Salisbury Humphreys, who at first hailed the *Chesapeake* to stop and then sent a boat over with the demand to return the escapees. When Barron refused, Humphreys fired seven broadsides at close range causing Barron to tell the ship's captain, Charles Gordon, to strike his colors after firing only one shot in return.[262] Not only that, three Americans were KIA and 18 wounded including Barron himself.[263] British sailors then boarded the crippled American ship, arrested the four sailors and sailed for Halifax. Barron and Captain Gordon took the *Chesapeake* and its demoralized and humbled crew with the ship in shambles and returned to Portsmouth/Norfolk where Barron was court-martialed and suspended from command for being unprepared for battle. Captain Gordon and a Marine Lieutenant were also reprimanded.

The public outrage at the incident was so intense that war was barely averted. President Thomas Jefferson banned all British warships from American ports and subsequently urged Congress to pass the Embargo Act of 1807 which devastated the American economy at the time. Simply stated the act prevented U.S. merchant ships from carrying goods of any kind to foreign ports and no foreign ships could carry American merchandise out of the country. What President Jefferson wanted was fair treatment from the warring parties of England, France, and Spain. What he got instead was a severe depression of the American economy and a near secession of some of the New England states of the union. In an attempt to enhance the embargo

---

262 Mariner's Museum, Newport News VA, https://www.marinersmuseum.org/sites/micro/usnavy/08/08b.htm

263 Hickman, Kennedy, War of 1812, available online: http://militaryhistory.about.com/od/shipprofiles/p/War-Of-1812-Uss-Chesapeake.htm

act in 1809 Jefferson urged Congress to pass the Force Act which allowed the federal government to seize any American vessel on just the suspicion that it might be headed for a foreign port. It was really an unusual stance for the conservative Jefferson and was much more like that of a Federalist leader. The outrage among merchants particularly those in New England, was such that Jefferson was forced to sign a repeal of the Embargo Act just before his second term ended in March 1809.[264] Author Richard Zacks in his excellent book *The Pirate Coast* noted that Jefferson had squandered seven years of popularity on an unproved economic theory and essentially labeled him an unconfessed pacifist.[265]

For the next three years, with President Madison now at the helm, the British continued to impress American merchant seamen into their Navy and made things worse by a series of economic sanctions on U.S. free trade particularly with France. The French were also being difficult with things not having really improved since the Quasi-War. In addition, Britain was encouraging Native Americans to resist expansion of the Western frontier, and that situation culminated in the Battle of Tippecanoe fought on the night of November 7-8, 1811.[266]

Although Thomas Jefferson had expanded the frontier by purchasing land from the Native Americans, treaties were not always honored by the frontiersman and new settlers often occupied Indian lands illegally. In 1808 Shawnee Indian Chief Tecumseh and his brother set about organizing the Native Americans by building an intertribal village north of Lafayette, Indiana. For the next three years Tecumseh traveled extensively meeting with other tribal leaders building up the intertribal alliance which has been labeled by historians as the Indian Confederacy. Tecumseh also warned his brother, a somewhat mystical and religious leader of the tribe, not to engage or start any fights with the settlers or American forces while he was gone on his travels.

In November, 1811, a U.S. Army expeditionary force under the command of Major General William Henry Harrison, who was also Governor of the Territory of Indiana, approached the intertribal vil-

---

264 Zacks, Richard, *The Pirate Coast*, pages 362-68.
265 ibid.
266 Encyclopedia Britannica, the Battle of Tippecanoe.

lage with the intent of encouraging a breakup of the Indian tribes living there by a show of force. Harrison had been given a great deal of latitude by President Madison who did not want an Indian war but had instructed Harrison to use defensive measures if necessary. As Harrison's expedition approached the town a sentry fired at them giving him the excuse he needed to attack. Instead, a group of villagers led by Tecumseh's brother, called the Prophet, met Harrison and requested a powwow.[267] The Prophet, the brother of Tecumseh, was also known by the Indian names of Tenskwatawa (Ten-Squaw-Taw'wa), or Laulewasikau.[268]

The Prophet requested a cease-fire to which Harrison agreed but moved his force to the high ground near an old Catholic mission. When an assassin who had defected from the American forces and was intent on killing Harrison was captured by the guards, Tenskwatawa, the Prophet, launched his attack on the Army encampment. After a diversionary attack on the north end of the camp was quickly repelled by the Americans, the main body of Indian Militia, called the Yellow Jackets, hit the south. With dawn approaching, the Native Americans could see they were outnumbered and quickly retreated back to their village. At that point Harrison's U.S. Army Expedition had 62 KIA and 126 WIA out of approximately 1100.[269] The Indian Confederacy's losses were unknown. The estimates varied from 40 KIA (Harrison's estimate)[270] to 35-40 KIA and 70-80 WIA by others.[271]

Another source stated that the Native Americans attacked the encampment of the Army force, which was surprised by the 4:30 a.m. night attack but quickly organized and defeated the Indian Confed-

---

267 Blodgett, Dr.Brian, *Tecumseh His Role and Conduct in the War of 1812*, Blodgett's Historical Consulting (Internet Source) https://sites.google.com/site/blodgetthistoricalconsulting/tecumseh.

268 Hickman, Kennedy, *Tecumseh's War: The Battle of Tippecanoe*, http://military-history.about.com/od/battleswars1800s/p/tippecanoe.htm

269 Native American Encyclopedia: http://nativeamericanencyclopedia.com/history-the-battle-tippecanoe/

270 Ohio History Central: http://www.ohiohistorycentral.org/w/Battle_of_Tippecanoe?rec=482

271 Hickman

eracy, and subsequently burned the Indian village. Tenskwatawa escaped to Canada.[272]

Thus the combination of trade restrictions on the United States by Great Britain, the continued impressment of American merchant sailors into the British Navy, plus the belief by many Americans that the British had supported Native American aggressiveness against the frontier settlers resulted just over six months later in President Madison signing a declaration of war against Great Britain on June 18, 1812.

Although some sources[273] consider the battle of Tippecanoe as the first battle in the War of 1812, the first actions after war was declared were riots breaking out in Baltimore during June, July, and August of that year in protest of the war. The public and their representatives in Congress were split on Madison's decision. The New England states in particular did not want their economy further devastated by the inability to trade overseas and were considered opponents to the declaration of war. The hawks of the declaration tended to be from the frontier territories, those violently opposed to British impressment of American merchant sailors, and those who felt that the expansion of the U.S. frontier should extend into Canada which was then currently occupied by British settlements and military forces. The Federalists of New England were the most vocal opponents.

The population in Baltimore which was generally in favor of the war became angered when a local newspaper published an editorial condemning the war; the result was mob violence.

The Public Domain Review, a Project of The Open Knowledge Foundation, St John's Innovation Centre, Cowley Road, Cambridge CB4 0WS, United Kingdom, printed an article titled *An Exact and Authentic Narrative of the 2nd Baltimore Riot (1812)* with the following subtitle:

"An exact and authentic narrative, of the events which took place in Baltimore, on the 27th and 28th of July last. Carefully collected from some of the sufferers and eyewitnesses. To which is added a narrative of

---

272 Encyclopedia Britannica, the Battle of Tippecanoe.
273 269 Public Broadcasting System, http://www.pbs.org/wned/war-of-1812/timeline/

Mr. John Thomson, one of the unfortunate sufferers; 1812; Printed for the purchasers.

[Public Domain Review then described the narrative as:]

"A small book giving various eye witness accounts of the "Second Baltimore Riot", one of the most violent anti-federalists attacks during the War of 1812. The first riot took place just over a month before when the Baltimore based "pro-British" Federalist newspaper The Federal Republican denounced the declaration of war. On the night of June 20th a mob stormed the newspaper's offices destroying the building and its contents. A truce was eventually negotiated and the owner of the paper, Alexander Hanson, and his employees were taken into protective custody. In July, after spending a few weeks in Georgetown, Hanson brought his newspaper back to a building in Baltimore and continued to write editorials denouncing the war. Once again, a mob lay [sic] siege to the building but this time Hanson and his employees fought back with gunfire, reportedly killing two of the mob. A military force intervened and again escorted Hanson and his supporters to jail for their protection. The following night the mob broke into the jail and nine Federalists, including Hanson, were hauled out into the street and given a severe three-hour beating, including being stabbed with penknives and having hot candle wax dropped into their eyes. Eventually the authorities intervened. One of the paper's employees, a Revolutionary War veteran named James Lingan, had been killed while Hanson was to die only seven years later never having fully recovered. No one ended up being brought to justice for the attacks."[274]

The first few months of the War of 1812 were not anything to brag about for the United States. One of the most tragic tales involved a former Revolutionary War veteran and hero, William Hull, the uncle of Commodore Isaac Hull, former commander of the *USS Enterprise*, hero of Tripoli and the one who gave great support to William Eaton at Derna. The senior Hull, i.e., William, was a hero in his own right during the Revolutionary War. A graduate of Yale University in 1772, William was a practicing lawyer in the short years before the Declaration of Independence. During the Revolutionary War he served in multiple

---

274 Library of Congress, Internet archive available online :http://publicdomain-review.org/collections/an-exact-and-authentic-narrative-of-the-2nd-baltimore-riot-1812/

battles with exemplary conduct noted by George Washington, and thereafter served as both a judge and a senator before being appointed as territorial governor of Michigan by then President Thomas Jefferson.[275]

Uncertain as to whether he should stay in politics during the upcoming War of 1812 with Great Britain or accept a proffered commission as a Brigadier General, William Hull, the former Lt. Colonel, accepted the commission. At the age of 58 it was probably the worst mistake of his life. He spent the next several weeks in Ohio territory raising an 1100 man army which was later supplemented by a 400 man militia of U.S. Army regulars from the 4th infantry Regiment.

On July 12, 1812, General Hull, three weeks after his 59th birthday, crossed with his 1500[276] man militia[277] east over the Detroit River into Canada without opposition and started to head south along the east bank of the River. His initial intent was to attack Fort Amherstburg, (later called Fort Malden) a British stronghold 20 miles south of Detroit on the east bank of the river that held about 300 Canadian militia as well as approximately 150 British regulars and 250 Indians.[278] Instead, according to historians of the time and later, Hull stopped the main body of his force and *"issued a bombastic proclamation to the people of Canada announcing their imminent liberation from 'tyranny and oppression,' but he stayed at the river landing almost opposite Detroit. He sent out several small raiding detachments along the Thames and Detroit Rivers, one of which returned after skirmishing with the British outposts near Fort Malden [today part of Amherstburg in upper Canada]"*[279]

---

275 Ridler, Jason, War of 1812, available online: http://www.eighteentwelve.ca/?q=eng/Topic/10

276 Matloff, Maurice, editor, American Military History p-136, originally a U.S. Army publication, available online: http://www.conservapedia.com/War_of_1812.

277 Hickey, Donald R. The War of 1812, A Forgotten Conflict, University of Illinois Press, 2012, pgs. 80-83. Hickey says about 2000 men minus 200 Ohioans who refused to serve outside of U.S. territory.

278 Matloff, page 136.

279 Matloff, page 137.

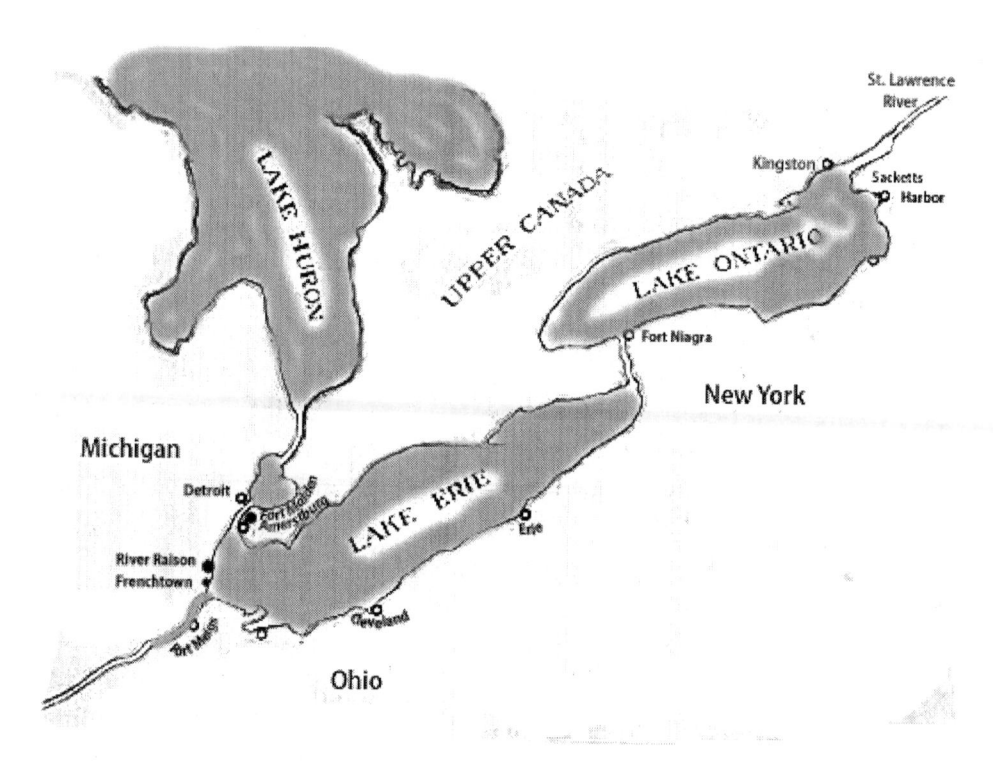

Map of significant towns and military posts in 1812 during early months of the War of 1812.

There were several issues against success for Hull:
- The first and likely most significant was the fact that he had suffered a stroke of some consequence the year prior to his recommissioning. He could not speak without slurring his words, a problem exaggerated by his consumption of alcohol and chewing tobacco which caused him to drool.
- The enemy commander, British General Isaac Brock, was a brilliant young officer who was experienced and aggressive. He was at least two steps ahead of Hull during the entire campaign, as you will see.
- Communications were a problem due to the distances from the central government of the U.S. to its commanders in the field. Hull was not even aware that war had been declared when he first crossed into Canada.
- The British however, were not only aware of the declaration of war but had acted on it and captured a ship, the *Cuyahoga*, that General Hull had dispatched ahead of his force on the Detroit River, carrying medical supplies and other necessary equipment. Unfortunately it also included his orders and his personal journal. The documents included the size of his force, the plans for his invasion of Canada, his route of travel, the supply lines and just about every other vital piece of information that he could not afford to lose to the enemy.
- Aside from the U.S. Army regulars from the fourth infantry regiment, the militiamen he recruited in Ohio were an undisciplined and inexperienced bunch of rascals not used to following orders and quick to make their own decisions. Their demeanor would come close to causing a mutiny.
- Tecumseh and his Indian Confederacy, also called the First Nation, had decided to embrace the British and were about

to become seriously involved in the U.S. campaign to invade Canada.
- And finally a number of civilian dependents including his own son and daughter and her children[280] were ensconced in Fort Detroit and for whom the General felt responsible. Their presence would hamper any rational decisions that he would have to make.

Hull's first action on the east side of the Detroit River resulted in the first casualty of the War of 1812. A skirmish between British defenders of a bridge over a tributary of the Detroit River, the Canard River, just south of Sandwich, and a combined American unit sent out by General Hull of light infantry and light cavalry commanded by Colonel Lewis Cass of the 4th Infantry and Lt. Colonel James Miller respectively occurred on July 16, 1812. The site of the battle is marked at the current hamlet of Canard River, which today is a town of about 500 people and is now a part of the north side of Amherstburg, Ontario, Canada. The casualties included a British private by the name of John Hancock who was KIA, and another private, John Dean who was WIA and captured by the Americans. Dean was wounded in the shoulder, had an arm amputated and later died at Fort Detroit.[281]

General Brock, the British commander, upon hearing of the American invasion and early skirmishes, immediately set out from York, (today part of Toronto, Ontario) to Amherstburg, a distance of about 280 miles, with a force of 300 British regulars and some militiamen to meet the invaders. When Brock finally arrived at Amherstburg, his forces totaled just over 1500 which included his regulars, 400 militiamen (including those already stationed at Amherstburg) and some 800 Native American warriors led by Tecumseh.

Meanwhile, General Hull, having heard of the British triumph over the Americans at Mackinac near the mouth of Lake Michigan, and rumors of British enforcements that were on the way with Tecumseh's Native Americans, beat a hasty retreat back to Fort Detroit. This deci-

---
280 Elting, John R., *Amateurs to Arms*, page-33. Da Capo Press, Chapel Hill, 1995
281 Colautti, Heather, Windsor Community Museum, Ontario, Canada. http://www.citywindsor.ca/residents/culture/windsors-community-museum/documents/war%20timeline%20for%20city%20website.pdf

sion caused his troops to lose confidence in the General whose own militia officers advised him of the growing unrest. Unknown to them General Hull's fear of being scalped by the Native Americans was documented in his personal journal, which was captured by the British. It would later be used by General Brock as a form of psychological warfare.

Brock staged an attack that made Hall's worst fears appear to come true on August 15, when Brock's British regulars and his band of militia and Native Americans crossed the Detroit River 3 miles south of Detroit and demanded the Americans' surrender. Hull was smart enough to know that although he could likely repulse an initial assault from the Fort, he would not be able to survive a long siege. When Brock let it be known that he would not be able to control the American Indian Warriors once fighting started, Hull's fear of the possible atrocities that would be performed on his family and the civilians in the Fort were enough for him to surrender the Fort without firing a shot. He did this on the next day August 16, 1812. A few rounds of Brock's artillery plus the whoops and noise made by the Native Americans at the gates of the Fort were enough to hasten his decision.[282]

Author Mark Thorburn[283] points out that ironically while General Hull was one of the first to surrender a major American post in the War of 1812, his nephew, U.S. Navy Captain Isaac Hull in command of the *USS Constitution* garnered the first American naval victory in the war by defeating His Majesty's Ship *(HMS) Guerriere* on the open ocean approximately 400 miles south of Halifax, Nova Scotia just three days later.

The aftermath of the surrender of Fort Detroit was at first disbelief and then outrage by the general public, and by Congress and the President. His own men labeled Hull a coward as did former President Thomas Jefferson.[284] It's possible, likely even, that the outrage was fueled by the delusion that the invasion of Canada would be a cakewalk. The administration and military were totally unprepared for the resistance they met. At the time most politicians believed that

---

282 Thorburn, Mark. "General William Hull Court-Martial: 1814." <u>Great American Trials</u>. 2002. Internet Source, http://www.encyclopedia.com/doc/1G2-3498200047.html
283 ibid.
284 Thorburn

Britain and its colonies in Canada were obsessed with Napoleon and his war and would not pay much attention to the protests and war declared by the U.S. They were wrong. They also did not accept their own responsibility in assigning an older disabled veteran like Hull to command a major portion of the attack on Canada. As a result General Hull became a scapegoat, a process no doubt also fueled by his own actions.

On August 17, General Hull and 582 of his men, all Army regulars, were taken aboard the ship the *Queen Charlotte* to await transport to Québec City as POWs.[285] A week later the remainder of Hull's force which had not already deserted was also escorted aboard commercial ships back to Ohio as far as Cleveland, out of danger of Native American reprisals, and released.[286]

After arriving in Québec City on September 16, Hull was released on parole (along with all married American officers) by then Governor General of Canada, Sir George Prevost. The single officers were also released on parole but kept in nearby Charlesbourg (today a borough of Quebec City) to await prisoner exchange. The enlisted men were confined to two transport ships on the St. Lawrence River also awaiting prisoner exchange.[287] Hull went to his home in Massachusetts,[288] where the disgraced general requested an investigation into his own conduct, and which resulted in a scheduling of his own court martial for early 1813. That trial was canceled by President Madison and rescheduled for January 1814. Hull would have to face prosecution charges of treason, cowardice, neglect of duty, and conduct unbecoming of an officer.[289]

---

285 Yanik, Anthony J., *The Fall and Recapture of Detroit in the War of 1812* page 102, Wayne State University Press, 2011.
286 ibid. page 102-103.
287 ibid.
288 ibid. page 106.
289 Thorburn

There is good evidence that the proceedings were stacked against Hull. Consider these facts:[290]
- No military defense counsel was appointed for Hull.
- His civilian lawyers, Robert Tillotson and C.D. Colden could not cross-examine any witnesses in court; nor could they discuss points of law with members of the court. As a result General Hull had to defend himself for which he was not prepared. The rulings were made by the presiding judge, Major General Henry Dearborn.
- The prosecutors were also civilians hired and appointed by the administration, an unusual departure from military protocol. Both of these lawyers were prominent politicians and famous lawyers in the country. One was Martin Van Buren, a future President of the United States, and the other was Philip S. Parker.
- The documents vital to Hull's defense such as communications with the war department, his orders, his journal, his daily logs and operations, letters from Ohio's and Kentucky's governors went missing after the surrender and he was denied access to copies from the official records.
- Presiding over the court appointed by the administration was Major General Henry Dearborn, Commander-in-Chief of the Army and the very same officer who struck a truce with the British forces near Niagara at the same time Hull's forces were threatening Amherstburg. Dearborn's truce allowed Isaac Brock and his British forces to come to the aid of their colleagues at Amherstburg and eventually forced the surrender of Fort Detroit. Therefore it could be presumed that Dearborn himself had a stake in the outcome of the trial in protecting his own reputation if Hull was acquitted.
- Procedural irregularities of court were allowed during the trial that would not be tolerated today. Witnesses were allowed to hear each other's testimony and opinions were allowed as part of the testimony and they were not necessarily those

---

290 Yanik pages 107-112

of experts. Even allegations were allowed without evidential proof.
- And finally, the majority of members of the court were recently promoted officers that had served under Dearborn, but were still of lesser rank than the officer charged. In fact all of the officers under Hull who were willing to testify against him at the trial had been promoted. Few were battle tested.

The verdict at the end of the three-month trial found General Hull guilty of all charges with the exception of treason over which the court felt they did not have jurisdiction but indicated they did not think he was guilty. His sentence was death by firing squad. That same day President Madison remitted the execution order and Hull was dishonorably discharged from the Army. He spent the rest of his life trying to clear his name.

William Hull circa 1795-1801, portrait by artist James Sharples, Senior. Photo credit Wikipedia, public domain.

There were other setbacks for the United States that had their origins in 1812 extending into 1813. In October 1812, Lieutenant Colonel Solomon Van Rensselaer, an American veteran of the Indian wars of the 1790s,[291] which were fought primarily in the Ohio Valley against the Miami Indians, was one of the officers involved in the Battle of Queenston Heights, a British stronghold across the Niagara River.

Solomon Van Rensselaer was the junior officer and aide to his older (by 10 years) cousin Major General Stephen Van Rensselaer, who commanded elements of a New York militia and supposedly was supported by Brigadier General Alexander Smyth a regular Army officer. Smyth however held the militarily untrained Van Rensselaer in contempt and refused to obey his orders or answer his summons. General Van Rensselaer was under pressure from President Madison to show accomplishments in the Niagara area, and although in theory his forces outnumbered the British nearly 3 to 1, in fact without the support of the regular Army his numbers advantage was not nearly as good as it seemed on paper.

On October 13, 1812, Van Rensselaer attacked the British outpost at Queenston Heights. At his first attempt in crossing the Niagara the small boat carrying the oars of the other vessels went missing. The Brits across the river spotted the floundering loose boats and watched as Van Rensselaer regrouped his forces on his side of the river. Thus his first mistake was losing the element of surprise. Clearly he did not have enough boats or enough ammunition to supply his forces and his lack of planning turned what should have been a relatively routine assault into a disaster.

The opposing British general was the indomitable Isaac Brock who had forced the defeat at Detroit. Brock was killed during the battle and the junior Van Rensselaer, who was the senior Van Rensselaer's cousin Solomon, was wounded several times.[292] After the resounding defeat Major General Stephen Van Rensselaer resigned his commission and returned to politics to become lieutenant governor of the state of New York.

* * *

---

291 Internet source: *Official Indian Wars of the United States*, http://www.thelatinlibrary.com/imperialism/notes/indianwars.html

292 Bielinski, Stefan, *The New York State Museum*, Internet source: http://www.nysm.nysed.gov/albany/bios/vr/solvr5113.html

CHAPTER NINE

January 18, 1813

"We have met the enemy and they are ours"-Commodore Oliver Hazard Perry

After General Hull's dismissal from the Army, command of the Army of the Northwest was given at first to General James Winchester. He was quickly replaced with and became second-in-command to General William Henry Harrison when that popular officer was promoted to Major General. A political process initiated by the Kentucky Militia had put pressure on the administration and Secretary of War William Eustis to make the change. Eustis wanted Winchester in charge but Eustis was about to be replaced by John Armstrong so he didn't offer much resistance. In a letter from the Secretary of War dated September 17, 1812, Harrison was informed of his promotion.[293]

Well into January 1813 the setbacks for the United States were still not over. Following the debacle of the loss of Detroit, Harrison was determined to retake the city and fort. Winter, however, was about to prevent any major campaign that Harrison had in mind. Before he ordered his troops to button up for the winter he sent his second-in-command, General Winchester, with a force of about 300 men,[294] to protect an American settlement called Frenchtown, on the Raisin River at the present site of Monroe, Michigan. Before Winchester arrived, the settlers, approximately 700 strong, had driven off a small

---

293 Hickey. Page 84 paperback edition 2012, University of Illinois Press
294 Hickey. ibid.

British force of unknown strength on January 18, 1813. Four days later on January 22, a British force commanded by Colonel Henry Proctor, accompanied by Tecumseh's warriors, arrived from Amherstburg and counterattacked. Author Donald Hickey, citing Harrison's papers, states that some 900 Americans were killed, missing, or captured during the action.[295] Winchester himself was captured.

Proctor, the British Colonel, knowing that Harrison's main force wasn't too far away, took the American prisoners who were able to travel and beat a hasty retreat back to Fort Amherstburg, leaving the wounded prisoners behind. The next day, January 23, Native American warriors attacked the settlement again killing an estimated 30 survivors of the previous day's battle with the usual desecration of the dead typical of the Native warriors of the day. From then on it was known as the River Raisin Massacre and triggered the American settler's rallying cry of *"Remember the Raisin."*

Actually the supposedly three-pronged invasion of Canada proposed by the administration failed at every level. In an 1812 to 1813 time frame, the surrender of Fort Detroit in the Northwest Territories was the first failure blamed on General Hull. The second major failure was the lackluster result of Major General Henry Dearborn's attack on Montréal November 20, 1812.[296] The attack had been ordered by the administration through Secretary of War Eustis. As often happens in wartime when the politicians tell the generals what to do (usually for political capital) instead of listening to the generals' advice, the results are equivocal at best, and disastrous at worst.

Although it is not always the case witness the more modern outcomes that were influenced by politicians during the Vietnam War and more recently in Afghanistan, Iraq, Syria, and the Middle East with the rise of ISIS.

At any rate the third failure was the attack ordered by the administration in November 1812 and was led by Colonel Zebulon Pike. Pike, with a detachment of about 500 men from Dearborn's army, surrounded a British block house on November 12th, before dawn

---

295 Hickey. Page 85
296 Hickey. Page 88.

about 42 miles south of Montréal on the Lacolle River, a tributary of the Richelieu.[297]

What followed was the Battle of LaColle Mills and according to one source[298] either Pike split his attacking force or there was another detachment of American militia from Dearborn's army that Pike was not aware of, using a different approach to the block house. Whatever the truth, one group entered and occupied the facility after a brief skirmish in the dark with the defenders.

When the Americans who had surrounded the block house were spotted by those already within, a firefight ensued pitting Americans against Americans. The Brits and a band of Native American and Canadian defenders under the command of Major Charles de Salaberry and of similar strength to the Americans had vacated the facility following the earlier skirmish. De Salaberry's men heard the firefight in the dark and were as confused as those firing the shots. It was not until full daylight appeared when five Americans were found to be KIA and another five wounded that the horrible truth was revealed to the Americans. Today the incident would be called "friendly fire."

Major de Salaberry's scouts soon discovered the truth as well whereupon the Major launched a counterattack with his Canadian volunteers and some 300 Caughnawaga[299] Indians. After a short engagement Colonel Pike, realizing there was no will to fight amongst his disheartened troops, disengaged from the action and retreated back to Dearborn's camp. Three days later Dearborn withdrew his entire force from Canada.[300]

---

297 USwars.com. Battle of Lacolle Mills, Internet source: http://www.mywarof1812.com/battles/121120-lacolle-mills.html
298 ibid.
299 also spelled Kahnawake
300 ibid.

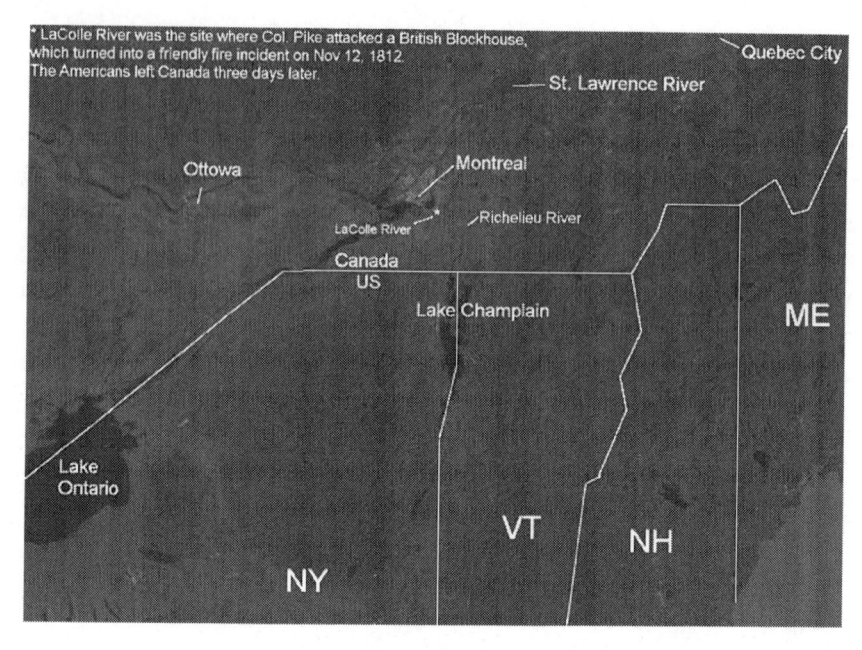

Map by Paul Hook

In stark contrast to the Army, the American Navy fared much better in 1812-13, probably because the United States Administration officials followed the recommendations of senior Navy Officer Commodore John Rodgers. The decision by Administration, which included President Madison, Secretary of the Treasury, Albert Gallatin, and Secretary of State James Monroe resulted in very practical orders to Secretary of the Navy Paul Hamilton. On June 22, 1812 the Secretary of the Navy was instructed to: *"operate his sources as two (later there were three) separate squadrons to cruise off the Atlantic coast for the protection of American commerce."*[301]

Make no mistake however, as always there were some differences of opinion amongst the senior Navy captains and Commodores regarding strategy. Stephen Decatur and William Bainbridge, both senior officers, advised sending Navy ships abroad to cruise separately.

---

301 *Proceedings of the United States Naval Institute, volume 32, 1906, page 84. Original University of Minnesota digitized October 23, 2013.*

At least on this occasion the politicians in the President's cabinet had some options and listened to one of the senior officers.

Secretary of the Treasury Gallatin was instrumental in encouraging the adaption of Commodore Rodgers' plan.[302] It was probably the best decision. Not only was it the least expensive strategy, of which secretary Gallatin was well aware, but the communication delays between the Secretary of War and his squadrons were significantly shortened, the enemy targets were plentiful, and their locations were often known.

The results of the strategy included Captain Isaac Hull's and the USS Constitution's victory over HMS Guerriere on August 19, 1812, mentioned previously; the USS United States' (commanded by Stephen Decatur) capture of the British frigate HMS Macedonian on October 15; and the 18 gun sloop, WASP's defeat of HMS Frolic on October 18. That particular victory according to author Hickey[303] cost the British almost 80 percent of Frolic's crew in casualties.

As much as we as United States citizens condemn piracy in this modern era, we are not without our own history of privateering. Some historians say that more damage was caused to the British by American privateers in the War of 1812 than was caused by our own Navy. Shortly after the declaration of war against Great Britain, the United States Congress approved rules for privateering and began issuing commissions for such.[304] There was no moral high ground however since British and Canadian privateers took prizes as well. There was also no question that American privateers were given added incentive by the then legal piracy against the enemy and that they also provided a service to their country as a private Navy at no cost to the taxpayers.

The U.S. Navy's victories gave the American public something of which to be proud. However the ground war did not start to turn around until April 27, 1813, when a large American force vastly outnumbering the defenders which included British regulars, Canadian

---
302 Hickey, page 92.
303 ibid. p-95.
304 Annals of Congress, debates and proceedings, 1789-1824, 12th Congress-first session. The source refers to the act of June 26, 1812 quoted in Hickey, page 97.

militia, and native North American Indians of the Chippewa and Mississauga tribes, landed in the Parkdale section of today's Toronto and soundly defeated their opponents. The Americans were supported by naval gunfire which accompanied the amphibious invasion fleet on Lake Ontario.

The American amphibious force was led by General Henry Dearborn who was in charge of the eastern portion of the three-pronged attack planned by the American administration. This was the same general officer who had arranged a truce with the British that allowed General Isaac Brock to go to the rescue of the British settlement at Amherstburg which, in August 1812 was being threatened by American General William Hull. Brock's arrival forced the surrender of Fort Detroit as previously described.

Dearborn was supposed to attack Kingston which was the main British naval base on Lake Ontario, but he apparently felt that Kingston was too strong a fortress for his initial assault and instead elected to attack the poorly defended city of York which would become modern day Toronto.[305] General Dearborn was supported in his decision by Commodore Isaac Chauncey[306] who was commander of the amphibious fleet that deposited Dearborn's army on the outskirts of York. Chauncey was the same naval officer who had commanded the *USS John Adams* after the frigate had delivered Commodore Morris home from the Mediterranean. He also had fought with Commodore Preble and John Rodgers in the second assault on Tripoli in 1804.

Although not as strong a base as Kingston, York, Ontario's provincial capital was known to have a 30-gun frigate under construction for the British and two British warships were based there as well. Dearborn felt that it was an opportunity to inflict considerable damage on the British Navy without much risk and apparently Commodore Chauncey concurred. The only problem was Dearborn and/or Chauncey, having heard rumors of the strength of the British forces at Kingston of 6,000 to 8,000 men, convinced Secretary of War Arm-

---

305 Rickard, J (25 November 2007), Battle of York, 27 April 1813, http://www.historyofwar.org/articles/battles_york_1813.html

306 ibid.

strong that York was a better target even though it was strategically much less important.

When the initial American amphibious forces debarked from Chauncey's 15 amphibious assault boats they were led by Brigadier General Zebulon Montgomery Pike. Pike was the same officer who had led the attack on the block house 42 miles south of Montréal the previous autumn, in which two detachments of American soldiers fought each other in the dark. General Dearborn never left the safety of Chauncey's warship until he was forced to go ashore and take command when Pike was killed.[307]

Leading the defenders was Major General Roger Hale Sheaffe, an experienced British officer who had replaced General Brock when that officer was KIA in the defense of Queenston Heights on October 13, 1812. Sheaffe was also the provincial administrator (Colonial Lt. Governor) of the Canadian province of Ontario. He had at his disposal about 300 British regulars, 45 Indians of the Mississauga and Ojibway tribes, about 250 Canadian militia, an unknown number of provincial Marines and about 40 artificers* who were assisting shipbuilders working on the new British frigate.[308] (Ridler says it was *"a force of 700 British regulars and Canadian militia and perhaps 100 Aboriginals against 1700 Americans;"*[309] and Hickey says it was 1000 British troops and 50-100 Indians against 1800 American soldiers, and 800 seamen and marines).[310]

General Sheaffe, having suffered about 200 casualties and even more (about 275) of his men captured after four hours of battle, ordered the destruction of the ammunition dump of his embattled garrison upon his retreat. Whether or not by design (the British flag was still flying over the Garrison) the explosion of the magazine caught

---

307 Malcomson, Robert and Thomas, original article Military History (magazine) Oct. 1998. Internet source: http://www.historynet.com/war-of-1812-battle-of-york.htm.

*Artificer was an enlisted rank in charge of a unit's equipment.

308 ibid.

309 Ridler, Jason, bio of Roger Hale Sheaffe, War of 1812 Internet source: http://www.eighteentwelve.ca/?q=eng/Topic/94

310 Hickey, page 134.

the Americans by surprise and was so severe that it was heard some 30 miles away in Fort Niagara.[311]

The explosion caused the majority of the 320 casualties[312] (Hickey says 310 casualties) the Americans suffered in the engagement. Of the 265 WIA, 250 were caused by the exploding ammo dump.[313]

Brigadier General Zebulon Montgomery Pike was one of the KIA casualties. The explosion also forced the American Army combat surgeons to work steadily without food or sleep for two days treating the wounded. A surgeon, Dr. William Beaumont, mentioned this in his journal which has been researched and recorded by author Donald Hickey.[314]

Because of the devastation caused by the explosion on the ranks of the Americans who were just standing around after the British retreated, the survivors blamed the British and the British commander.

After General Pike's death, command of the American forces was passed to Colonel Cromwell Pierce (before the arrival of General Dearborn) who although he didn't know the cause of the explosion, expected a British counterattack and ordered his forces into a defensive position. When no counterattack came after an appropriate wait, Pierce sent a team forward under a white flag to negotiate a British surrender. He was upset to find out that his negotiators were dealing with Canadian militia and not General Sheaffe.

Things got worse when a column of smoke in the distance proved to be coming from the British Navy Yard where General Sheaffe had ordered the destruction of the yard and the British gunboat under construction. Sheaffe's orders were carried out after peace negotiations had a started. I could not find any research evidence showing that Sheaffe was aware of the peace negotiations.

The anger of the American troops regarding Sheaffe's actions resulted in the sacking and looting of the town of York (now part of

---

311 ibid. page 135.
312 Malcomson, Robert and Thomas, original article Military History (magazine) Internet source: http://www.historynet.com/war-of-1812-battle-of-york.htm.
313 ibid.
314 Hickey, page 135.

Toronto). All the government buildings were torched. The looters were also joined by locals and order was not restored until a local clergyman, John Strachan, convinced General Dearborn, (who arrived the next day), to get control of his troops. Dearborn did so, but reluctantly, since General Sheaffe's actions were not considered honorable by the Americans, who were convinced Sheaffe gave his orders after the peace negotiations had started. In addition, Sheaffe had taken all the British and Canadian surgeons with him leaving the Canadian militia with their wounded to fend for themselves.[315] Sheaffe himself would later be relieved of command and administrative authority and was essentially branded as *persona non grata*, at least in that part of Canada.

There were several other battles in the spring of 1813 in which a lot of lives were lost on both sides but without much strategic advantage. They included the siege of Fort Meigs in Ohio, the Battle of Sackets Harbor on Lake Ontario from where Chauncey and Dearborn launched their amphibious fleet in the Battle of York, and the Battle of Fort George on the Canadian side of the Niagara River where it empties into Lake Ontario. This latter engagement should have been of strategic value to the victorious American forces because they would then control the entire frontier of the Great Lakes, but British General John Vincent was able to regroup his forces at the western end of Lake Ontario and therefore was still a threat to the frontier.

Probably the most significant event of the war in 1813 was Captain Oliver Hazard Perry's defeat of the British on Lake Erie in September of that year.

Before I describe what happened, we will start with a little background. Keep in mind that the background information presented here is a year earlier than Chauncey's and Dearborn's victory at York (Toronto) just described.

In July 1812 the British captured Fort Mackinac, an American outpost at the mouth of Lake Michigan. It was an easy operation for the British since the American commander of Fort Mackinac had not been notified that the United States had declared war on Great Britain. At

---

315 *Malcomson*

the time of the surprise capture, an American merchant ship under the command of Captain Dan Dobbins was delivering salt to the outpost and was also captured by the British. Since he was a merchant mariner and not a member of the military post, Dobbins managed to obtain his release and headed for Detroit, which had also just been captured by the British. There he was detained and released again. He finally made his way to his home in Erie and reported the events to the commander of the Pennsylvania Commonwealth militia, General George Meade, who urged Dobbins to go immediately to Washington, D.C. to brief President Madison. Back then travel between Erie and Washington, D.C. took at least a week.

After contacting the President and briefing him and his cabinet over a 10 day period, Dobbins, on September 15, 1812, was appointed as a sailing master in the United States Navy, given $2000 in government funding and sent back to Lake Erie to build four gunboats near Presque Isle,[316] just off Erie's shoreline. Dobbins knew Presque Isle had a large harbor secured at its entry by sandbars which would prevent any enemy warship's admission. Dobbins was knowledgeable enough to know that shallow draft gunships could be extracted over the sandbars' one fathom depth after being built. The decision to build gunships was made by President Madison. The American side of the Lake Erie shore was totally defenseless and control of the Great Lakes was basically in the hands of the British.[317]

Three days earlier, on September 12, 1812, Captain Isaac Chauncey was ordered from New York by the secretary of the Navy to go to Sacket's Harbor on the east end of Lake Ontario. Chauncey was appointed as the commanding officer of the upper Great Lakes and his mission was to gain control of Lakes Huron, Ontario, and Erie. Chauncey's second-in-command was Navy Master Commandant James D. Elliott who was also the commander of Naval Forces on Lake Erie.

Dobbins was supposed to report to Chauncey but he had difficulty communicating. He even went to Black Rock, a naval facility near

---

316 *Presque Isle is not really an island but a peninsula.*
317 *Knoll, Adm. Denys (Ret), Battle of Lake Erie: Building the Fleet in the Wilderness, Navy Department Library, Washington DC, 1979, Oct. 1998, page 12. Internet source:// ww3w.history.navy.mil/library/online/battle_lake_erie.htm*

Buffalo to talk with Chauncey but he was not available. However, he did talk with one of Elliott's assistants and received a letter from Elliott himself some days later. Elliott was apparently convinced that Presque Island was totally unsuitable for building gunboats (probably because of the sandbars) and stated that Dobbins would hear from him later. Elliott then proceeded to ignore follow-up communications from Dobbins, who by mid-December was so frustrated that he wrote directly to Secretary of the Navy Paul Hamilton.[318]

Dobbins, although extremely knowledgeable about sailing the Great Lakes, was not a ship designer or builder which likely accounted for most of his frustration. He was also running out of federal money, but his friends and the people he had hired persuaded him to continue with the construction of gunboats. His letter to the Secretary of the Navy apparently lit a fire under the britches of Captain Chauncey (and probably Master Commandant Elliott too after Chauncey's rear end was burned by Secretary Hamilton) because Chauncey showed up at the Presque Harbor Isle shipyards on New Year's Eve, December 31, 1812, with a ship designer, Henry Eckford, in tow. He stayed just one day and left in a huff just 24 hours later on New Year's Day and never returned to Erie or Presque Isle. According to retired Admiral Denys Knoll[319] Chauncey's visit resulted in the following:

- A master shipwright from New York City, Noah Brown, was ordered to the Presque Isle (Erie) shipbuilding sites to supervise construction. He made it in the record travel time of 10 days and arrived in February 1813.
- Two of the ships under construction were considered too small, by ship designer Henry Eckford, to sail the Great Lakes safely, and their length was increased by 10 feet.
- Two additional ships, the *USS Lawrence* and the *USS Niagara*, were authorized for construction by Secretary of the Navy Hamilton. Hamilton also contracted and provided the funds for arming the two new brigs (two masted vessels) with eighteen 32 pounder carronades each, plus one long-range 12

---
318 Knoll, page 14.
319 ibid, page 17.

pounder cannon mounted in the bow of each brig for chasing fleeing enemy ships.
- Captain Chauncey requested the assignment of Captain Oliver H. Perry to command the new Erie squadron.
- Many other unspecified alterations in the ship constructions that Dobbins had started.

On February 22, 1813, 28-year-old Oliver Perry was promoted to Commodore and left his ship from Newport, Rhode Island. Along with 150 of his best crewmen and his younger brother Alexander, he started out under orders to report to his new assignment in Erie. It took him over a month to get there because of the harsh winter traveling conditions plus a two week delay at Sackets Harbor at the insistence of Commodore Chauncey who also kept Perry's crewmen because he was afraid of an attack by the British on Sackets Harbor.[320]

Perry, a mover and shaker himself, had the support of the new Secretary of the Navy William Jones, (who had replaced Secretary Hamilton on January 19, 1813) and quickly assessed the situation at Erie and Presque Isle. Appreciating the military weakness along the south shore of Lake Erie, Perry consulted with the Army commander General Meade, who agreed to reinforce Erie with 1,000 Pennsylvania militiamen. Perry then set off for Pittsburgh on the first of several trips to obtain supplies and recruit skilled workmen to complete construction of the gunboats.

By September of 1813, Perry had completed construction of two of the gunboats at Presque Isle and set about cruising Lake Erie. The British opposing commander, Captain Robert H. Barklay, a one-armed experienced officer who had fought with Lord Nelson at Trafalgar, had at his disposal a fleet of six ships, the best of which was *HMS Detroit*. The *Detroit* was said by some authorities to be the *USS Adams* which had been captured by the British on October 8, 1812. Actually the British ship *HMS Detroit* was built in 1810 by master shipwright Wil-

---

320 ibid, page 21.

liam Bell at Amherstburg specifically to enhance the British fleet on Lake Ontario.[321]

Perry, on the other hand, commanding the 20 gun *USS Lawrence* with a squadron of nine vessels held the advantage of numbers but not of firepower since he was outgunned 63 to 54.[322] His second-in-command was Jesse Elliott, the commander of the Lake Erie squadron and the same fellow who had ignored the pleas of Captain Dan Dobbins to help with the building of gunboats at Presque Isle. On September 10, 1813, the two fleets would sail within sight of each other, but first Dobbins and Perry had to get the new gunboats out of Presque Harbor over the sandbars. Here's how they did it:

Dan Dobbins had long anticipated and planned for getting the largest gunboats, built as identical ships, the *USS Lawrence* and the *USS Niagara* over the sandbar. He had carefully sounded and mapped the best route over the sandbar and marked the route with buoys. Unloaded, both ships had 6 foot drafts, and the shallowest part of the route marked over the bar was three feet.

---

[321] Tucker, Arnold, Wiener, Pierpaoli, & Fredicksen, *The Encyclopedia of the War of 1812, Volume 1, p 191-2.* ABC-CLIO, Santa Barbara, CA, 2012.
[322] Knoll, page 27.

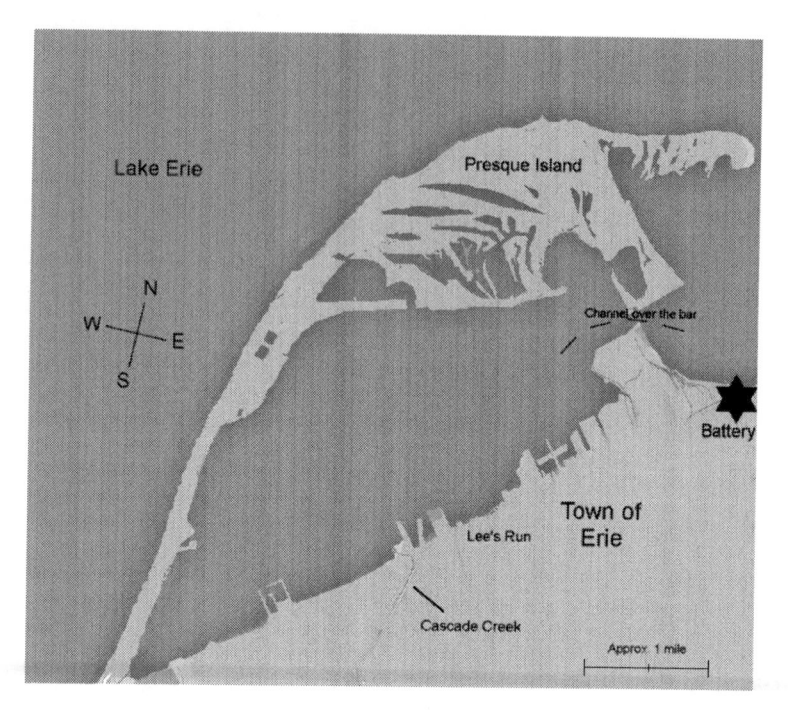

Presque Isle Erie, PA circa 1814. Cartography by Paul Hook

Now all they had to do was get the ships into position. On August 2, 1813, Dobbins was the pilot aboard the *Lawrence* and the sister ship *Niagara*, with guns loaded in case the British showed up, was standing by. The *Lawrence* was stripped of its heavy guns, ballast, and equipment and advanced along the sandbar as far as possible by a process called kedging. Kedging was simply throwing an anchor with its cable ahead of the ship and then hauling on the anchor cable until the ship was at the entry of the buoy-marked channel.

The next step was indeed ingenious, but a trick well-known by experienced mariners. Two flat keeled barges were positioned on each side of the *Lawrence*, timbers that passed through the gun ports on each side of the gunboats were then lashed to the gunwales (gunnels) of each barge.

The barges were unique in that each had been designed and built by the Brown brothers, Noah and Adam, had jigsaw-puzzle type plugs built into their flat bottom keels, and had been flooded with water so that they were exhibiting a draft of 6 feet when the timbers were lashed to their gunnels and advanced through the gun ports of the *Lawrence*. Called camels, the two barges were designed specifically for the purpose they were now being utilized. All the Brown brothers had to do once the timbers were in place was to replace the plugs in the camels' flat bottom keels, pump the water out of each barge and allow the natural buoyancy of the barges to lift the *USS Lawrence* enough to float her over the sandbar.[323] Because the water level in Lake Erie was low on this particular occasion the process had to be repeated during the night, but by August 4, was successful. The heavy guns and equipment were then reloaded. Commodore Perry was aboard and the *Lawrence* was anchored in position to protect a repeat process for the *USS Niagara*.[324]

By August 6, Perry's fleet of five gunboats and four converted merchants was ready to sail. It would have been a fleet of 10 except the converted merchant ship *Amelia* was found to be un-seaworthy. One of the major problems Perry had was a lack of experienced seamen to man the vessels. He had pleaded with Commodore Chauncey to have Master Commandant Elliott release the crew he had detained to help man the two new gunboats without success. He had finally given up and written to the secretary of the Navy, going over Chauncey's head. The strategy apparently worked, because Elliott showed up with 89 of Perry's original crew, on August 10. Elliott was given command of the *Niagara*. Perry had just a month to get his squadron in shape for battle.

The fateful day of September 13, 1813, favored Perry's squadron with the wind at their backs. Around noon both squadrons were closing for action. When the first shot was fired by British Captain Robert H. Barkley aboard *HMS Detroit*, Commodore Perry's flagship the *USS Lawrence* hoisted her new battle flag with the words *"Don't Give Up the Ship"* boldly emblazoned in white against a blue background. The banner reflected the last deathbed order of Perry's best friend, Captain James Lawrence for whom Perry's flagship was named. Lawrence had been killed in battle just three months earlier when the

---

323 *Knoll, Page 24.*
324 *ibid.*

USS Chesapeake was captured by *HMS Shannon* near Boston Harbor on June 1, 1813.[325]

Barclay's opening shot from his long guns fell short, convincing Perry to close the distance to take advantage of his own carronades, at the same time hoping to come inside the effective range of Barclay's long guns. While this was happening it was noted by Perry and others that Master Commandant Elliott in the *USS Niagara* was hanging back from the rest of the squadron effectively out of range of the action. No explanation was ever provided by Elliott other than there was some confusion about Perry's signals.

After exchanging fire over a period of two hours, Perry's flagship, the *Lawrence,* had taken the brunt of the British long guns and firepower from Barclay's flagship the *Detroit* and the 17-gun *HMS Queen Charlotte*. Every single gun of Perry's starboard batteries had been disabled, and her superstructure damaged to make the ship effectively disabled. At this point looking for a ship to transfer his flag, Perry noted the undamaged *Niagara,* and promptly called for a small boat and four oarsmen to transfer his flag. Accompanied by his brother Alexander, Perry headed for the *Niagara*. One can only imagine the words exchanged when Perry boarded the undamaged vessel. The British, meanwhile anticipating a probable surrender by Perry when he boarded the small boat, ceased firing upon the American squadron.[326] They were to be sorely disappointed.

Author and former naval officer Alexander Slidell Mackenzie's (1803-1848) classic work* quoted below gives a graphic tale taken from eyewitness accounts of the experiences of those who were there including the only physician healthy enough to treat the wounded during Perry's two-hour struggle against Barclay's squadron before he transferred his flag to the *Niagara*.

---

325 US Naval History and Heritage Command, Internet source: http://www.history.navy.mil/photos/events/war1812/atsea/ches-sn.htm

326 Knoll page 30.

* Mackenzie was a midshipman cadet in 1815, who served with participants of the Battle of Lake Erie and later with Perry himself. He eventually rose to the rank of Commodore, and became Perry's biographer. His work was copyrighted in 1910, long after his death in 1848.

"Overwhelming as was the superiority of the force directed against the Lawrence, being in the ratio of thirty-four guns to her ten in battery, she continued, with the aid of the Scorpion, Ariel, and Caledonia, to sustain the contest for more than two hours, her fire being kept up with uninterrupted spirit, so long as her guns continued mounted and in order. Never was the advantage of thorough training at the guns more exemplified than in the case of the Lawrence.

"The surgeon remarks that he could discover no perceptible difference in the rapidity of the firing of the guns over his head during the action; throughout, the actual firing seemed as rapid as in exercise before the battle. By this time, however, her rigging had been much shot away, and was hanging down or towing overboard, sails torn to pieces, spars wounded and falling upon deck, braces and bowlines cut so as to render it impossible to trim the yards or keep the vessel under control. Such was the condition of the vessel aloft; on deck the destruction was even more terrible. One by one the guns were dismounted, until only one remained that could be fired; the bulwarks were so entirely beaten in that the enemy's round shot passed completely through. The slaughter was dreadful, beyond anything recorded in naval history.

"Of one hundred well men, who had gone into action, twenty-two were killed and sixty-one wounded. The killed were hastily removed out of the way of the guns, and the wounded passed below and crowded together on the berth deck. It was impossible for Doctor Parsons, the assistant surgeon of the Lawrence, the only medical officer who was in health to perform duty in the squadron, to attend to such a press of wounded; bleeding arteries were hastily secured, shattered limbs supported by splints, and those that were nearly severed by cannon-balls hastily removed.

"Owing to the shallowness of these vessels, the wounded were necessarily all above the water-line, and exposed to be, again, struck by cannon-balls passing through the vessel's side; thus, midshipman Laub, while moving away from the surgeon, with a tourniquet on his arm, to resume his duties upon deck, was struck by a cannon-ball, which traversed his chest; and a Narraganset Indian, named Charles Poughigh, was killed in like manner by a cannon-ball after his leg had been taken off.

"Perry had a favourite spaniel on board the Lawrence, which had been left in a state-room below to be out of the way. The confinement, the noise, and the groans of the wounded, terrified the poor animal, and at each discharge it growled and barked with affected rage, or howled most piteously. In the course of the action, a shot passed through the bulkhead and left a large hole, through which the dog immediately thrust its head, yelping terribly for release. Its strange manoeuvres were too much for the gravity even of the suffering wounded, and some of them broke forth into loud and intemperate laughter.

"Mean time Perry continued to keep up a fire from his single remaining carronade, though [in order] to man it he was obliged to send repeated requests to the surgeon to spare him another hand from those engaged in removing the wounded until the last had been taken. It is recorded by the surgeon, that when these messages arrived, several of the wounded crawled upon deck to lend a feeble aid at the guns. At length the commander's own personal aid, with that of the purser, Mr. Hambleton, and chaplain, Mr. Breese, was necessary to fire this sole remaining gun, and it, too, was at last disabled.

"The conduct of Perry throughout this trying scene was such as to inspire the most unbounded confidence in his followers, and to sustain throughout their courage and enthusiasm. Free from irritation and undue excitability, the necessary orders were given with precision and obeyed with steady alacrity."[327]

Elliott, undoubtedly anticipating Perry's ire, may have been surprised when Perry boarded the *Niagara* with no side boys attending, and offered this reply to Elliott's sarcastic query of how his day had gone:

"Badly," Perry replied, "my ship is a wreck and I've lost most of my men. Why are the gunboats so far astern?"

---

327 Mackenzie, Alex S. USN, Commodore Oliver Hazard Perry, Superior Printing Co. Akron, 1910. Pages 181-183. Courtesy Allen County Genealogy Ctr., Fort Wayne, IN. Available online: https://archive.org/details/allen_county.

"I don't know," answered Elliott. Then, seeing an opportunity to avoid an immediate confrontation he offered, *"Perhaps I could round them up for you."*

"Why don't you do that, Captain? I'll take over here. Watch for my signals."

"Aye Aye, sir," replied Elliott who then quickly hopped into the awaiting boat and was off on his duty.

Perry's first orders aboard the *Niagara* were to back off the topsail, slow the vessel down and avoid running out of the action. At the same time he ordered signals for close action, hoisted top gallant sails (also called top garrant sails pronounced "t'garn'sls")[328] and with his battle flag, *"Don't Give Up the Ship"* flying, Perry altered course toward the enemy. As the answering signal flags appeared along the line they were accompanied by loud cheers of the Americans whose gunboats in line astern had been held back by the actions of the *Niagara* when it was under the command of Elliott.[329]

When the British observed the *Niagara* heading straight for them they intended to hold their fire until it was effective. *HMS Detroit*, under the command of Barklay, began to maneuver to present her undamaged starboard guns as a broadside to the advancing *Niagara*. Unfortunately for the Brits the *Queen Charlotte,* trying to maneuver similarly was not quick enough and collided with *Detroit,* the two vessels thus rendering themselves relatively helpless as the *Niagara* passed slowly by within pistol shot of both ships. Not only did the *Niagara* devastate the rigging of both vessels with canister and grape[330] but her port carronades also came to bear on the sterns of the British ships *Lady Prevost*[331] and *Little Belt* causing similar murderous damage. Tacking back on the next pass, Perry continued to pour grape and

---

328 Underhill, Harold (1986). *Masting and Rigging.* Glasgow: Brown, Son and Ferguson, LTD.

329 Mackenzie, page 192.

330 Canister consisted of sharp flints packed in a tin or brass container which burst on impact for a shotgun effect. Grapeshot was one solid package of small metal balls packed into a canvas sack which was very effective as anti-personnel weaponry but also devastated the rigging of sailing vessels.

331 Most sources spell it Prevost but some including Knoll, spell it Provost (page 27).

canister shot into the *Queen Charlotte* and the *Hunter* which lay astern of her. Some of the shot passed through *Queen Charlotte* into the *Detroit*. Army sharpshooters, acting as Marines aboard *Niagara*, cleared the enemy decks of any able-bodied men still standing. Shortly thereafter the smaller gunboats of Perry's squadron provided the *coup de grace* and all resistance ceased.[332]

The Battle of Lake Erie has been called by some historians the most important action of the War of 1812. Author Donald Hickey said it changed the balance of power in the region.[333]

Perry became a national hero. His battle flag is still exhibited at the U.S. Naval Academy at Annapolis, Maryland. Congress voted Perry and his men $260,000 in prize money which was shared by all involved. The largest share went to Commodore Chauncey ($12,750), and Perry got a similar amount ($12,140). Even Elliott was decorated and got over $7,000.

Perry reported 27 KIA and 96 wounded.[334] (Hickey says total American casualties were 125). British casualties were heavier with 41 KIA and 94 WIA as reported by British commander Barclay. (Hickey agrees with Barclay's numbers).

After the battle, Perry sent the famous terse message quoted in the epigram of this chapter to General Harrison, *"We have met the enemy and they are ours."* See the epilogue for the ultimate fates of Perry and Elliott. There is no doubt that the victory Perry won in the Battle of Lake Erie was the turning point of the war.

The British loss at The Battle of Lake Erie jeopardized the supply lines providing sustenance to the British and Canadian armies. The British commander, General Henry Procter, who had also fought at the Siege of Fort Meigs and the assault on Fort Stephenson, both in Ohio, decided it would be best for his troops if he withdrew along the west flowing Thames River in Ontario. Procter's decision gravely

---

332 Mackenzie, page 193.
333 Hickey, page 130-31.
334 Knoll, page 31.

aggravated Tecumseh's Indians who felt the British were abandoning them.

General Harrison took advantage of the situation and raised additional troops primarily from Kentucky exceeding 3,000 in number.[335] They crossed into Canada in pursuit of Procter's army. Harrison caught up with Procter in early October 1813 and sorely defeated him in what became known as the Battle of the Thames in which Native American warrior Tecumseh lost his life.

∗∗

---

335 *Hickey, page 131-31.*

CHAPTER TEN

September 19, 1813

"War is a blessing compared with national degradation."- Andrew Jackson

Major General James Wilkinson was a man of questionable reputation who was involved in the Aaron Burr conspiracy in 1806 and who had lost about half of his men by desertion in 1809 to apparent mismanagement of his command. He was such a controversial character in the southwestern United States, that by 1813, the Madison administration had him transferred to the Canadian frontier to avoid a political confrontation with the Louisiana Senators who insisted that there were soldiers in the Louisiana militia who absolutely refused to serve under the general.[336]

General Dearborn was educated as a physician. He became a hero at Bunker Hill during the Revolution, was imprisoned by the British, and was held for a year and a half before being exchanged. He served under Benedict Arnold before he was captured and fought multiple other battles before spending the winter of 1777–78 at Valley Forge, Pennsylvania, with General Washington. He also served as Secretary of War (see Chapter 3) under Jefferson and held the post until 1809. When the War of 1812 was declared on Great Britain, Dearborn, now in his 60s, was recalled and promoted to Major General. He was given command of the Northeast territory from the Niagara River to the Atlantic Coast. He was likely responsible for much of the administra-

---

336 Hickey, page 142.

tion's strategy concerning Amherstburg, Fort Niagara, Kingston, and Montréal.[337]

Some of Dearborn's actions, including those at the trial of General William Hull, have been discussed previously and when this true American hero's weaknesses and failures became apparent he was transferred from command of the Northeast territories and given an administrative assignment in New York.

The result was that General James Wilkinson became commander of the entire eastern frontier. It created another controversy with Major General Wade Hampton, the officer next in line whose opinion of Wilkinson was so low he refused to take any of his commands.[338] Secretary of War Armstrong had little hope that the two would cooperate.

Although there is some controversy as to who was actually in charge of the administration's strategy, at least one source[339] states that Secretary of War John Armstrong had directed Wilkinson and Hampton via orders from the War Department to begin a two-pronged attack targeting Montréal. General Wade Hampton's force of 6,000 men (Hickey says 3,800 because most of Hampton's state militia refused to cross into Canada) was supposed to head north from Lake Champlain toward Montréal. Wilkinson's force of 8,000 (Hickey says 7,300) was to move northeast (down river) along the shores of the St. Lawrence with the same target in mind.

General Wade Hampton, whose reputation was not nearly as tarnished as Wilkinson's, was also called a scoundrel by military historian Kennedy Hickman. General Hampton had crossed the Canadian border on September 19, 1813, after moving his army by boat from Plattsburgh to the northern end of Lake Champlain.[340] Lack of fresh water forced Hampton to veer west along the shores of a small river called the Châteauguay south of Montréal. He was still there on October 25, 1813, when he was confronted by a defending force of

---

337 Wikipedia
338 Hickey, page 142.
339 Hickman, Kennedy, War of 1812, Battle of Crysler's Farm, Internet Source: http://militaryhistory.about.com/od/warof1812/p/War-Of-1812-Battle-Of-Cryslers-Farm.htm.
340 Hickey, page 142.

Canadian militia accompanied by Kahnawake Indian warriors. The defenders were under the command of a French-Canadian Lieutenant Colonel with the long name of Charles-Michel d'Irumberry de Salaberry, and were dug in along a line of abatis[341] on the north banks of the Châteauguay and English Rivers. Lieutenant Colonel Salaberry was not only a commissioned officer of the Canadian militia but a British officer as well.[342]

Part of the problem for the Americans was that Hampton had sent out about 1,500 of his men under the command of Colonel Robert Purdy to try to get behind the Canadian defenders. Purdy's guides were less than reliable and they got lost in the woods. Another part of the problem was observed by the Canadian and British defenders who reported seeing many of the American officers abandoning their men during the firefight and seeking higher, safer ground for themselves.

Without the help of Purdy's men, the frontal assault initiated by Hampton was much less effective than was anticipated. After several hours Hampton realized he would not be successful. He had recently received a note from Secretary of War Armstrong that winter quarters were being constructed for his men near the head of Lake Champlain. He Interpreted this to mean it was okay for him to abandon the assault on Montréal for the winter. By 3 o'clock that afternoon Hampton had ordered the withdrawal. Later, British and Canadian writers described the retreat as "panicked." There may have been some truth in that since Purdy's lost soldiers were pursued throughout the night by Kahnawake warriors.[343]

In the meantime, Wilkinson, with his force of somewhere between 7,000 and 8,000 soldiers, left Sacket's Harbor on October 7 but did not reach the shores of the St. Lawrence until November 1. Eleven days after Wade Hampton's retreat from the Châteauguay River, on

---

341 Kennedy Hickman defines abatis as a field fortification consisting of tree branches positioned in a row with sharpened ends facing outwards toward the enemy. Internet source: http://militaryhistory.about.com/od/glossaryofmilitaryterms/g/Abatis.htm.

342 Laferty, Renee, Battle of Châteauguay, Internet source: http://www.eighteentwelve.ca/?q=eng/Topic/49

343 ibid.

November 6, Wilkinson learned of the defeat but decided to continue with his part of the two-pronged strategy to attack Montréal albeit with little enthusiasm. He did send Brigadier General Jacob Brown with a small scouting force ahead along the St. Lawrence to clear the way and report back, but before Wilkinson could get the main body moving he learned he was being pursued by a force of somewhere between 650 and 900 British and Canadian militia under the command of Colonel Joseph Morrison.[344]

On the morning of November 11, 1813, Wilkinson got a report from Colonel Brown that Brown had defeated a small British force at Hoople's Creek on the eve of November 10, and that the way was clear for Wilkinson's main body to advance northeast along the shores of the St. Lawrence. Wilkinson, however, decided to clear any threat approaching his forces from the rear before embarking his troops aboard small amphibious boats to advance along the St. Lawrence. Little did he know that Morrison's troops had camped just two miles away the night before.[345]

The result of what became known as the Battle of Crysler's farm was that Wilkinson, suffering from dysentery and incapable of command because of taking drugs including opium and alcohol to treat the intestinal disorder, turned over command of the Americans to Brigadier General John Parker Boyd. Boyd attacked the pursuing British and Canadian troops, but lacking enough ammunition, and according to one source[346] also lacking *"adequate guidance"* the Americans were soundly defeated.

Military expert Hickman called the victory by the British and Canadians with their Mohawk and Mississauga warriors a stunning defeat of the Americans who suffered 102 KIA, 237 WIA, and 120 captured. Morrison's much smaller force of about 900, (another source, Renee

---

344 Hickman, http://militaryhistory.about.com/od/warof1812/p/War-Of-1812-Battle-Of-Cryslers-Farm.htm.

345 ibid. (If Hickman's figures are correct the British/Canadians were outnumbered by 7 to 1!).

346 Hickey, page 144.

Lafferty,[347] says no more than 2,400) suffered 31 KIA, 148 WIA and 13 missing.[348]

Other sources refer to Crysler's Farm as the battle that saved Canada,[349] but whatever you call them, the two battles, Châteauguay and Crysler's Farm[350] effectively ended the 1813 American campaign in Canada.

Things were relatively quiet in Canada during the last part of 1813 and the early months of 1814, but the War of 1812 in the South involving Alabama, Georgia, Mississippi, and Louisiana was still active. Although the British had anticipated allying with the Creek Indians, particularly in Georgia and Alabama, they had not done so by early 1814.

One particular band of troublesome Creeks, called Red Sticks because of the colorful war clubs they carried, had been visited by Tecumseh in 1811. They had taken his oratory against the white settlers seriously[351] and were causing the most trouble. Ironically, the Red Sticks and many other Creek Indians were a band of mixed white and Native American bloodlines, and were led by a warrior named Peter McQueen.

After they had attacked several white and mixed settlements along the Gulf Coast, including burning the plantations of owners with Creek ancestors, Sam Moniac and James Cornells, McQueen and his Red Sticks were returning from a trading visit to Pensacola on July 27, 1813, when they were waylaid by a force of Mississippi Militia led by Colonel James Caller.

In a battle which was later labeled by historians as the Battle of Burnt Corn, the fighting took place about 80 miles north of Pensacola probably in Escambia County of Alabama near the Conecuh Coun-

---

347 Laferty, Renee, Battle of Châteauguay, Internet source: http://www.eighteentwelve.ca/?q=eng/Topic/49

348 Hickman.

349 http://www.cryslersfarm.com/battle.htm

350 The British headquarters was at John Crysler's farm but the actual battle was fought on neighboring farmlands. ibid.

351 Hickey, page 145.

ty line.[352] The Mississippians made off with most of the trading loot, which was Spanish arms and ammunition the Red Sticks had gotten from the Spanish governor in Pensacola. The Red Sticks obtained the guns and ammunition by trading their loot from the raids and ransoming the wife of James Cornells whom they had kidnapped. The Mississippian's success was only temporary, however, because the Red Sticks quickly reorganized and counterattacked driving off the Mississippians.

Although the Mississippians still retained possession of most of the firearms and ammunition they were soundly routed by the counterattacking Red Sticks, and had to flee on foot or aboard the pack animals since their horses had been unattended during the surprise counterattack. The embarrassing defeat was later satirized in a poem by Lewis Sewall, "The Last Campaign of Sir John Falstaff the II; or, The Hero of the Burnt-Corn Battle (1815)," The embarrassment caused by the poem is said to have resulted in the immediate resignation from the Mississippi Militia of those who participated. They were also subject to public ridicule for years after.[353]

Just over a month later on August 30, 1813, the Creeks, led by a Scottish/Cherokee Native American named William Weatherford, retaliated again by attacking an American stockade called Fort Mims about 40 miles north of Mobile, Alabama. They massacred most of the 400 civilians and 140 Militia who occupied the fort. The slaughter included many women and children and the only people to escape were a few that were able to flee into the nearby woods. Others who survived included a few black slaves and some Native Americans who were carried off by the victorious Creeks. [354]

The Fort Mims Massacre, as it became known, essentially converted what was a series of Red Stick raids against the whites and their own mixed settlements into what was called the Creek War. The Creek War was a punitive effort by the people in Georgia and Mississippi as well as Tennessee and Alabama to destroy the Creeks. Although

---

352 Kaetz, James P. Auburn University, Encyclopedia of Alabama: http://www.encyclopediaofalabama.org/face/Article.jsp?id=h-3081
353 ibid.
354 ibid.

the Red Sticks were responsible for most of the violence against both peaceful Creeks and whites, the retaliation by the white settlers of the South did not discriminate peaceful Creeks from the Red Sticks.

In Georgia and Mississippi recruits were quick to join the effort led by Captain Sam Dale. This legendary Indian fighter was said to have jumped into a Creek dugout canoe and killed several of the native warriors in hand-to-hand fighting. Other legendary Indian fighters, Brigadier General John Floyd of the Georgia militia and Brigadier General Ferdinand L. Claiborne[355] of Mississippi led their forces in devastating attacks on the Creeks. Part Cherokee (some say Creek) William Weatherford (also known as Red Eagle) was one of the last of the Native American warriors to be seen during a battle on the Alabama River when he escaped by riding his horse off a cliff into a river in December 1813.[356]

Because the British were not initially allied with the Native American forces in the South, the fighting against the Creeks established legendary reputations amongst the Indian fighters of the admittedly racist white Americans. These included such famous historical figures as Davy Crockett, Sam Houston, and Andrew Jackson.

Jackson, a Major General in the Tennessee Militia, earned his legendary status and nickname of Old Hickory, by demonstrating his toughness in battle ("as tough as old wood") and his willingness to support his men even to the extent of giving up his horses for the sick.[357] The Native Americans had another name for Old Hickory, Sharp Knife.[358] (One source[359] says the Indian name was Long Knife).

The campaign against the Creeks headed by Jackson culminated in the Battle of Horseshoe Bend, Alabama, on March 27, 1814. At the

---

355 Hickey, page 148.
356 ibid.
357 National Park Service, U.S. Department of the Interior web source: http://www.nps.gov/natr/historyculture/andrew-jackson-gains-his-nicknames.htm
358 ibid.
359 America's Library: http://www.americaslibrary.gov/jb/nation/jb_nation_ft-jack_1.html

time of the battle, Horseshoe Bend was in an area of Mississippi Territory which later became Alabama.

By this time it was fairly well accepted that both the British and the Spanish had not only been supplying the Red Sticks, but had encouraged them to continue assaulting American settlements and forces. This accepted belief was supported by the obvious European architecture of the Red Sticks' fortifications at their defensive stronghold along the Tallapoosa River, called Tohopeka by the Native Americans, but widely known as Horseshoe Bend.[360]

Andrew Jackson, portrait courtesy Library of Congress

Horseshoe Bend was actually a peninsula which caused the river to take a typical horseshoe configuration around it. The hostile Red Sticks who occupied the fortification numbered about 1,000 and had cautiously arranged their canoes on one side of the peninsula in case they had to flee an attack.

At about 6:30 a.m. Jackson split his force ordering his second in command General John Coffee to take his force of 700 mounted riflemen and another 600 friendly Creek Indians to surround the Indian village on the south end of the peninsula. Coffee was also responsible for the prevention of Red Sticks escaping the trap and seeking refuge on the 15 acre river island just northwest of the Tohopeka village.

[360] ibid.

September 19, 1813   151

He sent Lieutenant Jesse Bean and 40 of his Tennessee militia to take care of that problem.

Around 10 a.m. on March 27, 1814, during an attack on the fort, and using the only two good cannons Jackson had, three members of his friendly Creeks swam the river and stole the Red Sticks' canoes. While the big guns were firing, Jackson's friendly Indians paddled the stolen canoes around the peninsula to attack the stronghold from the rear on the southeast side of the peninsula. When the artillery barrage was over, Jackson and his force of approximately 3,000 began a frontal assault on the fortifications from the north.

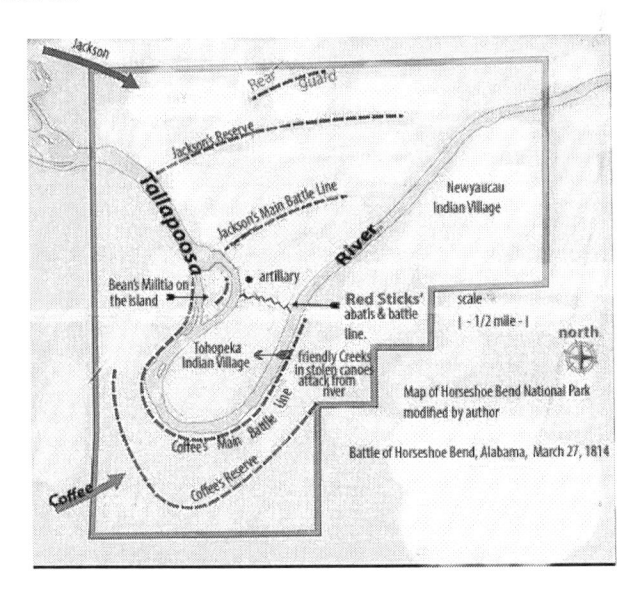

Battle of Horseshoe Bend, Alabama, March 27, 1814

During the frontal assault by Jackson's infantry a young Lieutenant by the name of Sam Houston was one of the first ones over the barricades. He was severely wounded three times during the battle. One source[361] said the arrow wound was in one of his shoulders and another source said the arrow wound was in his right leg, but that he

---

361 Hickman, Kennedy: http://militaryhistory.about.com/od/warof1812/p/battle-of-horseshoe-bend.htm

took a bullet in his right shoulder.[362] All historical sources indicate that Houston's wounds were severe.

The whole episode turned into a vicious slaughter with over 557[363] Red Stick defenders killed,[364] and an unknown number wounded or missing. William Weatherford (Red Eagle) was again one of the defenders who was said to have escaped. Some months later Weatherford walked into Jackson's camp to surrender. Jackson was so impressed with his bravery that he released the half breed warrior to carry a message of peace to other survivors.[365]

The aftermath of the Battle of Horseshoe Bend was basically created by the indomitable will of Andrew Jackson and his hard line approach to solving the Creek Indian problem. Ignoring the peace treaty recommendations of Congress and the Madison administration, Jackson forced not only the Red Sticks but the pro-American Creeks, Cherokees and other Native Americans to sign a peace treaty forcing them to cede approximately 23 million acres[366] (Hickey says 36,000 square miles which would be 23,040,000 acres[367] and Sanderson Beck[368] says 36 million acres) to the United States. Congress was so outraged by the severe terms Jackson forced on the Indians that they would not approve the so-called Treaty of Fort Jackson, signed on August 9, 1814. The treaty was approved several months later when public opinion and Jackson's victory at New Orleans forced them to do so.

Remember that treaties are now basically the purview of the U.S. President, although the rules imposed by the Constitution allows the Senate with a two thirds majority to give its advice and consent to treaties created by POTUS, the President of the United States. That

---

362 *The Life of Sam Houston*, http://www.graceproducts.com/houston/life.html
363 Hickman, Kennedy: http://militaryhistory.about.com/od/warof1812/p/battle-of-horseshoe-bend.htm
364 Hickey, page 150 says 800 killed.
365 ibid.
366 Hickman, Kennedy: http://militaryhistory.about.com/od/warof1812/p/battle-of-horseshoe-bend.htm
367 Hickey, page 151.
368 Beck, Sanderson: https://history.state.gov/milestones/1801-1829/barbary-wars.

was not necessarily true in 1813, when Congress not only could but did create or approve treaties.

One of the latest rulings occurred in 1956 and is interpreted by ex-law professor and constitutional scholar Rob Natelson of the University of Montana and Senior Fellow in Constitutional Jurisprudence, Independence Institute of Colorado:

Professor Natelson basically said that although Congress could exercise certain authorities not on its list, it still could not violate the rules of the Constitution. For instance, Congress could not pass a law that would make an act illegal *when* it was legal at the time the act occurred. Nor could Congress consent to a treaty that violated a right guaranteed in the Bill of Rights. Professor Nielsen cited the Supreme Court case of 1956 in *Reid versus Covert*.[369]

Abrogation, or nullification, of treaties is another matter and probably still to be decided by the courts.

As for Jackson, he became even more famous because of the Battle of New Orleans which he led, fought, and won decisively on January 8, 1815. The battle was fought after a peace treaty had already been signed with the British a month before on Christmas Eve 1814, in Ghent, Belgium. Of course the communications delay between Europe and United States took weeks because the telegraph was not invented until 1837. Jackson would later become seventh President of the United States. His portrait is engraved on our twenty dollar bill.

The War of 1812, which actually lasted until January 1815, was full of other significant events in its last year. These included the blockade of the Atlantic Coast which had a significant depressive effect on U.S. foreign trade, British raids in the area of Chesapeake Bay and Hampton, Virginia and some naval engagements. It also included the occupation of Washington D.C. by the British and their retaliatory burning

---

369 Natelson, Rob, U. of Montana: Our American Constitution: http://constitution.i2i.org/2014/07/20/how-much-authority-http://constitution.i2i.org/2014/07/20/how-much-authoritydoes-congress-have-under-the-treaty-power-the-question-the-supreme-court-dodged/http://constitution.i2i.org/2014/07/20/how-much-authority-

of the White House in Washington D.C. which occurred as revenge for the Americans' sacking of York (Toronto).

One of the most interesting stories in the history of the War of 1812 was the origin of the Star-Spangled Banner. Francis Scott Key was a lawyer who practiced in Georgetown. Even though he was a pacifist he nevertheless served as a volunteer in Georgetown's Light Field Artillery. Because of his negotiating skills as a lawyer, Key had been sent by his commanding officer, Captain George Peters, under a flag of truce aboard an American diplomatic vessel to negotiate the release of a physician, Dr. William Beane.[370] The good doctor, who had been captured by the British during their assault and occupation of Washington, D.C., was being held aboard a British ship in Baltimore Harbor.

Key and the U.S. government prisoner exchange officer, Colonel John Skinner, were well treated by the British who had already decided to release Dr. Beane. They would not, however, release him until the British artillery assault on nearby Fort McHenry, some four miles away (another source[371] says eight miles away) was over. Therefore Skinner, Key, and Doctor Beane returned to their own ship to await the outcome of the British artillery barrage, as they had promised the British negotiators.

Three of the common myths often reported about Francis Scott Key and the Star-Spangled Banner were debunked recently in an ABC radio broadcast as described by Scott Wilson on July 4, 2014.[372]

- Quoting University of Michigan Associate Professor (of Music) Mark Clague at a recent Library of Congress symposium on the origins of the anthem, Wilson said that Key was actually aboard an American ship during the Battle of Baltimore and

---

370 Multiple sources also spell it Beanes, and multiple sources also spell it both ways.

371 Another source is: Fort McHenry National Monument: http://www.nps.gov/fomc/historyculture/francis-scott-key.htm

372 Wilson, Scott: http://abcnews.go.com/blogs/politics/2014/07/star-spangled-banner-myths-debunked/

not held as a prisoner aboard a British ship as is commonly stated.
- Professor Clague also debunked the belief that Key wrote the words to the anthem as a poem which was later set to music by somebody else. He said that Key intended the words to be sung to a melody of the time called *"When a Warrior Returns"* which had a unique rhythm called *"con spirito"* meaning with spirit." Another source[373] states that Key wrote the lyrics while staying in the Indian Queen Hotel in Baltimore on September 15, 1814, from notes he made during the bombardment of Fort McHenry on September 13-14.
- The third myth debunked by Professor Clague was the common belief by many other sources that the melody was actually a common bawdy drinking song called *"The Anacreontic Song."*

Clague, according to Clark Wilson's article, claimed *"The Anacreontic Song"* although first performed at the Crown and Anchor, which was indeed a tavern in London, was actually adopted by The Anacreontic Society, a high-class gentlemen's club, and used as an opening song for its meetings. Clague's theory is that Francis Scott Key's modeling of the anthem after the rhythm of *The Anacreontic Song* was intentional.

At any rate most sources agree that Francis Scott Key paced the deck of whatever ship he was on which was indeed most likely the American vessel, until dawn when he was inspired to write the words, or at least the notes of his observations. He also knew that when he visualized the American flag that the British artillery barrage had failed, and that the Americans were still in possession of Fort McHenry. When the British abandoned their anchorage in Chesapeake Bay while Doctor Beane was still aboard the Ameri-

---

373 Kershner, Michelle. *Museums and Historic Sites*, 2013: http://www.visitfrederick.org/what-to-see-and-do/10-key-facts-about-the-star-spangled-banner-and-its-author

can vessel, Key and Skinner knew the British had failed to take Fort McHenry.

Keys' original title to the lyrics he wrote as a song and not a poem was *"The Defense of Fort McHenry."* The song was used as an American symbol for many years but not without its critics, who felt both the melody and lyrics were difficult to sing. In 1916 President Woodrow Wilson declared that the song should be used to open all official events, but it did not become the official national anthem until 1931, when President Herbert Hoover made it so.

When word of the Peace Treaty of Ghent, Belgium, ending the War of 1812 finally reached the United States in January 1815, the war was officially declared over by President Madison. The way was now open for the United States to create a final solution to the extortion by the Barbary Coast Pirates.

CHAPTER ELEVEN

February 23, 1815

"Slavery is such an atrocious debasement of human nature that its very extirpation, if not performed with solicitous care, may sometimes open a source of serious evils." -Benjamin Franklin

The Treaty of Tripoli supposedly ending the first Barbary war was signed on June 4, 1805 when Tobias Lear took over the negotiations at Derna and ended the yearly tributes paid to Yusuf Karamanli, the Pasha of Tripoli. When the Mediterranean Squadron was withdrawn in 1807, the Barbary Powers resumed their piratical ways capturing American merchant ships.

The United States Navy and government however had their hands full with the actions of the British and French fleets, the policy of impressment, and other serious problems as already shown. During the British naval blockade of the Atlantic Coast the American merchant fleet was pretty much bottled up in ports and unable to get out to trade with foreign countries. As a result their exposure to the Barbary Coast atrocities was reduced. Not all American ships, however, were safe.

One particular example was the capture of the merchant brig *Edwin* out of Salem, Massachusetts. It was enroute from Malta to Gibraltar when it was seized by Algerian pirates on August 25, 1812. Captured along with its Captain, George C. Smith and his crew of 10 was an American passenger, Mister Pollard.[374] All were imprisoned in Algiers and although an offer of $3,000 in ransom per captive was made by the United States, it was rejected.[375]

When the war was declared on the U.S. by the Dey (or Bey) of Algiers, Hajji Ali, he rejected the tribute that the United States had negotiated in the previous Treaty of 1795 as insufficient.[376] Hajji Ali also expelled Tobias Lear from the American Consulate in Algiers, along with his staff. Lear arrived back in the United States on April 9, 1813,[377] aboard the USS Allegheny, the very ship which was to have delivered the rejected tribute.

There was not much the U.S. could do about a confrontation. Nor after the exile of Tobias Lear could we negotiate ransoms for captured merchantmen who were serving as slaves until the War of 1812 was over. When President Madison became aware that the War of 1812 was over in February 1815, he did indeed petition Congress on February 23 to support armed intervention against Algiers.

Copied from the Congressional record of March 1, 1815 is the following:

"In secret session-

"A confidential message was received from the House of Representatives, by Mr. Gaston and Mr. Forsyth, two members of that body; Mr. Gaston, Chairman:

Mr. President: the House of Representatives have confidentially passed a bill entitled 'An act for the protection of commerce of the United

---

374 Chronology, Richard Somers website: http://www.richardsomers.org/rsomers%20page2.html

375 McClellan, Maj. Edwin N. Hist U.S.M.C. 11st Ed. Chap II, page2. Internet source: https://www.mcu.usmc.mil/historydivision

376 US Department of State, Office of the Historian, Internet Source: https://history.state.gov/milestones/1801-1829/barbary-wars.

377 Tobias Lear papers, William L. Clements Library, The University of Michigan: http://quod.lib.umich.edu/c/clementsmss/umich-wcl-M-1044lea?view=text

States against the Algerine cruisers' in which they request the concurrence of the Senate.

"The said bill was twice read by unanimous consent, and passed to the third reading."[378]

On March 2, 1815 the Congressional record showed thus:
"In secret session-
"The Bill from the House of Representatives entitled 'An act for the protection of commerce in the United States against Algerine cruisers' was read for the third time.

"On the question, 'Shall this bill pass?' it was determined in the affirmative-yeas 27, nays 2, as follows:"[379]

The rest of the quote listed the voters' names under the proper column for yea or nay. Although it was not a formal declaration of war, many historians considered it as such. At any rate Congress approved President Madison's request and the first of two squadrons of Navy ships left New York on May 20 headed for Algiers.

The first squadron to leave the states was commanded by a name that should by now be familiar to the reader, Commodore Stephen Decatur. He had 10 ships available to him which included:
- Three frigates, the 54 gun *Guerriere*, the 48 gun *Macedonian*, and the 48 gun *Constellation*.
- One sloop, the Ontario with 28 guns.
- Four brigs, the *Epervier* with 18 guns, the *Firefly* with 14 guns, the *Flambeau* with 12 and the *Spark* also with 12.
- Two schooners, the *Spitfire* with 12 guns and the *Torch* with 10.

At least two of the ships were British vessels captured in 1812, the *Macedonian*, captured by Decatur himself when he was Captain of the USS *President*, and the *Epervier*. Another was named after an American- destroyed British ship, the *Guerriere*.

The 14 gun *Firefly* sustained storm damage a few days out of her departure from New York on May 20 and was forced to return for refitting.[380]

---

378 *Annals of Congress, Senate, 13th Congress, 3rd session page 284*. Available online: http://memory.loc.gov/cgi-bin/ampage/
379 ibid. page 291.
380 Tucker, Spencer, et al. editors. *Encyclopedia of the War of 1812*.Vol. 1, ABC-CLIO, Santa Barbara, 2012, page 9.

In his flagship the *USS Guerrier*, commanded by Captain Lewis, Decatur and the rest of his squadron arrived in Gibraltar on June 15. Many historians have quoted remarks by others that Decatur's rapid departure from New York was due to his eagerness to get into the action and his desire to avoid operating under the orders of the senior commander, William Bainbridge. Captain Bainbridge was commanding the squadron that was supposed to be the first one to reach the Mediterranean.

Regular officers in the Army, Navy, or Marines are career officers, usually graduates of West Point or Annapolis, or some other college or military Academy. Other officers, especially in wartime, are usually reserve officers or draftees with a much shorter duration of service. Of the regular officers, many have gone to school together or served together for years during their service. It becomes a fleet wide family in the Navy with all the competition and "sibling" rivalry typical of a large family. Most of it is good-natured but once in a while petty jealousies arise, particularly when a junior officer in rank or duration of service does something to help promote himself (or herself) over the other regular officers.

In the early 1800s some regular Navy officers disparaged Decatur with remarks that may have been the result of a fleet wide jealousy of the young hero who had been promoted over others of more senior rank after his exploits in the first Barbary War.[381]

Even Bainbridge may have harbored a hidden resentment and jealousy toward the younger Commodore. Bainbridge, if you will remember, was the former commander of the *USS Washington* who was forced to carry the Dey of Algiers' cargo of gifts and slaves to Constantinople in 1800 after having delivered the annual tribute from the U.S. He was also forced by the fear of imprisonment to fly the Algerian flag during that journey. That was not the only humbling experience for this officer who also had his heroic moments.

Bainbridge is probably most infamous for running his ship, the *USS Philadelphia*, aground on October 21, 1803, while chasing a Tripolitan Corsair. And of course a junior officer, Stephen Decatur was the young hero who led the mission to destroy the *USS Philadelphia* so it could not be used against us. Meanwhile Bainbridge had been held captive by the Tripolitan Pasha, Yusuf Karamanli. He was not released

---

[381] ibid.

from prison until the bombardments of Tripoli in 1805 which ended the first Barbary war.

Another episode of embarrassment for Bainbridge had been when he commanded the first ship to be surrendered to the French during the Quasi-War, the *USS Retaliation*.

Bainbridge had enjoyed much better success as a young merchant sailor. At the age of 19, while in port in Bordeaux, he responded to a request for help from a nearby ship that was experiencing a mutiny. He helped put it down sustaining a wound that nearly killed him, all the while being outnumbered by seven mutinous sailors. For that heroic feat he was given command of a small merchant vessel, the *Hope*.[382]

He'd also had several successful commands including one as Commanding Officer of the *USS Essex*, one of the original frigates of Commodore Dale's first Mediterranean squadron. Bainbridge also had command of the *USS President* in 1809, and the *USS Constitution* during the early months of the War of 1812. On December 29, 1812 while in command of the *Constitution*, Bainbridge was wounded in action against *HMS (His Majesty's Ship) Java*, but still managed to destroy the enemy vessel. His own ship was also badly damaged losing its own helm in the exchange of fire. To this day the still commissioned *USS Constitution* retains the helm from the *Java* that Bainbridge recovered before the enemy vessel sank.[383] Three months after the victory over the *Java*, Bainbridge was presented with the Congressional Gold Medal by President Madison.

Bainbridge, who was supposed to be the senior commander of the two squadrons, had been in Boston since the spring of 1814 with his squadron. Citizens of Boston had complained about the location of the Navy squadron which they felt was an obvious target for British guns. They were also worried about their own structures and citizens should the British open fire on the squadron. Bainbridge had been requested to move his squadron to an unprotected part of the harbor to spare any damage to Boston itself. Bainbridge refused the request and told Boston officials that if they surrendered to the British

---
382 Wikipedia.
383 ibid.

without resistance he would fire upon them himself.[384] The animosity that Bainbridge probably stirred up with those remarks may have been responsible for the delays in outfitting his squadron and may have been caused by the offended Boston merchants and officials.

Decatur, having heard of Bainbridge's problems in mid-May, anticipated his delay and may have given the young Commodore another reason to leave without waiting for Bainbridge's squadron. He had wanted to leave on the 15th of May but adverse weather and winds forced him to wait until the 20th.

When Decatur's squadron arrived in Gibraltar on June 15, well ahead of Bainbridge, the consulates said that Admiral Rais Hammida[385] and his Algerian corsairs were most likely waiting along the southern Spanish coast off Cape de Gata for the half-million dollar tribute promised them by the Spanish government to continue the peace between the two countries. The Algerians of course were Decatur's first target, since Morocco had been behaving since the renewal of its treaty with the United States forced by Commodores Preble and Rodgers in 1805. If Decatur could isolate the Algerian Navy from the port of Algiers where the Muslim shore batteries would constitute a distinct threat, the safety level for American vessels would be greatly improved.

Sure enough, two days later on June 17, Captain Charles Gordon's lookouts aboard the *USS Constellation,* spotted the sails of the *Meshuda,*[386] Hammida's flagship, just off Cape de Gata as they had been told.[387] Remember, the *Meshuda* was originally an American merchant ship, *Betsy*, captured by Tripolitan pirates in 1796. Armed by the Arabs, she wound up in Gibraltar's harbor guarded by Captain Hugh Campbell in the *USS Adams* of Commodore Morris' squadron, "lest she escape and prey on American shipping." The *Meshuda* and her

---

384 Hickey, page 268.
385 Also spelled Hamidu
386 Also spelled Meshouda, or Mashouda.
387 Tucker, et al page 9.

pirate crew were released from quarantine when Campbell was ordered by Commodore Morris to join the Tripoli blockade.

The *Meshuda* was recaptured by Campbell and the *USS Adams* shortly thereafter in July, 1803, then flying a Moroccan flag. She was kept as a prize by the Americans until Commodores Preble and Rodgers returned her to Mulay Suleiman, the Emperor of Morocco, in September 1803. The ship was given back to the thieves who had stolen it as a goodwill gesture but only after our show of force convinced Suleiman to end his demand of additional tribute and renew his father's previous peace agreement.

Now the *Meshuda* was back in the mix flying a British flag when she was first spotted by Gordon's lookouts. She was now part of the Algerian fleet commanded by the so-called Admiral of the Algerian Navy, Rais Hammida.

Decatur was on the *USS Guerriere* and receiving "enemy located" flag signals[388] from Captain Gordon aboard the *USS Constellation* and ordered battle stations for his squadron as they went in pursuit. Hammida, seeing the ships approach, was not expecting the Americans and most likely believed they were British. He kept a neutral course. Decatur was about to order his squadron to fly the British colors as well, suspecting the Algerian admiral was thinking exactly what he was thinking. Then the mistake happened.

Charlie Gordon, the Master of the *Constellation*, raised the American flag over his stern flag mast. Decatur, recognizing the mistake, quickly signaled for all ships in the squadron to raise the British flag** but it was too late. Admiral Hammida quickly changed course and headed for his home port of Algiers on the African coast. The *USS Constellation*, the closest of the Americans, opened fire and the rest of the squadron gave chase. When Admiral Hammida realized he had no chance to outrun the *Constellation*, he reversed course and headed for the Spanish coast. The maneuver took him on a course headed directly for the *USS Ontario* which was lagging behind most of the

---

388 Tinniswood, Adrian, Pirates of the Barbary: etc. Penguin, NY, Nov 11, 2010.

squadron on a course between the *Constellation* on Decatur's starboard side and the *Epervier* on his port.[389]

Decatur, recognizing an opportunity, had Lewis move his ship in so close to the *Meshuda* that their musket fire was able to reach the *Guerriere*, wounding four of her American crew, one fatally. On the positive side, *Guerriere* was close enough to inflict devastating damage and did so with two strong broadsides directly into *Meshuda's* quarterdeck and superstructure.

The first broadside literally cut the opposing admiral's body in parts. Admiral Rais Hammida was sitting in a chair on his quarterdeck for a better view of the action when *Guerriere's* broadside cut him down. He was hit by a 42 pound cannonball that struck him in the chest.[390] The second broadside delivered the *coup de grace*, although the crew of the *Meshuda* failed to strike their colors most likely because there was no one alive on deck with the authority to do so.

Decatur's losses however were not over. With no one visible on *Meshuda's* deck, Decatur had Captain Lewis maneuver his ship to allow for a boarding party onto the Meshuda. While he was doing so one of his cannons exploded killing three more of the *Guerriere's* crew and wounding another seven.[391]

As all this was happening Captain** John Downs of the *USS Epervier* arrived in range of *Meshuda's* starboard quarter, saw some of the survivors manipulating *Meshuda's* helm and opened fire with nine additional broadsides. Decatur, noting the problems Captain Lewis was having after the cannon exploded, had to abandon the immediate boarding maneuver. Fortunately Captain Downs' skillful handling of his 16 guns forced the striking of *Meshuda's* colors.

Decatur then ordered Captain Lewis, who was the commanding officer of his flagship, Midshipman Hoffman, who was Decatur's aid,

---

389 Hannings, Bud, The War of 1812, a Complete Chronology, McFarland, 2012 page 299.

390 ibid.

391 ibid.

* It was common practice in those days for warring nations or pirate ships to fly false colors

** Downs' rank was Master Commandant. Regardless of rank, Masters of Navy vessels are addressed as "Captain".

and another officer by the name of Howell, to lead the boarding party and take possession of the *Meshuda*.[392]

Bud Hannings, author of *The War of 1812, a Complete Chronology*, describes the scene on board the *Meshuda* as "gruesome." There was blood everywhere and Admiral Hammida's body was splattered with his parts scattered from the epicenter of his destroyed quarterdeck chair along with the parts of 30 of his crewmen. There were 406 survivors of the *Meshuda's* crew who were taken prisoner.

Decatur then ordered Captain Jacob Jones and the *USS Macedonian* to tow[393] the *Meshuda* with its prisoners under guard to Cartagena. He then called in the captains of the remainder of his squadron and distributed souvenirs from the *Meshuda*, giving Captain John Downs first choice. He then set sail for a cruise along the Spanish coast for other marauders.[394] He found one two days later.

The Algerian ship *Estedio* was a 22 gun brig[395] sighted by the lookouts in Decatur's squadron off the Spanish coast of Cape Palos in the early morning hours of June 19, 1815. Decatur gave the order to pursue the corsairs' vessel, but in the pursuit his squadron found themselves approaching shallow water. Fearing that the heavy frigates might run aground, Decatur ordered the smaller ships with shallower drafts to continue the pursuit while his heavier ships stayed in deeper water.

The smaller ships that pursued the *Estedio* were the *Epervier*, the *Spark*, the *Spitfire* and the *Torch*.[396] While continuously firing on the fleeing pirate brig, the smaller vessels ran her aground on Cape Palos. Some of the pirates lowered lifeboats from their davits and started rowing away. Others waded to shore and disappeared. A shot from one of the American gunboats destroyed one of the escaping lifeboats. Others got away. Still, the Americans took 80 prisoners and

---

392 ibid.
393 Janssens, Jean Claude, (Translated by Gerald Hawkins), Confederate Historical Association of Belgium, the first operations of the U.S. Navy in the Mediterranean Sea: Internet source: http://www.chab-belgium.com/pdf/english/Barbary%20wars.pdf.
394 Hannings, page 299.
395 Tucker, Spencer, et al. editors. page 10
396 ibid.

counted 23 of the enemy KIA.[397] The Americans had no casualties. Decatur ordered the prisoners under guard and towed his second prize in two days to Cartagena. The capture of the *Estedio* was the last shooting battle of the second Barbary War which involved Americans.

On June 28, 1815, Decatur and his squadron sailed boldly into Algiers Harbor. Having captured two enemy ships, thus avoiding more bloodshed, he had urged his squadron to travel as quickly as possible to Algiers before the remnants of Admiral Hammida's fleet could get there. The *Guerriere* was also flying a Swedish flag signaling the Swedish consulate onshore that a meeting was requested.[398] Sweden was at best a half-hearted ally of the United States, but she was a neutral nation whose consulate could dampen tempers in negotiations.

Shortly after the *Guerriere* dropped anchor, a small boat from shore approached with two apparent dignitaries as passengers. These were the port Captain, and Swedish Consul Johan Norderling.

Through these two gentlemen, Decatur, showing admirable confidence, notified them that he had captured the *Meshuda* and the *Estedio*, and that the Algerian Admiral had been killed in the battle. Decatur also presented the port Captain with a letter from President Madison to the Dey. The letter, while showing the Muslim the respect the Dey expected by addressing him as "Omar the Great, son of Mohammed the Conqueror," declared that he would be happy to level the city of Algiers with gunfire if Omar did not immediately release all of the U.S. sailors he held in captivity![399]

The Algerian port Captain, as might be expected, expressed doubt regarding Decatur's claims. Decatur then pulled the ace from his sleeve and had one of the captured Muslims, who was actually Admiral Hammida's Lieutenant,[400] brought forth for the Captain of the

---

397 ibid.
398 Hannings, page 300.
399 Hannings, page 299.
400 Waldo, Samuel P, *The Life and Character of Stephen Decatur*, PB Goodsell, Hartford, 1821 page 249

port of Algiers to interview. After that there was no doubt in the port Captain's mind about what had happened.

You can imagine the shock and consternation Omar Agha (also called Umar ben Muhammed), felt when he was faced with such an ultimatum. Omar had ruled the Algerian Regency for just 3 months since March 23, 1815,[401] when he achieved the throne by the assassination of Dey Hadji Ali and earned the name Omar the Terrible.[402] His reign would last just two years.

Decatur had on board his vessel an American diplomat, by the name of William E. Shaker who had been sent by Secretary of State Monroe and President Madison. Shaker's job was, along with Commodore Decatur, to negotiate a peace treaty with the Dey of Algiers.

Historians reviewing the events in Algiers of June 28-July 3, 1815, agree that Decatur handled it very well refusing to accept the Dey's delaying tactics, showing his resolve and insisting on an answer to his ultimatum within three hours.[403]

When Omar Basha, the Dey of Algiers, capitulated, the result was the peace treaty shown in Appendix B. It is really a remarkable document in the nation's history, incorporating most of the 10 Commandments of Muslim Diplomacy discussed near the end of this chapter.

With the signed treaty in the possession of Captain Williams, Decatur dispatched Williams and the *USS Epervier* home to the United States.[404] Other changes included transferring Master Commandant John Downs, who had been captain of the *USS Epervier*, to take over as captain of Decatur's flagship the *Guerriere* and sending his own First Lieutenant, John Templer Shubrick to become the new master of the *Epervier*. Additional passengers dispatched on the *Epervier* were Lieutenants Benedict Neale and John Yarnall. Yarnall, one of *Guerriere's* Lieutenants, had been wounded during the battle with the *Me-*

---

401 McClellan, Maj. Edwin N., Hist., U.S.M.C., 1st Ed. Chap II, page 7. Internet source: https://www.mcu.usmc.mil/historydivision

402 McClellan, page 7.

403 Janssens, Jean Claude, (Translated by Gerald Hawkins), Confederate Historical Association of Belgium, the First Operations of the U.S. Navy in the Mediterranean Sea: Internet source: belgium.com/pdf/English/Barbary%20wars.pdf

404 Waldo, page 251.

shuda and Decatur, being ever mindful of his crew, sent him home to recover. They would never reach home.

Decatur left Algiers Harbor on July 8 and arrived in Tunis three weeks later on July 29. There the American Council in Tunis, Mordechai Noah, rowed out to meet with Decatur on his flagship.[405] Decatur's demands were similar to those he instituted in Algeria, namely:
- Tunis was to refrain from further attacks on American vessels.
- Tunis was to pay a reimbursement of $46,000 for letting the British recover two prize merchant vessels captured by an American privateer, the *Abellino*.
- The Dey had 12 hours to comply or Decatur would level the city.

Mordechai Noah took these demands ashore to meet with the Muslim leader. The first question out of the Dey's mouth asked what a hostile squadron from America was doing anchored in the bay. With that Noah presented the demands listed above. After consultation with a number of his colleagues, Dey Mahmoud replied that he was agreeable to stopping harassment of American merchant shipping, but he was reluctant to pay $46,000 (in gold),[406] probably thinking that his ally Great Britain, would help with the problem.

Mordechai Noah cleverly pointed out that more than one of the ships anchored with the American squadron was captured from the British. He then handed a telescope to the Dey, and had him focus on the *Macedonian*, which Decatur had captured himself, the *Guerriere*, an American built ship but one that was named after a British ship which the Americans had destroyed, and the Ontario, which Noah labeled as the *Peacock*, a known British loss to the Americans. Although Noah broke one of the future 10 Commandments of Muslim Diplomacy with this fabrication, it was effective. Noah then reminded Dey Mahmoud of Commodore Decatur's reputation concerning his actions in Tripoli and the burning of the *Philadelphia* with which Mah-

---

405 De Kay, James, *Chronicles of the Frigate Macedonian, 1809-1922*, W.W. Norton Co. NY, London 2000. Page 123.

406 Minor, Benjamin, & Wells, JD, *The Southern Literary Messenger*, JW White, Richmond 1835, digitized by Oxford University press November 28, 2006. Available online: https://books.google.com/books?id=XE4FAAAAQAAJ&pg=PR5&focus=viewport&output=text#c_top

moud was familiar.[407] He also informed him of what had recently happened in Algeria and pointed out that Decatur's guns were already trained on the Dey's palace.

It wasn't long after that that the Dey of Tunis capitulated, and agreed to the terms of a new Treaty. Decatur sailed from Tunis on August 2,[408] 1815, and arrived in Tripoli on August 5, having successfully if not forcefully, negotiated new treaties with two of the Barbary States.

Decatur anchored in Tripoli where *"he once more beheld the batteries and the castle under the guns of which, more than eleven and one half years before, he destroyed the frigate Philadelphia – and but two days from eleven years since he, with the gallant MacDonough and a little crew, fought the unparalleled battle with gunboats – slew double their own number – captured two full-manned boats with one boat less than half- manned, and avenged the death of Lieutenant [Steven's brother James] Decatur."*[409]

Anchored near Decatur's *Guerriere*, was the *USS Macedonian*, now captained by Jacob Jones whom Commodore Preble and Decatur had freed from captivity in this very port so many years ago. Captain Jones could stand on his own quarterdeck and view the castle in which he had been kept prisoner. It must have been a nice feeling for that gentleman to be a party to the Navy squadron which now held the upper hand.

Decatur, having communicated with the American Consul in Tripoli, Mr. Richard B. Jones, learned that the Pasha of Tripoli, Yusuf Karamanli, had permitted a British ship to take two American vessels from his harbor during the War of 1812, and refused protection of an American cruiser. This was in violation of the treaty previously negotiated. Decatur immediately demanded restitution of $25,000 and dispatched the American Consul Jones to confront the Pasha. The Pasha

---

407 *De Kay, page 125.*
408 *Waldo, page 252.*
409 *ibid.*

in return sent his governor back to the *Guerriere* to request a reduction in the amount of money demanded by the Americans.[410]

Here is the actual correspondence from Consul Richard B. Jones to Decatur and subsequently to the Pasha as well as Decatur's report to the Secretary of the Navy and his letters to Yusuf Karamanli's prime minister and the King of the Two Sicilies. The first letter below is referred to as *"enclosure No.1"* by Decatur in his later letter to the secretary of the Navy. Note the intestinal fortitude that Jones shows in his communication to Decatur:

"U. S. Consulate at Tripoli, in Barbary, August 6, 1815.

"Commodore Stephen Decatur,
Onboard the United States Frigate Guerriere, off Tripoli.

"Sir:
"I have the pleasure of now laying before you all the documents relative to the unlawfully seizing, in the port of Tripoli, and under the guns of the forts, two American prizes, captured by the Abellino, and taken out by the English brig Paulina. I have fully addressed the United States' Government on this affair, and hope you have come fully prepared to demand and obtain ample satisfaction.

"It is a case attended with such a flagrant violation of the United States' treaty with this regency, and our neutral rights, that it calls for the most prompt and energetic conduct on the part of the United States, which will not only convince this Power, but all others, that our rights' and privileges cannot be invaded with impunity. If, however, the Bashaw, contrary, to my opinion, should refuse us that satisfaction we are justly entitled to, it is my determination to leave the regency by this occasion.

"I shall have the pleasure of seeing you, and will detail more fully the events as they have taken place. In the interim,

---
410 ibid, page 253.

"I have the honor to be, &c.

[signed]

"RICHARD B. JONES."[411]
[American Consul in Tripoli]

The next letter is the one sent by Decatur to Yusuf Karamanli's Prime Minister:

"Commodore Stephen Decatur
U. S. Ship Guerriere, off Tripoli, August 6, 1815.

"His Excellency the Prime Minister of His Excellency the Bashaw of Tripoli.

"Sir: [This letter is referred to as 'enclosure No.2 by Decatur to the Secretary of the Navy].
"I have been officially informed that the Bashaw of Tripoli has permitted a British sloop of war, pending hostilities between that nation and the United States, to take from out of his harbor, and from under the guns of his castle, two American prizes, and refused protection to an American cruiser lying within his waters, in direct violation of the treaty which existed between our two nations. As soon as I had settled with Algiers for her aggressions, and with Tunis for a similar outrage to the one now complained of, I hastened to this place with a part of the squadron under my command.

"With ample power to take satisfaction for the violation of our treaty above stated, I only follow the invariable rule of my Government, in first making a demand of justice. I have, therefore, to inform your excellency that I require that immediate restitution be made of the value of the vessels taken from the harbor of Tripoli as before stated, and also compensation for the loss occasioned by the detention of the American cruiser, in violation of the treaty. Your Excellency will perceive the necessity of

---
411 Naval Operation's Against the Barbary Powers in 1815; Communicated to the Senate, January 11, 1816. http://www.ibiblio.org/pha/USN/1816/18160111Pirates.html

making known to me the determination of His Excellency the Bashaw, in relation to the above demands, with the least possible delay.

"I have the honor to be, with great consideration, your Excellency's most obedient servant,

[signed]
STEPHEN DECATUR."[412]   **

Portrait of (unnamed) Prime Minister of Tripoli 1815-1817 by London born artist Augustus Earle, 1793-1838

Author Samuel Putnam Waldo, Decatur's biographer, put forth this imaginary but probable conversation when Decatur met with the Prime Minister [Governor]:[413]

---
412 ibid.
413 Waldo, Page 253

Karamanali's Governor:	*"Most potent Chief,"* the governor, who spoke very good English said, *"my master, the son of the Profit, eleven years past, demanded of the great Preble, $600,000 as tribute and ransom but received just $60,000."*
Decatur:	*"Your demand arose from your wickedness in enslaving American citizens – ours rises from justice in demanding indemnification for your violation of our treaty. The American government paid $60,000 out of compassion to your master and we demand about half of it back as a matter of right – the money must be paid immediately to the American Consul."*

The money was paid and in addition Decatur demanded the release of two Danish citizens and eight Neapolitan's whom his own American Consul had said were imprisoned by the Pasha. When they were freed the happy men came on board to thank Decatur. Later after dropping the released prisoners off in Messina, Decatur proceeded to Naples where he addressed the King of Naples, Ferdinand IV, through the Minister of Foreign Affairs with this correspondence:

"US Ship Guerriere, Naples September 8, 1815

His Excellency, the Marquis Cercello Secretary of State

Sir – I have the honor to inform your Excellency that in my late negotiation with the Basha of Tripoli, I demanded and obtained the release of eight Neapolitan captives, subjects of his Majesty, the King of the Two Sicilies. These I have landed in Sicily. It affords me great pleasure to have had it in my power, by this small service, to evince his Majesty the grateful sense entertained by our government, of the aid formally granted to us by his Majesty during our war with Tripoli.

With great respect and consideration, I have the honor to be your Excellency's most obedient servant.

[Signed] *Stephen Decatur*"[414]

* * *

Four days later Decatur received this reply:
His Excellency the Marquis Circello,
Secretary of State & Minister of Foreign Affairs

Commodore Decatur,
Commander of the Squadron
of the United States of America

Naples, September 12, 1815.

Sir:
Having laid before the King my master the papers which you have directed me, dated the eighth instant, in which you were pleased to acquaint me that, in your last negotiation with the Bey of Tripoli, you had freed from the slavery of that regency eight subjects of His Majesty, whom you had also set on shore at Messina. His Majesty has ordered me to acknowledge this peculiar favor, as the act of your generosity, which you have been pleased to call a return for the trifling assistance which the squadron of your nation formerly received from his Royal Government during the war with Tripoli.

In doing myself the pleasure of manifesting this sentiment of my King, and of assuring you, in his name, that the brave American nation will always find in His Majesty's ports the best reception, I beg you will receive the assurance of my most distinguished consideration.

[signed]
MARQUIS CIRCELLO,
Secretary of State, & Minister of Foreign Affairs.

---

414 ibid, page 255

Decatur had already received this acknowledgement from Consul Richard Jones:

> "U. S. Consulate at Tripoli, in Barbary, August 9, 1815
>
> "Commodore Stephen Decatur,
> "Commander-in-chief of the American squadron, off Tripoli.
>
> "Sir:
> "Permit me to congratulate you on the honorable adjustment of all differences which have existed between the United States and this regency. This arrangement may not only be considered as just and honorable for the United States, but also as highly advantageous to the interest of our citizens. I have no doubt this lesson will long serve to keep in the remembrance of the Bashaw the power, justice, and humanity of the United States. To your dignified, firm, and manly conduct throughout this affair, the United States are indebted for the standing we now have; and as the representative of our country here, permit me to offer the sincere homages of respect, esteem, and regard, with which I have the honor to be, &c.
>
> [signed] "RICHARD B. JONES"[415]

* * *

Portrait of Stephen Decatur, by Charles Bird King circa 1820; National Portrait Gallery

---

415 ibid.

Decatur had also already dispatched this letter to the Secretary of the Navy:

Com. Stephen Decatur, USN
U. S. Ship Guerriere, Messina, August 31, 1815.

Hon. Benjamin W. Crowninshield
Secretary of the Navy

Sir:
I have the honor to inform you that, immediately after the date of my last communication, I proceeded to Tripoli. Upon my arrival off that place, I received from our consul [Richard B. Jones] a letter, a copy of which (No. 1) is herewith transmitted. In consequence of the information contained in this letter, I deemed it necessary to demand justice from the Bashaw. The enclosure (No. 2) is a copy of my note to the Prime Minister of Tripoli. On the next day the Governor of the city of Tripoli came on board the Guerriere to treat in behalf of the Bashaw. He objected to the amount claimed by us, but finally agreed to our demands. The money, amounting to the sum of twenty-five thousand dollars, has been paid into the hands of the consul, who is agent for the privateer. The Bashaw also delivered up to me ten captives two of them Danes, and the others Neapolitans.

    I have the honor to enclose the letter of the consul, informing me of the conclusion of this affair. During the progress of our negotiations with the States of Barbary, now brought to a conclusion, there has appeared a disposition, on the part of each of them, to grant as far as we were disposed to demand. Any attempt to conciliate them, except through the influence of their fears, I should expect to be vain. It is only by the display of naval power that their depredations can be restrained. I trust that the successful result of our small expedition, so honorable to our country, will induce other nations to follow the example; in which case, the Barbary States will be compelled to abandon their piratical system. I shall now proceed with the squadron to Carthagena, at which place I hope to find the relief squadron from America.

I have the honor to be, with great respect, sir, your most obedient servant,

[signed]

STEPHEN DECATUR.

In the meantime during Decatur's remarkable summer in the Mediterranean Bainbridge, with the second squadron, did not sail from Boston until July 3, 1815. and did not arrive in the Mediterranean until August, too late to be of much help except as a show of force. His squadron included the *USS Independence*, the *USS United States*, the *USS Congress*, and smaller vessels. Bainbridge and his squadron visited Algiers, Tunis, and Tripoli and at each port found that Decatur had already accomplished peace. He finally caught up with Decatur's squadron in Gibraltar on his way home.

Fully believing that a residual force should be left in the Mediterranean,[416] Decatur left his ships under the command of Bainbridge and headed for home. He arrived there on November 12, 1815. His biographer, Waldo, indicated that Bainbridge accompanied Decatur home but another source, McClellan,[417] stated they arrived three days apart.

When Decatur arrived in the United States he heard some shocking news.

"All the Americans who had been held as prisoners were sent on board the Epervier and that vessel shortly after sailed for home carrying the [ten] released Americans, the Treaty and a joint letter signed by Decatur and Shaler. The Epervier passed Gibraltar on July 12, 1815, was never heard of [again] and to this day remains one of the [great] mysteries of the sea".[418]

"On board the lost man-of-war were Captain Lewis and Lieutenant [Benedict] Neale, who had married sisters on the eve of their departure for the Mediterranean and were now returning after a successful termination of the war. Lieutenant Yarnall (who had distinguished himself in

---

416 *ibid, page 258.*
417 *McClellan, page 9.*
418 *ibid.*

the Battle of Lake Erie), [and had been wounded again during the recent battle with the Meshuda], and Lieutenant Drury were also on board."[419]

There was a hurricane reported in the area of the *Epervier's* travel route on August 9, 1815. Some modern-day historians feel this could be in the area of the Bermuda Triangle,[420] but unless the wreck is discovered in the future we will probably never know. Besides the passengers listed above, most records including the Navy Department casualty lists[421] indicate there were 134 souls including two Marines and 132 sailors lost when the ship disappeared.

The aftermath of Decatur's triumph in the Mediterranean was not only rewarded by Congress in the form of reward and prize money in the amount of $100,000[422] for Decatur and his crews, but by the adoration of the public. One of the most significant tributes was made by President Madison himself in the seventh Presidential Address to Congress (now called The State of the Union) given on December 15, 1815, in this first paragraph of his speech:

"*Fellow-Citizens of the Senate and of the House of Representatives:*

"*I have the satisfaction on our present meeting of being able to communicate to you the successful termination of the war which had been commenced against the United States by the Regency of Algiers. The squadron in advance on that service, under Commodore Decatur, lost not a moment after its arrival in the Mediterranean in seeking the naval force of the enemy then cruising in that sea, and succeeded in capturing two of his ships, one of them the principal ship, commanded by the Algerine admiral. The high character of the American commander was brilliantly sustained on that occasion which brought his own ship into close action with that of his adversary, as was the accustomed gallantry of all*

---

419 Maclay, Stanton Edgar & Smith RC, A History of the United States Navy, from 1775 to 1893, D. Appleton, 1894, pages 98-99. available online: https://books.google.com/books?id=qblCAAAAYAAJ&dq=Lt.+Neale+us+navy+1815&q=Neale#v=snippet&q=Neale&f=false

420 Bermuda Triangle Famous Incidents of Disappearances: http://www.bermuda-attractions.com/bermuda2_000051.htm

421 Casualties: U.S. Navy and Marine Corps Personnel Killed and Injured in Selected Accidents and Other Incidents Not Directly the Result of Enemy Action http://www.ibiblio.org/hyperwar/NHC/accidents.htm

422 Tucker, Spencer, Stephen Decatur, a Life Most Bold and Daring, Naval Institute press 2013, chapter 10 title page.

the officers and men actually engaged. Having prepared the way by this demonstration of American skill and prowess, he hastened to the port of Algiers, where peace was promptly yielded to his victorious force. In the terms stipulated the rights and honor of the United States were particularly consulted by a perpetual relinquishment on the part of the Dey of all pretensions to tribute from them. The impressions which have thus been made, strengthened as they will have been by subsequent transactions with the Regencies of Tunis and of Tripoli by the appearance of the larger force which followed under Commodore Bainbridge, the chief in command of the expedition, and by the judicious precautionary arrangements left by him in that quarter, afford a reasonable prospect of future security for the valuable portion of our commerce which passes within reach of the Barbary cruisers."[423]

But of course, much like George W. Bush's "mission accomplished" speech during the second Gulf War, President Madison's speech was a bit premature. Like most negotiations with the Barbary Pirates, and today with radicalized and other fundamentalist Muslims, trust must be verified before conclusions are reached and statements of success issued.

When Bainbridge and Decatur left the Mediterranean in October 1815, Commodore John Shaw was left in charge of the Mediterranean Squadron composed of the frigates *Constellation* (38 guns, Captain Crane) and *United States* (44 guns, and Shaw's flagship) and the sloops *Ontario* (18 guns, Captain Elliott) and *Erie* (18 guns, Captain Rigely).[424] The squadron was later joined by Captain Perry, of Lake Erie fame, in the 44 gun frigate, *Java*, in late January 1816.

"Commander Shaw retained this command until the following year, cruising in visiting ports of that sea, until he was relieved by Commodore Chauncey in the [USS] Washington, 74 [guns].[425]

Decatur was absolutely right, continuous show of force by the United States Navy kept our merchant fleets and our citizens fairly

---

423 James Madison: "Seventh Annual Message," December 5, 1815. Online by Gerhard Peters and John T. Woolley, *The American Presidency Project*.
424 Cooper, James Fenimore, Bainbridge. Somers. Shaw. Shubrick. Preble, Cary &Hart, 1846, digitized by Google: page 74. https://books.google.com/books
425 ibid.

safe. European nations were not so lucky. Whenever the United States Navy was not around, Omar's corsairs from Algeria and some of the other Barbary powers started harassing other nation's ships on a routine basis again and even went so far as to make raids on European cities kidnapping fishermen for slavery and looting coastal towns. Small villages in England, Ireland, and even Iceland were not immune. Open slave markets in Algiers and Tunisia again prospered.[426]

Barely a year after Decatur's success a combined artillery bombardment by ships from Great Britain and the Dutch Navy on the Barbary Coast port of Algiers occurred on August 27, 1816. The attack occurred as punishment for the raids and slave trading of Dutch and English citizens by the Algerian Pirates. The bombardment is depicted on a photo of the canvas painted in 1823 by artist Martinus Schouman.

It wasn't until 1830, when France conquered Algiers and other European nations occupied North Africa, did the Muslim corsairs disappear from the North African coast. Lesson learned: allies are needed and should always be supported, which brings us to the 10 Commandments of Muslim diplomacy first published in 2012.[427]

Bombardment of Algiers, to Support the Ultimatum to Release White Slaves, August 26-27 1816, painted in 1823 by Martinus Schouman on orders of Ministerie van Marine-photo credit: Rijksmuseum Amsterdam.

---

426 Rijksmuseum Amsterdam internet source: http://www.sailingwarship.com/bombardment-of-algiers-by-anglo-dutch-forces- on-august-26-27-1816.html

427 Hook, Franklin, Desert Storm Diary, Fall River Publishing, Hot Springs SD, 2012, pages 163-66.

The 10 Commandments of Muslim Diplomacy

1. Be Confident.
2. Record Agreements, with Signatures (and/or other devices)
3. Use Measured Responses to Breaches of Agreement.
4. Keep your word.
5. Respect their laws.
6. Be Honest.
7. Support Your Allies.
8. Recruit Muslim Allies for Human Rights.
9. Be Resolute.
10. Trust U.S.A. Power. (In God we trust!).

"In more detail including the reasons for the rules:
1. Be confident. Show no fear. Muslims respect confident authority. On the other hand weakness is provocative, and they will likely test it so they can count coup.[428]
2. If you don't have it, get any agreements in writing, signed, sealed and delivered, or at least have some kind of visual recording which will prove what was agreed. Make sure the agreement is binding to any peaceful or democratic change in government.
3. Stand up for your rights (Human or otherwise). U.S. Embassies are U.S. Territory. When embassies are established, the host nation is responsible for their safety. If the walls are breached, immediately respond with a measured response regardless of who is responsible. If it's just a physical breach consider options; for example you could:

---

[428] *Webster defines coup as a highly successful act or move. Counting coup is an anthropological term applied to United States Plains Native Americans who liked to count daring deeds performed in battle. Here the author is applying the term to negotiations during Muslim Diplomacy, an experience he gained with the culture during Gulf War I. Desert Storm Diary. page 164.*

A) Expel their embassy and diplomats out of the States.
B) Freeze their assets
C) Deny our foreign aid, and
D) If any U.S. citizen is hurt or killed send our own assets into their territory to get the culprits. Back it up with force and mean it. Pershing did this with his (i.e. the U.S.'s) right to travel anywhere in the Philippines he wished.
E) Consider other options such as a naval blockade, and no-fly zones.

If the Muslims know a breach has occurred they will expect an equally appropriate reaction.

4. Keep your word. Don't promise reward or threaten punishment without meaning it. This includes statements like "All options are on the table."
5. While in their territory respect their laws. That means you may have to squelch your right of free speech while you are there, but remember our embassies are U.S. Territory and you can express your free speech from there.
6. Be honest without compromising U.S. security or intentions.
7. Let it be known that you support your allies to the point of waging war for them if necessary. They could be such an Ally too (If you have a signed agreement!).
8. Get good Muslims involved. Have clarity of purpose. Human rights are part of our nature. Let them know that. Get specific if they ask.
9. Emphasize your resolve.
10. Trust the might of your country. Our motto is still "In God we trust".

"One of the most critical of these rules is number 4. If you read about the Philippine-American war, abatement of the Bates agreement with certain Muslims resulted in disaster. So let's learn something from history, and not prove that "what is past is prologue."[429]

---

429 *Shakespeare The Tempest*

"What if," you may ask, "you get a signed agreement between two allies and then one of them attacks the other?"

"The answer may seem obvious to some. You simply write into the agreement what would happen if they did that. Then apply rule number 4. Granted there may be obfuscation as to who did what first, but that is why we have intelligence sources, and our policies should not limit or handicap them."[430]

---

[430] Hook, Franklin, Desert Storm Diary pages 163-166, Fall River Publishing, Hot Springs, SD, 2012

CHAPTER TWELVE

Spring 2015

"Remember, the change you want to see in the world, and in your school, begins with you." Joseph Clementi

Reflections: Besides the "day that changed the world" mentioned in the first prologue of this manuscript, British author Karen Armstrong published in a new preface to *The Battle For God, A History of Fundamentalism*, the same idea, i.e. an event that changed the world, for September 11, 2001, which we call 9/11.[431] Armstrong noted that although it was an attack against the United States, it was a warning to all of us in the West that nothing would ever be the same again. Armstrong blames it on an unchanging dynamic of fundamentalism which involves not only Muslims but also Christians and Jews who have been dedicated to bringing God back to center stage from the sidelines where a secular world has placed Him. A very dedicated detailed historian, Armstrong has indeed shown that fundamentalists in all three religions have cultivated fantasies of destruction and are sometimes deliberately self-destructive. She cites the attempt by a Jewish underground faction to blow up the Dome of the Rock in Jerusalem in 1979, an act that could have destroyed the nation.

---

431 Armstrong, page vii.

Others cite American anti-abortionist terrorist acts as examples of Christian fundamentalist terror.

Canadian author, Paul March, published in his own blog, *Celestial Junk,* on February 6, 2006, (according to Snopes), paragraphs that others on the Internet have subsequently attributed to Dr. Emmanuel Tanya, a naturalized American citizen and survivor of Nazi Germany. March's thoughts were published worldwide as an email letter supposedly authored by Dr. Tanya. A synopsis of those thoughts is listed below. They are indeed thought-provoking.

- We are told repeatedly by experts that Islam is a religion of peace and the vast majority of Muslims are peaceful. Blogger March thinks that is irrelevant "fluff" meant to diminish the fact that fanatics are rampaging across the globe in the name of Islam.
- It is fanatics that currently dominate Islam at this moment in history. March states that it is fanatics who wage any one of 15 shooting wars worldwide and have systematically slaughtered Christian or tribal groups throughout Africa. (Remember this was written in 2006!) There's no doubt that the rapid expansion of ISIS confirms his thought that fanatics are zealously spreading their violence, beheading and murdering infidels, rape victims, and homosexuals, and teaching their young to kill and become suicide bombers.
- March's blog also points out that most Russian Communists (like most German citizens during WW II) just wanted to live in peace, but again the majority of peaceful wannabes were irrelevant. Communists were responsible for the murder of about 20 million people, and the Nazis' holocaust responsible for 6 million or more. The peaceful silent majority didn't speak out. Although neither group showed a fundamentalist religious reaction to stress, the secular organization's (i.e. Communist's) success prove the point that evil succeeds in a goal, such as genocide, when a peace-loving majority remains silent.
- In recent years Islamic prayers have been introduced into Toronto schools in Ontario and in Ottawa. Yet the Christian Lord's Prayer was removed. There was very little outcry from objec-

tors who apparently wanted to remain silent, whether out of fear or for political correctness is speculative.
- Recently learned are the facts that in the U.K., Muslim communities refused to integrate and there are now dozens of "no-go" zones in communities across the nation and in France as well. We need to pay attention to the only group which counts, the fanatics that threaten our way of life.

Karen Armstrong gives us hope though. She notes that it is still only a tiny percentage of even the fundamentalists, i.e. the radicalized factions, which take part in acts of terror. It is necessary though for the good, peaceful loving citizens, including Muslims, to speak up. We are beginning to see that happen by Islamic leaders such as Iyad Ameen Madani, and Mehmet Gormez:

Iyad Ameen Madani is the Secretary General of the Organization of Islamic Cooperation, which is second in size only to the UN in international organizations desiring to cooperate with each other. In a Vatican Radio Interview, as reported by Reuters, Rome, Madani was definite in his condemnation of radical elements of Islam (ISIS) who had persecuted Christians in Iraq and proclaimed themselves a new Caliphate. He further stated that ISIS has nothing to do with Islam, a religion that represents kindness, justice, and fairness. Madani's group operates in some 57 countries and represents an estimated 1.4 billion Muslims.[432]

Another Islamic voice of authority is Turkey's Mehmet Gormez, as reported by Ankara's Daily News. Gormez is Turkey's top Islamic cleric who flatly stated that Jihadists who commit atrocities in the name of Islam cannot belong to the faith. The Islamist State of Iraq and Syria (ISIS) and The Islamist State of Iraq and Levant (ISIL) have recently renamed themselves the Islamic State or simply IS. Gormez soundly

---

432 Vatican Radio, 7/25/2014 as reported by Reuters, http://en.radiovaticana.va/news/2014/07/25/worlds_muslim_leaders_condemn_attacks_on_iraqi_christians/1103410

condemned the militant Muslims who have forced thousands of Yazidis to flee their ancient homeland of Sinjar in northern Iraq.[433]

At the end of Armstrong's book there is a Reader's Guide including a conversation with the author. Karen Armstrong was interviewed by Jonathan Kirsch, a book columnist for the Los Angeles Times. In that conversation Armstrong stated that fundamentalism cannot be defeated and indicated we should, instead of dismissing fundamentalists as lunatics, listen to what they have to say. I am all for listening but I am not so sure that anyone can carry on a meaningful conversation with a religious fanatic. When the actions of the fanatics threaten the world's desire for peace and result in mass murder and other atrocities, then it's time to put a stop to it. I believe this true narrative has shown that when a nation has the ability and presents a show of force and keeps its word, it can effectively deal with lawless perpetrators or aggressors.

Stephen Decatur and the U.S. Navy's example of how to successfully use United States' power without firing a shot was not the first time it was done. Commodores Rodgers' and Preble's impressive deal with Moroccan Emperor Suleiman in the fall of 1803 was probably the first. The British and the French observing the result of the U.S. Navy's ultimatum with Tripoli and the other Barbary states delivered their own ultimatums to Algiers less than a year later. The bombardment of Algiers by the Dutch and British navies in August 1816, as punishment for Algiers refusing to cease their slave trading involving citizens of those two countries, put the *coup de grace* on pirate activity along the North African coast. A decade and a half later, after France invaded and occupied Algiers in 1830, pirate activity completely disappeared from the Mediterranean. Lessons learned. Now is the time to use those lessons once again.

You be the judge, dear reader. We have the ability, the means and the power to be successful again. All we need is a strong national leader to recognize the danger and use history's lessons to protect the country, our lives and our future. Time is short and we are not

---

433 Daily News, Ankara, Turkey: http://www.seznam.name/rss-clanek-13216638/2014-08-19/isil-s-actions-have-no-place-in- islam-turkey-s-top-cleric-mehmet-gormez-says.html

likely to negotiate or talk our way out of this problem. Experience has shown that you cannot reasonably trust nor can you successfully negotiate with religious or political fanatics. My feeling is that now is the time for not only peace loving Muslims to speak up, but those of us of all faiths, or no faith, to step forward. We must join together to put a stop to this evil. If we don't and if one of these radicalized factions gets ahold of a nuclear weapon, we could indeed see what Armageddon is really like.

END
* * *

Epilogue -What Happened to the Major Players

"Wars are made by politicians who neglect to prepare for it."- Wild Bill Donovan, First Director of the Office of Strategic Services, the forerunner of the CIA.

Adams, John
John Adams, the second man to hold the office of President of the United States, was born October 30, 1735 in what is now Quincy, Massachusetts. Trained as a lawyer, he graduated from Harvard in 1755, earned a Master's degree in 1758, and married Abigail Smith in 1764. They had five children; the second child, John Quincy, became the sixth president of the United States. Revered for his plain speaking and intellect, Adams was also noted for his independence, even from his own chosen political party, the Federalists. After his presidency, Adams lived quietly on his farm in Quincy and continued to write and defend his policies as President. He also corresponded with Thomas Jefferson and they apparently became good friends, even though their policies disagreed to a certain extent. John Adams had one of the longest retirements for a President, nearly 25 ½ years, before he died. Both Adams and Jefferson died within hours of each other appropriately on the nation's Independence Day, July 4, 1826.[434] He was 90 years old.

Bainbridge, William
Bainbridge was the captain of the *Philadelphia* when it ran aground off Tripoli in the first Barbary war and was taken prisoner by the corsairs. He also commanded the second squadron in the second Barbary

---

434 *John Adams.* (2015). The Biography.com website. Retrieved 01:59, Feb 21, 2015, from http://www.biography.com/people/john-adams-37967#related-video-gallery

war and was delayed leaving the states for the Mediterranean. In 1820, Bainbridge served as Stephen Decatur's second in a duel with Commodore James Barron. He later was instrumental in establishing a school for naval officers and the first board of examiners for officer promotion. Bainbridge also commanded several navy yards in the latter part of his career. He has been called one of America's unluckiest sea captains by historian Thomas Jewett. Bainbridge died of pneumonia in 1833, He was 59 years old.[435]

Barron, James
After his court-martial and suspension from the Navy for five years for the *Chesapeake-Leopard* Affair, Barron went to the merchant fleet and was caught in a Danish port while he was in command of a merchant ship, *Portia*, when the War of 1812 was declared. Barron was refused passage home by the neutral Danes until the war was over. An avid inventor, Barron supported himself in Denmark by his inventions which included a rope spinning machine, a cork cutter, a dough kneading machine and a new type of mill.[436] When he finally got back to the States he sought a naval command and through his correspondence became involved in an argument with Stephen Decatur. The argument resulted in a duel in which Decatur succumbed and Barron survived. Afterwards Barron was the subject of a Naval Board of Inquiry in 1821, but the decision of the Board was noncommittal. He was, however, reinserted to active duty and in 1824 became commander of the Philadelphia Navy Yard. He also commanded the Gosport Navy Yard in Virginia and then returned to Philadelphia to the same post he previously had. After that he ran a retirement home in Philadelphia for naval officers for a period of time and subsequently returned to the Norfolk area where he lived until his death in 1851.[437] He was 83 years old.

---

435 Jewett, Thomas, William Bainbridge: America's Unlucky Sea Captain, http://www.earlyamerica.com/review/2005_summer_fall/sea_captain.htm

436 William and Mary special collections database, Earl Gregg Swem Library, James Barron Papers, http://scdb.swem.wm.edu/?p=collections/findingaid&id=6725&q=&rootcontentid=176236

437 ibid.

Epilogue - What Happened to the Major Players

Barron, Samuel
"In 1805 he turned over command of his squadron to John Rodgers and returned to the United States due to poor health. He was then assigned command of the Gosport Ship Yard in Virginia. His health [from his liver disease] never fully recovered and Commodore Samuel Barron died in 1810 at the age of 45. Samuel Barron's son, also named Samuel, served with distinction in the United States Navy, until he resigned his commission in April 1861 to join the Confederate Navy during the Civil War."[438]

Burr, Aaron
Burr, the third vice president of the United States, and the one who killed Alexander Hamilton in a duel, spent four years after his trial traveling through Europe, trying to gain support for a revolution in Mexico for freeing the Spanish colonies. He returned to the United States in 1812, and reopened his law practice, but was virtually broke in the beginning. Back in 1783, he had married a widow, Theodosia Prevost, who was 10 years older than he. They produced a daughter, also named Theodosia. Burr's wife died after 10 years of marriage in 1794, and the daughter, Theodosia, was tragically killed in a shipwreck in 1812. Three years after his daughter's death Burr remarried. The bride was a wealthy widow, Eliza Jumel, but the marriage ended in divorce three years later. Following the divorce, Burr suffered a series of strokes and passed away on September 14, 1836, in Port Richmond, New York, a small town on Staten Island.[439] He was 80 years old.

Cathcart, James Leander
James Cathcart was a sailor on the American ship *Maria* cruising along the Portuguese coast in July, 1785, when the schooner was boarded and captured by Algerian corsairs. He was a slave for the next 11 years. Highly intelligent, Cathcart quickly learned the Arab language and curried favor among his captors. Over the 11 years he worked himself to as high a position in the Arab Regency as one could imagine, becoming the Dey's chief assistant. During his years of

---
438 Wikipedia, http://en.wikipedia.org/wiki/Samuel_Barron_(1765%E2%80%931810)
439 Aaron Burr. (2015) The Biography.com website. Retrieved 09:58, Feb 21, 2015, from http://www.biography.com/people/aaron-burr-9232241#final-years

captivity and increasing freedom as the Dey's clerk, he was also able to accumulate wealth. He even bought a ship of his own. Cathcart in his own words[440] described one of the ways he accumulated wealth. When he became the clerk of the Bagnio Galera, a mustering station of the prison he was working in, he was allowed to keep a tavern but had to pay only half of the profit to the Regency. His duty as the clerk of the station was to muster slaves in the prison every evening, report when any of them were ill or missing, and see that they got medical treatment.

According to his own words,[441] Cathcart saw to their needs and even purchased their coffins out of his own stash. Bubonic plague and its other form, the less common pneumonic variety, were both deadly diseases in those days. Caused by bacteria, *pasteurella pestis*, plague has a reservoir of the bacteria in rats, and the vectors, or transmitters, are rat fleas for the bubonic variety. In the pneumonic variety the disease is spread by airborne droplets from man-to-man. Plague is known as the Black Death because of the swollen, matted and hemorrhagic (black and blue) discolored regional lymph nodes, called bubos, which occur near the flea bite. Thus, the label bubonic. The disease usually runs its course in five to six days but can extend up to two weeks.

Half-way through his years of imprisonment, Cathcart reached the position of clerk of the Bagnio Galera. His promotion was partly due to the number of clerks who died of the plague in a short time. Three of them died in less than a month just before Cathcart took over. Why he was fortunate enough not to get the disease, Cathcart could not explain. I suspect however that his wealth provided the circumstances which allowed him to sleep in quarters not occupied by rats and fleas. He also bought a tavern (some say more than one) outside of the walls of prison that provided him with even more money. In 1796, after 11 years of captivity, Cathcart was sent home to America on his own ship along with 12 survivors of the captured American ships. The purpose of this release was have Cathcart collect and send back the

---

[440] Baepler, Paul, ed. *White Slaves, African Masters*, pgs 137-138, University of Chicago Press, 1999
[441] ibid.

tribute negotiated by Joseph Donaldson, which had never been paid by the United States.

Cathcart was successful in his discussions with the U.S. government and the U.S. Senate ratified a treaty with Algiers in March 1796, paid a substantial tribute, and delivered a six gun frigate to the Dey in 1798.[442] A month after the ratification, Cathcart was appointed as a diplomat to assist William Eaton in the Mediterranean. The rest of his diplomatic history has already been discussed. Cathcart married Jane Bancker Woodside in Washington, D.C. in 1798. Some sources (Wikipedia, and Find a Grave.com) report that they had 12 children. After his diplomatic service Cathcart returned to Washington in 1817. He held several government positions until his death in 1843. Both he and his wife are buried in Rock Creek Cemetery, Washington, D.C. He was 76 years old.

Dearborn, Henry
Dearborn left the United States Army in 1813 and married his third wife, Sarah Bowdoin. He was then nominated and withdrawn for the post of Secretary of War in 1815. He served as minister to Portugal from 1822-1824, and died peacefully in Roxbury Massachusetts on June 6, 1829.[443]

Decatur, Stephen Jr:
"After returning home, [from the second Barbary war] he became a member of the Board of Navy Commissioners in Washington, D.C. In 1820 the strong-willed and spirited Decatur was challenged to a duel by a brother officer, Commodore James Barron. The contest, which took place at Bladensburg, Maryland, on 22 March 1820, resulted in wounds to both men. Barron survived, but Stephen Decatur died of his injuries shortly afterwards. The U.S. Navy has named five ships in honor of Stephen Decatur, including: USS Decatur (1840-1865); USS Decatur (Destroyer # 5), 1902-1920; USS Decatur (DD-341), 1922-1945; USS Decatur (DD-936,

---

442 St. John, R. B., Libya and the United States, Two Centuries of Strife, page 22, University of Pennsylvania Press March 2 013

443 US Army Center of Military History, http://www.history.army.mil/books/CG&CSA/Dearborn-

later DDG-31), 1956-2004; and USS Decatur (DDG-73), 1998-____."[444] He was just 41 years old.

Eaton, William
After the first Barbary War, Eaton returned to the United States to a hero's welcome, but he was deeply disappointed and felt betrayed by the naval commanders, Tobias Lear, and his own government. He was especially concerned that Hamet Karamanli, had been thrown under the bus so to speak, and that an unnecessary tribute in the amount of $60,000 had been paid to Tripoli for the release of *Philadelphia's* crew. On top of all that, the U.S. Government owed him money. The issue became a partisan debate within Congress and although the Federalists wanted Eaton to be rewarded with a medal or a tract of land, he never received so much as a thank you from the federal government. Massachusetts, however, rewarded him with 10,000 acres of land which today lies inside the boundaries of the state of Maine. Eaton returned to Brimfield, Massachusetts and was elected to the state legislature. After his testimony in the Aaron Burr trial in 1807, he only served one term which was blamed on his outspokenness about his treatment by John Marshall in the Burr trial, thus losing him the Federalists' vote. His health deteriorated rapidly after that probably exacerbated by heavy drinking. In his own words, Eaton described his last days in this letter to a Mr. Humbert, a friend from Tunis:

"Brimfield Jan 10, 1810

"My dear friend,

"Fortune has reversed her tables – I am no more Eaton. I live, or rather stay, in obscurity and uselessness. The wound I received on the coast of Tripoli, and others more early, have deprived me of an arm's use and the use of a leg. – Want of economy, which I never learned, want of judgment in the speculative concerns of private life, which I never studied, and,

---

444 *Naval History and Heritage Command: http://www.history.navy.mil/our-collections/photography/us-people/d/decatur- stephen.html*

what is more, privatization of the consideration of a government which I have served, have unmanned me.

"A fellow first fed on horse chestnuts and then on charity, now bestrides the world, and fattens on gore [Eaton was referring to Napoleon]: we Americans venerate him because we have lost our national character; perhaps it was never well fixed. We can shew you citizens who fly to mountains and caves for a hiding place; but our wars are on paper. Free presses, but no heavy metal.

"I am glad you are well; when I am so I will write you more. Death has laid himself alongside, and throwing his graplings [sic] upon my quarter and forecastle, but I keep him off midships yet."[445]

[signed William Eaton]

Born in Woodstock, Connecticut February 25, 1764, Eaton died in Brimfield, Massachusetts on June 1, 1811. He was 47 years old.

Elliot, Jesse Duncan, "On January 6, 1814, he and Perry were each honored with a Congressional Gold Medal [as] the Thanks of Congress. This was the first time in history when an entire British naval squadron surrendered.

"Even before the medals were given, Elliott and Perry became embroiled in a thirty-year-long controversy over their respective conduct and fault in the Battle, extending even beyond Perry's death. Perry claimed that Elliott had failed to offer timely support; Elliott decried lack of communication and signals. Indeed, charges were filed, although not acted upon.

"Elliott commanded the sloop USS Ontario during the Second Barbary War and was promoted to Captain in 1818, serving on a naval commission selecting sites for navy yards, lighthouses, and other coastal fortifications, until 1822. In 1820, Elliott was second to Commodore James Barron when the latter fatally shot Stephen Decatur in a duel. He was transferred to the Brazil Squadron in 1825, served as captain of the USS

---

445 Prentiss, Chas, editor, The Life of the Late Gen. William Eaton, pages 425-426,, E. Merriam & Co., Brookfield, 1813.

Cyane for two years, and later commanded the West Indies Squadron from 1829 to 1832.

"He was appointed commander of the Boston Navy Yard in 1833 and of the Mediterranean Squadron in 1835. During the Mediterranean assignment, he was charged with minor offenses by several of his junior officers, and was recalled to the United States in 1838. Elliott was politically unpopular at the time (possibly stemming back to his performance during the Battle of Lake Erie and subsequent feud with Perry), and was convicted of these charges and suspended from duty for four years until the remaining charges were dismissed by President John Tyler in October 1843. Appointed commander of the Philadelphia Navy Yard in December 1844, Elliot remained there until his death on 10 December 1845. He is buried in Mount Moriah Cemetery in Pennsylvania. After being overgrown for many years, his grave was re-identified in 2012."[446] He was 63.

Harrison, William Henry:
The aftermath of the Battle of Tippecanoe made William Henry Harrison a hero of the settlers and earned him the nickname *Tippecanoe*. In September of 1813, Harrison added to his legend by recapturing Detroit which had been surrendered a year earlier by William Hull. Although he was defeated in the presidential elections of 1836 Harrison's fortunes were reversed in 1840 when with his Whig running mate John Tyler he won the election made famous by his slogan of *"Tippecanoe and Tyler Too"* over Democratic incumbent Martin Van Buren by an electoral college vote of 234 to 60. The popular vote was much closer, with only a 145,914 vote difference out of 1,387,928 total votes (10.5%). Born in 1773, at the time of the election he was the oldest elected president of the United States at age 67. He also served the shortest term of a president when he caught a cold and died of pneumonia on April 4, 1841 after having served just over 30 days in office. His wife had not even yet moved to Washington D.C. He was the first president to die in office.[447]

---

446 Wikipedia, http://en.wikipedia.org/wiki/Jesse_Elliott#cite_note-4
447 William Henry Harrison. (2015). The Biography.com website. Retrieved 09:58, Mar 20, 2015, from http://www.biography.com/people/william-henry-harrison-9329968#presidency-and-sudden-death

Hamilton, Alexander:
Hamilton was born on the Caribbean island of Nevis in the British West Indies on an unknown date, circa January 1755-1757, the bastard son of a Scottish trader named James. His father had an adulterous affair with his mother, Rachel Fawcett Lavine, who was married to someone else. After the breakup of the marriage, Rachel moved in with Hamilton who then abandoned the family when Alexander was still a baby. When he was 16 years old Hamilton was sent to New York for an education by two benefactors, Nicholas Cruger, his first employer, and Reverend Hugh Knox, his minister. In 1775 Hamilton left school to join the revolutionary Continental Army, fought in battles in White Plains, Trenton, and Long Island and earned a battlefield commission. He came to the attention of George Washington because of his writing skills and obvious intelligence and served as his aid for the rest of the war. Hamilton was instrumental in the final battle at Yorktown. After the war he left Washington's service and went to law school passing the bar. He left his practice in New York to become the nation's first Secretary of the Treasury, serving from 1789 to 1795. Hamilton was very active in politics, as was his father-in-law. Alexander Hamilton was killed in a duel with Aaron Burr, on July 11, 1804. He was about 48 years old.

Hull, Isaac,
Isaac Hull had a long and distinguished career in the U.S. Navy serving in the Quasi-War aboard the *USS Constitution* which he later commanded during the War of 1812. He is probably most famous for his defeat of *HMS Guerriere* on August 19, 1812, which excited the American public who all of a sudden realized that their small Navy could handle a British ship-of-the-line. Isaac Hull had also commanded *USS Enterprise* during Barbary War I and strongly supported William Eaton when he was Captain of the *Argus* during Eaton's march across the desert to Derna. After his defeat of *HMS Guerriere* in 1812, Hull ran Navy Yards in Maine and Boston and later commanded the Pacific Squadron operating in the waters of South America. After 1841, his health deteriorated and he passed away at age 69 in 1843,

in Philadelphia where he is buried. Hull had five ships named after him; the latest was a destroyer, the *USS Hull (DD 945)*.

Hull, William:
Hull was born in Derby, Connecticut on June 24, 1753, graduated from Yale University in 1772, and passed the bar in 1775. During the Revolutionary war he fought in several battles including White Plains, Trenton, Princeton, Stillwater, Saratoga, Fort Stanwix, Monmouth, and Sandy Point. It is interesting to note that he was a friend of Nathan Hale during the Revolution and may have been responsible for making Hale's legendary last words, "I only regret that I have but one life to give for my country"[448] famous. Although he was dishonorably discharged from the Army in disgrace after being sentenced to death following his court martial, he was subsequently pardoned by President Madison. He was somewhat vindicated following the publication of two of his books, *Detroit: Defense of Brigadier General William Hull 1814*, and *Memoirs of the Campaign of the Northwestern Army of the United States: A.D. 1812- 1824*. He was honored by a public banquet on May 30, 1825 in Boston,[449] and died peacefully at home on November 29, 1825. He was 72.

Jackson, Andrew
Andrew Jackson was elected as the seventh president of the United States in 1828. No stranger to the military, Jackson was a veteran of the Revolutionary War and with his brother Robert was captured by the British. Both of his brothers, Robert and Hugh, were lost in the war, one, Hugh, to action in the Battle of Stono Ferry in 1779, and the other to smallpox, which Andrew survived.[450] Orphaned at age 14, Andrew was raised by his uncles and studied law in Salisbury, North Carolina. He practiced law and became wealthy as a real estate and

---

448 There are many sources that omit the word "only" from the famous quote and many historians question the accuracy. Some sources also substitute "life to lose" for "life to give."

449 Wikipedia-cited source: Colonial Society of Massachusetts, 1907, page 366

450 Andrew Jackson. (2015). C Retrieved 10:16, Mar 20, 2015, from http://www.biography.com/people/andrew-jackson-9350991#related-video-gallery

plantation owner near Jonesboro, Tennessee prior to the War of 1812. He was a member of the Tennessee militia.

In 1796, he became active in politics and served in the U.S. House of Representatives from Tennessee. He was also a delegate to the Tennessee constitutional convention. Jackson was elected to the Tennessee Supreme Court and served until 1804. After the War of 1812, Jackson was re-elected to the U.S. Senate in 1822 (he had been elected in the late 1790s but resigned from the Senate shortly after being elected). He lost a presidential bid to John Quincy Adams in 1824, but won an overwhelming majority in 1828.

During the 1828 election his opponents called him *"jackass",* but Jackson turned the tables on them by liking the label and making it a symbol of his new political party, the Democrats. He was the first president to use the veto power. He did that against Second Bank of the United States when its charter was up for renewal. Jackson won his second term in 1832 with 56% of the popular and an overwhelming number of Electoral College votes. For other details of Jackson's life I refer the reader to the excellent biography by Jon Meacham, *American Lion, Andrew Jackson in the White House.*[451]

Jackson died on June 8, 1845. His death was blamed by at least one authority on lead bullets that had never been removed causing lead poisoning.[452] I would challenge that cause because manifestations of lead poisoning are colic, encephalopathy (degenerative brain disease), peripheral neuritis, and anemia. Meacham's book (noted above) cites a letter that Jackson's niece wrote describing his physical condition near his death. He was swollen all over, (peripheral edema), which is a condition of heart failure or renal failure. He had no signs of encephalopathy (dementia or other dysfunction) or peripheral neuropathy. He did have symptoms of colic (abdominal pain) but his was associated with diarrhea which would not be common with heavy metal poisoning. He may well have had some degree of lead poisoning but I don't believe it was of his cause of death. He was 78 years old.

---

451 Random House, New York, 2008
452 The Biography.com website

Jefferson, Thomas

Jefferson, the third President of the United States and author of the Declaration of Independence, began building his own private estate, Monticello when he was only 26 years old. When he was 29 he married Martha Wales Skelton, the young widow with whom he lived for 10 years and produced six children, only two of whom survived to adulthood. After his wife's death, Jefferson never remarried, but there is strong evidence of a conjugal affair, with his wife's mulatto half-sister, Sally Hemings, one of the slaves he had inherited from his wife's parents' estate and who was the illegitimate child of his father-in-law, John Wales. The Jefferson-Hemings affair may have produced as many as six children. After he left office as President, he returned to Monticello, and besides the management of the estate, set about founding the University of Virginia. In addition, he sold his book collection to the United States government with the purpose of founding the Library of Congress. Jefferson died on July 4, 1826, just a few hours before his friend John Adams, whom he had succeeded as President. He was 83 years old.[453]

Karamanli, Hamet

After the peace treaty negotiated by Tobias Lear, Hamet remained in exile on the southeast coast of Sicily in the city of Syracuse until U.S. Consul Dr. George Davis heard about the secret clause in the Treaty with Tripoli that Lear had placed. The clause allowed Yusuf Karamanli to detain his brother Hamet and his family as virtual prisoners for a period of two and a half years. Dr. Davis confronted Yusuf and informed him that the U.S. Senate had not ratified the treaty's secret article and that it would not be honored. Yusuf reluctantly agreed to free his brother in October 1807, and Hamet was joined by his family on Syracuse shortly thereafter at the expense of the U.S. government. Due to the previous efforts of William Eaton, Congress did approve $2,400 for Hamet, but with the presence of his wife and a dozen servants that were still working for the family, Hamet could not afford to maintain his lifestyle. He fled with his family to Malta to escape

---

[453] *The Jefferson Monticello* website: http://www.monticello.org/site/jefferson/thomas-jefferson

his debtors. Shortly thereafter, when the governor of Derna passed away, Hamet was appointed to replace him. Yusuf was apparently influenced by urging from Dr. Davis and no doubt saw a way to keep Hamet away from his own throne. Although Hamet apparently was a good ruler of the city, his brother, Yusuf with typical criminal fanatic treachery, tried to kill him two years later. Hamet fled again, this time to Alexandria, where he died in 1811.[454] Hamet, Yusuf's older brother, was about 47 years old.

Karamanli, Yusuf
After Karamanli signed the Treaty with the United States he behaved himself in reference to U.S. ships but continued to harass other nations and settlements as far north as Iceland. With declining revenues from America there was also a collapse of the economic status of Tripoli and the other Barbary states, especially after the combined bombardment of Tripoli by the Dutch and British Navies. As the economic status of Tripoli declined, Yusuf Karamanli lost control of his empire and abdicated the throne to his son, Ali in 1832.[455] A Civil War followed in which the Ottoman Sultan, Mahmud II, offered to help Ali, but with typical treachery, turned on Ali and deposed and exiled him. In 1835 the Karamanli dynasty was over and Mustafa Negib became the new Pasha of Tripoli. Yusuf died on August 4, 1838 at age 72, cause unknown.[456]

Key, Francis Scott
Francis Scott Key was born August 1, 1779 in Frederick County Maryland, and was educated at home for the first 10 years. He later attended St. John's College and was trained as an attorney. He married Mary (Polly) Taylor in the early 1800s (circa 1821) and they had 11 children. During the War of 1812, he composed the lyrics of the nation's national anthem. After the war, he opened a law practice in Washington, D.C. and was an advocate of the abolition of slavery. He

---

454 Zachs, pages 372-373.
455 Boddy-Evans, Alistair, African History, http://africanhistory.about.com/od/militaryhistory/ss/Yusuf-Karamanli-2.htm
456 Tucker, Spencer page 348

contracted pleurisy and died January 11, 1843 at the age of 63. He is buried in Mount Olivet Cemetery near Frederick, Maryland.[457]

Lear, Tobias
A man of questionable integrity, Lear was known to have stolen rent money from his employer, George Washington.[458] After negotiating the peace with Tripoli, Lear and his new third wife, Frances Henley, stayed in Algiers until 1812, when he was expelled from the country by the Dey because the United States was behind on tributes and refused to pay. The Lears arrived back in Washington in the middle of the War of 1812. Appointed to a post in the Department of War, Lear was in Washington, D.C. when the British attacked the city and burned the White House. Lear died on October 11, 1816, due to an apparent self- inflicted gunshot to the head. He was 54 years old.

Madison, James
After leaving office in 1817, James and Dolley Madison returned to their estate, Montpelier, and kept themselves busy. Besides running the plantation Madison and close friend Thomas Jefferson served on a board planning to create the University of Virginia. The school opened in 1825, and Madison followed Jefferson's leadership of the new University after Jefferson's died in 1826. In the 1820s he was a delegate to the state's constitutional convention and became such a significant contributor that he is often called the father of the U.S. Constitution. Madison died June 28, 1836, 10 years after Thomas Jefferson passed. There is no doubt that this quiet intellectual was instrumental in creating a new government with new ideas that allows people to enjoy the freedoms they have today.[459]

---

    457 Francis Scott Key. (2015). The Biography.com website. Retrieved 09:34, Mar 20, 2015, from http://www.biography.com/people/francis-scott-key-9364165#song-becomes-national-anthem

    458 Zachs, page 217 http://www.biography.com/people/andrew-jackson-9350991#related-video-gallery

    459 James Madison. (2015). The Biography.com website. Retrieved 03:47, Mar 18, 2015, from http://www.biography.com/people/james-madison-9394965

Marshall, John
John Marshall served the longest of any Chief Justice of the Supreme Court, 34 years, from 1801 to 1835. A lifelong Federalist, he was the nemesis of Thomas Jefferson's administration but without doubt shaped the judicial branch of government as the Constitution intended, giving the judiciary equal, if not slightly more power than either Congress or the executive branch of government. Marshall died of an undisclosed ailment at age 79 on July 6, 1835, in Philadelphia where he had gone for treatment. He was the last surviving member of the Adams administration (Secretary of State).

Morris, Richard
After his recall to the United States, Commodore Richard Valentine Morris was judged by a Navy Board of Inquiry which decided Morris had not used due diligence and activity in annoying the enemy. He was summarily sacked by President Jefferson and Secretary of the Navy Robert Smith and dismissed from the Navy. He later became a Federalist politician and a member of the New York State Assembly, from Westchester County. He died May, 13, 1815, in New York City, at the age of 47 years and 66 days.[460]

Perry, Oliver Hazard
In 1798, at the tender age of 13, Oliver Perry became a midshipman on his own father's ship, the *USS General Greene,* which was a gunboat built during the Quasi-War with France. He spent his first year or so in the Caribbean learning the trade under his father. When the Navy downsized in 1800 prior to the Barbary War, Oliver's father, Captain Christopher Perry, was discharged from the Navy and Oliver was without an assignment for almost two years. In 1802, the Navy assigned Oliver to the *USS Adams* and the young midshipman then found himself in the Mediterranean for the next four years. At age 17, he was promoted and was the youngest naval officer ever commissioned a Lieutenant in the U.S. Navy up to that time. After the War of 1812, Perry once again found himself in command of a ship that he had supervised construction of, the *USS Java,* and again found himself in the

---

460 Political Graveyard.com, http://politicalgraveyard.com/bio/morris.html

Mediterranean. This true American hero courted trouble as master of the *Java* when he got into an altercation with the Marine Captain aboard his vessel and wound up slapping him. Both officers were mildly disciplined. After his second service in the Mediterranean, Perry's next assignment as Commodore was the *USS Nonesuch*, in the Caribbean. While there Perry contracted yellow fever and succumbed to the disease on his 34th birthday, August 23, 1819.[461]

Preble, Edward
In 1804, Preble's health deteriorated and he requested relief of command which was initially denied. He returned to the United States in February 1805 and worked at shipbuilding facilities in Portland, Maine. A Congressional Gold Medal was struck in March 1805 and presented to Commodore Preble for gallantry and good conduct of himself and his squadron at Tripoli. President Jefferson offered him control of the Navy Department in 1806, but the Commodore declined it due to poor health. He died of tuberculosis on August 25, 1807. He is buried in Eastern Cemetery, Portland Maine. He was 46 years old.[462]

Pike, Colonel Zebulon Montgomery
Pike, the officer in charge of General Dearborn's first skirmish near Montréal, was born on January 15, 1779 in Lamberton, (now considered a part of Trenton and not to be confused with Lumberton) New Jersey. He joined his father's regiment, the third U.S. infantry, and was commissioned a second lieutenant on March 3, 1799. As a commissioned army officer he was also an explorer and in 1806 was likely one of the first white men to attempt climbing a challenging mountain in Colorado which now bears his name. In his early career he was suspected of being a part of Aaron Burr's conspiracy to establish a new government in the southwestern United States. Conspiracy charges were never proven. He was promoted to Brigadier General in

---

461 Pennsylvania Book Libraries web site, PA. State U. http://pabook.libraries.psu.edu/palitmap/bios/Perry__Oliver_Hazard.html
462 Irving Family web site:http://irving-fam.com/tng/histories/Edward%20Preble%20Bio.pdf

1813, and was killed in action on April 27, 1813, at the Battle of York (Toronto).[463]

Procter, General Henry
Henry Procter was born in Wales, U.K. in 1787, and by age 25 was a colonel in the British Army. He served as commanding officer of the British troops in the Detroit River region of Canada during the War of 1812.[464] Procter was the commanding officer who accepted American General William Hull's surrender of Fort Detroit on August 16, 1812. He was also the officer who organized the counterattack for the British at the Raisin River massacre. He is most famous however for his role in the Battle of the Thames River, Ontario, Canada, in October, 1813, where Tecumseh was killed. Procter was court-martialed by the British for his mismanagement of the retreat of his forces who fled the battlefield and left Tecumseh and his force to fend for themselves. He received a sentence of suspension of rank and loss of pay for six months.[465] He returned to Great Britain where he died in 1859.

Rodgers, John
After serving in the Mediterranean during the first Barbary War, Commodore Rogers returned to the United States and took command of the New York flotilla which was a small fleet of gunboats designed to protect New York Harbor during the trade embargo with France and Great Britain in 1807. He had command of the North Atlantic fleet during the War of 1812 and became a popular hero for capturing some 23 enemy vessels. He was also instrumental in the defense of Fort McHenry during the bombardment by the British which inspired the Star-Spangled Banner written by Francis Scott Key. In 1815 he was appointed to the

---

463 Cutrer, Thomas W. "Pike, Zebulon Montgomery," *Handbook of Texas Online* (http://www.tshaonline.org/handbook/online/articles/fpi19), accessed November 26, 2014. Uploaded on June 15, 2010. Published by the Texas State Historical Association

464 Hurt, R. Douglas. *The Ohio Frontier: Crucible of the Old Northwest, 1720-1830.* Bloomington, IN: Indiana University Press, 1996. Cited by Internet source: http://www.ohiohistorycentral.org/w/Henry_Procter

465 ibid. Internet source.

Navy Board of Commissioners, a civilian government organization which was meant to support the secretary of the Navy. In 1823 Rodgers returned to active service to lead a support expedition to Thompson's Island (Key West) during a yellow fever epidemic. After that crisis Rogers returned to the Mediterranean in command of that squadron aboard his new flagship, *USS North Carolina*. Rodgers' presence in the Mediterranean with his squadron laid the groundwork for a new treaty with Turkey giving the United States access to the Black Sea. In 1827 Rogers returned to his position on the Navy Board of Commissioners where he remained until his death in 1838.

Sheaffe, Sir Roger Hale
Sheaffe was the British commander at the Battle of York (Toronto) who ordered the delayed explosion of the ammo dump and the destruction of the Navy Yard while peace negotiations were going on. He was born in colonial Boston before the American Revolution on July 15, 1763. One of 10 children, he was the third son of Harvard graduate William Sheaffe, who was a customs officer for the Crown. His father died when he was just eight years old and his mother opened a boarding house to support the family. One of the boarders was British Royalty, the Duke of Northumberland, who, impressed with the boy's intelligence and potential, offered to send him to military school in England. The highlight of his military career was his heroic actions at the 1813 battle of Queenston Heights when he replaced his commanding officer Sir Isaac Brock who had been killed in action. Following that British victory Sheaffe was promoted to Commanding Officer of Upper Canada and became the colonial administrator or governor of Ontario Province. Following the British defeat in the Battle of York (Toronto) Sheaffe was relieved of his command and administrative duties as governor. He was later recalled to Great Britain where he spent the rest of his life. He died in Edinburgh Scotland on July 17, 1851, two days after his 88th birthday.

Sterett, Andrew

Upset over the fact that Stephen Decatur was promoted over him Sterett resigned from the Navy and joined the merchant service. Secretary of the Navy, Robert Smith, reluctantly accepted Sterett's resignation. Sterett found work as the captain of the ex *USS Warren*, a U.S. Navy sloop of war that had been converted to a three masted merchant vessel. The primary owner was Lemuel Taylor who was an entrepreneur out of Baltimore. It was common practice in those days for exporters like Taylor to hire a private agent who would not interfere with the running of the ship but whose job was to represent the ship's owner of the cargo. In this case there was a definite squabble between the superintendent of the cargo called the "supercargo" whose name was Procopio Jacento Pollock, and the captain of the vessel, Andrew Sterett. Pollock was a man of questionable reputation who was suspected of being a smuggler and who had been accused as a cheat by others who had hired him. When the ship was south of Brazil headed for Cape Horn, Pollock produced a sealed letter from the owner, Lemuel Taylor, completely contradicting Sterett's instructions and instructing Pollock to take over the direction of the voyage. Sterett felt he had been betrayed and he even tried to shoot Pollock.

His reaction was so deranged that his fellow officers took away his pistols. The ship's crew was in an uproar for weeks. Sterett had threatened that he would be damned if he would follow the new instructions and that he would either blow out Pollock's brains or his own. He later calmed down and appeared to be rational to his crew and was given back his pistols. He then went on deck, took a few shots at some birds and returned to his quarters where he did indeed shoot himself in the head. He lingered for two weeks before he died on January 9, 1807. He was 28 years old. The ship continued around the horn to Chile where the cargo was moved to shore and placed in a warehouse where only Pollock and the local governor had keys. The crew was imprisoned in Chile. In 1808, fourteen of the survivors returned to Newport, Rhode Island. The ship became part of the Chilean Navy. Lemuel Taylor declared bankruptcy and moved to Cuba. Pollock stayed in Chile where he lived until his death.[466]

Truxton, Thomas
Thomas Truxton was one of the three senior officers of the U.S. Navy to be labeled as outstanding by author Christian McKee, Preble's biographer. There was no doubt that he was a competent senior Navy officer since he was the commanding officer of the *USS Constellation* when it defeated the French frigate *L'Insurgente* during the Quasi-War. Truxton was also the author of the flag signal book used by the U.S. Navy in the 18th and 19th centuries before that particular signal book was replaced by one authored by Captain James Barron. He had a command style similar to General George Patton, insisting that his crews be prepared for action at any minute. The only problem was that Truxton had an arrogant personality and a big ego also similar to Patton's. He lost his command when Secretary of the Navy Robert Smith sacked him after Truxton insisted that a flagship captain be assigned to the *Chesapeake,* which Truxton was commanding. No flagship captains were available at the time, so Smith accepted Truxton's threatened resignation without giving him a chance to respond and replaced him with Richard Valentine Morris.[467] Once again a civilian, Truxton entered politics and was unsuccessful in winning a position in the House of Representatives but did win an election as sheriff of Philadelphia County in 1816, and served for three years. He also authored a book on celestial navigation.[468] Some of the junior officers that served under Truxton included David Porter, Andrew Sterett, Isaac Hull, John Rodgers, and Isaac Chauncey. There are six United States U.S. Navy Ships, all of them christened *USS Truxton,* named after this very competent U.S. Navy officer. Truxton died and was buried in Philadelphia in 1822.[469] He was 67.

---

466 ibid
467 Toll, Page 172. The choice was one that Sec. Smith undoubtedly regretted.
468 http://www.united-states-navy.com/people/ttruxtun.htm
469 ibid

Washington, George

Washington and French General Rochambeau received Cornwallis's surrender at Yorktown October 19, 1781, ending the Revolutionary War. On December 23, 1783, two days before Christmas, Washington resigned his commission and headed for Mount Vernon, his estate in Virginia. He made it by Christmas Day. A very successful farm manager, Washington also became president of the Potomac Company in 1785, with a goal to improve transportation on the Potomac River.

In 1787, Washington presided over the Constitutional Convention, and was one of the original signers.

On January 10, 1789, he was elected as the first President of the United States. On March 4, 1793 he was inaugurated for a second term as President of the United States. A year into his second term in 1794, Washington donned his old uniform and led an army unit into western Pennsylvania to put down the Whiskey Rebellion, which was a revolt against paying taxes to the federal government. He passed away on December 14, 1799, a little over two months before his 67th birthday. He was said to have died of a severe throat infection[470] most probably complicated by pneumonia and accelerated by the medical treatment of the day, bloodletting.

Wilkinson, General James

James Wilkinson was the Army general who barely avoided prosecution for conspiracy in the Aaron Burr trial for treason and was regarded by his colleagues such as Winfield Scott and John Randolph as incompetent and a probable spy for the Spanish. He was also transferred to the Canadian frontier after Dearborn's removal. Wilkinson and General Wade Hampton were supposed to lead a two-pronged attack on Montréal with Wilkinson leading a force of 7,000 men downstream along the St. Lawrence from the West and Hampton approaching Montréal from the South along the Richelieu and Chateauguay Rivers north of Lake Champlain in Vermont. Neither commander was very enthusiastic. The campaigns resulted in the Battles of Chateauguay on October 26, 1813

---

470 *Mount Vernon website: http://www.mountvernon.org/george-washington/*

and Crysler's farm on November 11, both were failures. Wilkinson had one more foray into Upper Canada which was also a failure at the Battle of La Colle Mill.[471] After the battle, Wilkinson was relieved of command and discharged from the Army. In early 1815 he was appointed a diplomatic Envoy to Mexico, but while awaiting approval of the Mexican government, he died in Mexico City where he is buried. He was 67.

* * *

---

471 Hickey, pages 144-146

BIBLIOGRAPHY

Books:

A History of the United States Navy, from 1775 to 1893, D. Appleton, 1894, Maclay, Stanton Edgar & Smith RC

Almanac of American Military History, Vol. 1, ABC-CLIO, Santa Barbara, 2012, edited by Tucker, Spencer

Amateurs to Arms, Da Capo Press, Chapel Hill, 1995, Elting, John R

American Lion, Andrew Jackson in the White House, Random House, New York, 2008. Meacham, Jon

Blood and Faith, The Purging of Muslim Spain. New York: The New Press, 2009, Carr, Matthew

Chronicles of the Frigate Macedonian, 1809-1922, W.W. Norton Co. NY, London 2000, De Kay, James,

Commodore John Rodgers, a Biography, Arthur Clark Co. 1910, Cleveland, Paullin, Chas. O.

Commodore Oliver Hazard Perry, Superior Printing Co. Akron, 1910. Mackenzie, Alexander S.

Decatur's Bold and Daring Act, The Philadelphia in Tripoli 1804, Osprey Publishing LTD, Oxford, UK, 2011, Lardas, Mark

Desert Storm Diary, Fall River Publishing, Hot Springs, SD, 2012, Hook, Franklin

Edward Preble a Naval Biography, 1761-1807, Naval Institute Press 2014, McKee, Christopher

Encyclopedia Britannica, the Battle of Tippecanoe, W. Benton Co. Chicago, 1972

Encyclopedia of the War of 1812 Vol. 1, Tucker, Spencer, et al. Editors, ABC-CLIO, Santa Barbara. 2012

Gold Braid and Foreign Diplomatic Relations, US Naval Press 1988, Long, David, Foster

Graham's Monthly Magazine of Literature and Art, volume XXV,

Jefferson's War: America's First War on Terror, 1801-1805. Carroll & Graf 2003, J Wheelan, Joseph The Barbary Wars, Hill & Wang, NY, 2005, Lambert, Frank

Library of Universal History: Containing a Record of the Human Race. Library of the U. of Chicago Durrett Collection 1899, Clare, Israel Smith,

Make Your Life Worthwhile, Harper and Row, New York, 1946 Fox, Emmet

Masting and Rigging. Glasgow: Brown, Son and Ferguson, LTD, Underhill, Harold (1986).

Moroland, Tumalo Creek Press, Bend, Ore. revised 2009, Fulton, Robert A.

Naval History of the United States, vol.12, Union Book Co. 1899. Digitized by U. of California, 2013, Clare, Israel S.

Never Subdued, Create Space, 2011, Franklin Hook, Pub. Hook, Franklin

Our Navy and the Barbary Corsairs, Houghton, Mifflin & Co 1905, Allen, Gardner W. 1905 digitized By LOC

Our Navy and the Barbary Pirates, Library of Congress, A. G. Weld, digitized by Google Books, public domain.

Pirates of the Barbary Coast, Penguin, NY, Nov 11, 2010, Tinniswood, Adrian

Six Frigates, W.W. Norton & Company, Inc., New York, London, 2006, Toll, Ian W.

Stephen Decatur, a Life Most Bold and Daring, Tucker, Spencer, Naval Institute Press, 2013,

The Battle for God, Ballantine Books, Div. of Random House, 2000, Armstrong, Karen.

The American Historical Record Volume 1, P-55, (Preble's Diary) edited by Benson, John Lossing, Chase and Town Publishers, 1872. Preble, Commodore Edward.

The Fall and Recapture of Detroit in the War of 1812, Wayne State University Press, 2011. Yanik, Anthony J.

The Frigate Constitution, Houghton, Mifflin, Riverside Press, Cambridge, 1900, Hollis, Ira N

The Encyclopedia of the War of 1812 Vol. 1, Tucker, Spencer, et al. Editors, ABC-CLIO, Santa Barbara, 2012

Bibliography

The Encyclopedia of the Wars of the Early American Republic, ABC-CLIO, Santa Barbara, 2014, Tucker, Spencer, ed.

The Life and Character of Stephen Decatur, PB Goodsell, Hartford, 1821, Waldo, S. Putnam

The Life of the Late Gen. William Eaton, E. Merriam & Co., Brookfield, 1813, compiled by Chas Prentiss

The Lake Erie Campaign of 1813, History Press, Charleston 2012, Rybka, Walter P.

The Louisiana Purchase: A Historical and Geographical Encyclopedia, edited by Rodriguez, Junius P., Santa Barbara, July 2002

The Pirate Coast, Hyperion, New York, 2005, Zacks, Richard

The Quasi War, Scribner & Sons, NY, 1966, Deconde, Alexander

The Southern Literary Messenger, JW White, Richmond 1835, Minor, Benjamin, & Wells, JD digitized by Oxford University Press November 28, 2006. Available on line: See Internet Sources.

The War of 1812, a Complete Chronology, McFarland, 2012. Hannings, Bud

The War of 1812, a Forgotten Conflict, Youth. Illinois Press, 2012, Hickey, Donald R.

The Wars of the Barbary Pirates, Osprey publishing, Oxford, UK, 2006, Fremont-Barnes, Gregory

Thomas Jefferson's Qur'an, Alfred A. Knopf, a Division of Random House, NY, Toronto, 2013, Spellberg, Denise

Victory in Tripoli, John Wiley & Sons, Jan 7, 2011, Hoboken New Jersey, London, Joshua

White Slaves, African Masters, University of Chicago Press, 1999, Baepler, Paul, editor.

Victory in Tripoli, John Wiley & Sons, Jan 7, 2011, Hoboken New Jersey, London, Joshua,

Internet Sources:

Alkhateeb, Firas, Lost Islamic History website, http://lostislamichistory.com/granada-the-last-muslim-kingdom-of-spain/

Allen, Gardner W. Riverside Press, Houghton, Mifflin and Co., Boston 1905. *Our Navy and the Barbary Corsairs*. Library of Congress.

Available online at: Http://babel.hathitrust.org/cgi/pt?id=loc.ark:/13960/t3611fm4k;view=1up;seq=397

America's library: (Library of Congress) http://www.americaslibrary.gov/

America's Navy website, http://www.public.navy.mil/surfor/ddg104/Pages/namesake.aspx

Andrew Jackson. (2015). The Biography.com website. Retrieved 10:16, Mar 20, 2015, from http://www.biography.com/people/andrew-jackson-9350991#related-video-gallery

Annals of Congress, Senate, 13th Congress, 3rd Session http://memory.loc.gov/cgi-bin/ampage284

Bielinski, Stefan, The New York State Museum, Internet source: http://www.nysm.nysed.gov/albany/bios/vr/solvr5113.html

Bermuda Triangle Famous Incidents of Disappearances http://www.bermuda-attractions.com/bermuda2_000051.htm

Blodgett, Dr.Brian, Tecumseh His Role and Conduct in the War of 1812, Blodgett's Historical Consulting (Internet Source) https://sites.google.com/site/blodgetthistoricalconsulting/tecumseh

Boddy-Evans, Alistair, African History, http://africanhistory.about.com/od/militaryhistory/ss/Yusuf-Karamanli-2.htm

Casualties: US Navy and Marine Corps Personnel Killed and Injured in Selected Accidents and Other Incidents Not Directly the Result of Enemy Action: http://www.ibiblio.org/hyperwar/NHC/accidents.htm

Congressional web site, http://www.inaugural.senate.gov/swearing-in/event/thomas-jefferson-1801

Crawford, Michael, Naval Historical Center, http://www.history.navy.mil/research/archives/subject-collections/u-s-war-with-tripoli-and-war-on-terrorism.html

Cutrer, Thomas W. Handbook of Texas Online: www.tshaonline.org/handbook/online/articles/fpi19). Accessed November 26, 2014. Uploaded on June 15, 2010. Published by the Texas State Historical Association.

Daily News, Ankara, Turkey, *http://www.seznam.name/rss-clanek-13216638/2014-08-19/isil-s-actions-have-no-place-in-islam-turkey-s-top-cleric-mehmet-gormez-says.html*Duchy of Parma, http://www.almanachdegotha.org/id29.html

Bibliography 217

Fort McHenry National Monument: http://www.nps.gov/fomc/historyculture/francis-scott-key.htm

FoundersOnLine:http://founders.archives.gov/documents/Jefferson/01-36-02-0394

Francis Scott Key. (2015). The Biography.com website. Retrieved 09:34, Mar 20, 2015, from http://www.biography.com/people/francis-scott-key-9364165#song-becomes-national-anthem

Gonzales, Matthew, Morisco Expulsion 1609: http://mattgonzalez8947.umwblogs.org/aboutHeitman, Francis Bernard, Heitman, Francis Bernard, Historical Register and Dictionary of the United States Army, 1890. Source, http://books.google.com/books?id=m1zEG4ySqlsC&pg=RA5PA1864&dq=legion+of+the+us&hl=en&sa=X&ei=2 QRQVPH_KcWVyATptIDoBw&ved=0CD0Q6AEwBQ#v=onepage&q=legion%20of%20the%20us&f=false

Hickman, Kennedy, *War of 1812, Battle of Crysler's Farm*, Internet Source: http://militaryhistory.about.com/od/warof1812/p/War-Of-1812-Battle-Of-Cryslers-Farm.htm.

Hickman, Kennedy. http://militaryhistory.about.com/od/warof1812/p/battle-of-horseshoe-bend.htm

Hickman, Kennedy. http://militaryhistory.about.com/od/shipprofiles/p/ussus.htm

Hollis, Iran, The Frigate Constitution, Google book, Houghton, Mifflin, Riverside Press, Cambridge, 1900

Horseshoe Bend National Park website: http://www.nps.gov/hobe/planyourvisit/upload/HOBE_S2.pdf

Hurt, R. Douglas. The Ohio Frontier: Crucible of the Old Northwest, 1720-1830. Bloomington, IN: Indiana University Press, 1996. Cited by Internet source: Info Please: Records of the United States Government, Record Group 11;

Irving Family web site:http://irving-fam.com/tng/histories/Edward%20Preble%20Bio.pdf

Islamic website, http://islamicresponse.blogspot.co.uk/2008/07/purpose.html

National Archives http://www.ourdocuments.gov/doc.php?doc=4 US Dept. of Justice Memorandum: http://www.justice.gov/olc/docs/memoabmtreaty11152001.pdf

James Madison: "Seventh Annual Message," December 5, 1815. Online by Gerhard Peters and John T. Woolley, The American Presidency Project, http://www.presidency.ucsb.edu/ws/?pid=29457.

James Madison, The Biography.com website. Retrieved 03:47, Mar 18, 2015, from http://www.biography.com/people/james-madison-9394965

Janssens, Jean Claude, (Translated by Gerald Hawkins), Confederate Historical Association of Belgium, the First Operations of the US Navy in the Mediterranean Sea: Internet source: belgium.com/pdf/english/Barbary%20wars.pdf

Jewett, Thomas, William Bainbridge: America's Unlucky Sea Captain, http://www.earlyamerica.com/review/2005_summer_fall/sea_captain.htm

Jewett, Thomas, http://www.earlyamerica.com/review/2002_winter_spring/terrorism.htm

Jewish Virtual Library, http://www.jewishvirtuallibrary.org/ Kaetz James, Auburn U, *Encyclopedia of Alabama:*

Kaetz James P, Auburn U. http://www.encyclopediaofalabama.org/face/Article.jsp?id=h-3081.

Kaetz James P, Auburn University, Encyclopedia of Alabama: http://www.encyclopediaofalabama.org/face/Article.jsp?id=h-

Kershner, Michelle. Museums and Historic Sites, 2013: http://www.visitfrederick.org/what-to-see-and-do/10-key-facts- about-the-star-spangled-banner-and-its-author.

Kohen, Elizabeth. (original source) 2003. http://facts.randomhistory.com/interesting-facts-about-spain.html21. John 21. 21 21. Templer Shubrick, article by James Fenimore Cooper 1844, Graham's Monthly Magazine of Literature and Art volume XXV, page 270, Digitized by NY Public Library April 22, 2013. Available free on line.

Laferty, Renee, Battle Châteauguay, http://www.eighteentwelve.ca/?q=eng/Topic/49

Library of Congress Exhibition, http://www.loc.gov/exhibits/inaugural/exhibition.html#jefferson

Library of Congress, Internet archive available on line, http://publicdomainreview.org/collections/an-exact-and-authentic-narrative-of-the-2nd-baltimore-riot-1812

Library of Congress, Our Navy and the Barbary Corsairs, Houghton, Mifflin & Co 1905, Allen, Gardner, W.

Library of Congress, Our Navy and the Barbary Pirates, A.G. Weld, Internet archive by Google books, public domain, http://babel.hathitrust.org/cgi/pt?id=loc.ark:/13960/t3611fm4k;view=1up;seq=26

Mariner's Museum, https://www.marinersmuseum.org/sites/micro/usnavy/06/06a.htm

McClellan, Maj. Edwin N., Hist., U.S.M.C., 1st Ed. Chap II, page 2. Internet source: https://www.mcu.usmc.mil/historydivision

Military History (mag), Oct. 1998. http://www.historynet.com/war-of-1812-battle-of-york.htm, Malcomson, Rob't & Thomas

Minor, Benjamin, & Wells, JD, https://books.google.com/books?id=XE4FAAAAQAAJ&pg=PR5&focus=viewport&output=text#c_top

Mount Vernon website: http://www.mountvernon.org/george-washington/

Natelson, Rob, U. of Montana: Our American Constitution: http://constitution.i2i.org/2014/07/20/how-much-authoritydoes-congress-have-under-the-treaty-power-the-question-the-supreme-court-dodged/-

National Archives, Founders On line, http://founders.archives.gov/documents/Jefferson/01-36-02-0394

National Archives, Founders On line http://founders.archives.gov/documents/Madison/02-09-02-0159

National Park Service, US Dep't of the Interior //www.nps.gov/natr/historyculture/andrew-jackson-gains-his-nicknames.htm

Native American Encyclopedia: http://nativeamericanencyclopedia.com/history-the-battle-tippecanoe/

Navy Department Library: http://www.history.navy.mil/library/online/barbary_derne.htm

Navy Department Library: http://www.history.navy.mil/library/online/battle_lake_erie.htm. Knoll, Adm. Denys (Ret), Battle of Lake Erie: Building the Fleet in the Wilderness, Washington DC, 1979, Oct. 1998

Naval Historical Center, dictionary of fighting ships: history.navy.mil/research/histories/ship-histories/danfs

Naval Operation's Against the Barbary Powers in 1815; Communicated to the Senate, January 11, 1816. http://www.ibiblio.org/pha/USN/1816/18160111Pirates.html

Naval Warfare in the Age of Sail, http://mysite.du.edu/~jcalvert/hist/navalwar.htm.

Official Indian Wars of the United States, http://www.thelatinlibrary.com/imperialism/notes/indianwars.html

Ohio History Central: http://www.ohiohistorycentral.org/w/Battle_of_Tippecanoe?rec=482

http://pabook.libraries.psu.edu/palitmap/bios/Perry__Oliver_Hazard.html

Oregon PBS Web Site: http://www.pbs.org/opb/historydetectives/feature/british-navy- impressment/

Political Graveyard.com, http://politicalgraveyard.com/bio/morris.html

Political Vel Craft, http://politicalvelcraft.org/2013/05/27/memorial-1801-first-war-with-the-united-states-by-islam-remembering-those-who-were-enslaved-killed/

Public Broadcasting System, http://www.pbs.org/wned/war-of-1812/timeline

Register of Officer Personnel United States Navy and Marine Corps and Ship's Data 1801-1807.

Pennsylvania Book Libraries http://www.history.navy.mil/library/online/PERSONNEL%20AND%20SHIP%20DATA%201801-1807.pdf

Remember the Intrepid, http://www.richardsomers.org/TheIntrepid13.pdf

Richard Somers website http://www.richardsomers.org/rsomers%20page2.html

Rickard, J., *Battle of York, 27 April 1813*, (11/25/2007), http://www.historyofwar.org/articles/battles_york_1813.html

Spanish Fiestas web site, Moors in Spain: http://www.spanish-fiestas.com/history/moors/

Stiadi, Edwin, http://www.edwinsetiadi.com/2011/05/19-october-1469-day-that-changed-world.html

Symonds, Dr. Craig, video lecture online undated. Civil War Trust: http://www.civilwar.org/video/battle-of-hampton- roads.html.

The Biography.com website. Retrieved 09:58, Feb 21, 2015, from http://www.biography.com/people/aaron-burr- 9232241#final-years the Conrad and McMunn boarding house at New Jersey Avenue and C Street

The Historical Society of Pennsylvania, Rodgers' FamilyPapers, http://www2.hsp.org/collections/manuscripts/r/rodgers 1208.htm

The Jefferson Monticello website: http://www.inaugural.senate.gov/swearing-in/event/thomas-jefferson-1801

The Jefferson Monticello website: http://www.monticello.org/site/research-and-collections/first-inauguration

The Jefferson Monticello website: http://www.monticello.org/site/research-and-collections/physical-descriptions-jefferson

The Jefferson Monticello website: http://www.monticello.org/site/research-and-collections/meriwether-lewis

The Jefferson Monticello website: http://www.monticello.org/site/research-and-collections/first-barbary-war

The Jefferson Monticello website: http://www.monticello.org/site/research-and-collections/meriwether-lewis

The Jefferson Monticello website: http://www.starrhill.com/brews/brew_item/monticello-reserve-ale

The Life of the Late Gen. William Eaton, digitized by Google. http://books.google.com/books?id=4alDAAAAYAAJ&pg=PR1#v=onepage&q&f=false

The Life and Character of Stephen Decatur, https://books.google.com/books, Waldo, S.P. https://books.google.com/books,

The Life of Sam Houston, http://www.graceproducts.com/houston/life.html

The Mariners Museum: https://www.marinersmuseum.org/sites/micro/usnavy/04/04d.htm

Thorburn, Mark. Great American Trials. "General William Hull Court-Martial: 1814." 2002. Internet Source, http://www.encyclopedia.com/doc/1G2-3498200047.html

Trentinian, Jacques de, France's Contribution to American Independence, http://www.xenophongroup.com/mcjoynt/alliance2.htm

Tobias Lear papers, William L. Clements Library, The University of Michigan: http://quod.lib.umich.edu/c/clementsmss/umich-wcl-M-1044lea?view=text

U. of Virginia, Miller Center web page: http://millercenter.org/academic/americanpresident/jefferson/essays/biography/1

U. of Virginia, Miller Center web page: http://millercenter.org/president/jefferson/essays/firstlady/martha

US Army Center of Military History, http://www.history.army.mil/books/CG&CSA/Dearborn-H.htm

US Army publication, American Military History available on line: http://www.conservapedia.com/War_of_1812 Matloff, Maurice, editor

US Department of State: https://history.state.gov/milestones/1801-1829/barbary- wars. https://history.state.gov/milestones/1801-1829/barbary-wars

US History.org, http://www.ushistory.org/franklin/philadelphia/grave.htm

US Naval History and Heritage Command, http://www.history.navy.mil/photos/events/war1812/atsea/ches-sn.htm

US Naval Institute, Naval History and Heritage Command: http://www.navalhistory.org/2012/07/23/richard-dale-strikes- barbary-pilots

US Naval Institute, http://www.usni.org/magazines/navalhistory/2012-04/last-voyage-andrew-sterett US Naval Institute, http://www.usni.org/magazines/navalhistory/2012-04/last-voyage-andrew-sterett

USS Boston: http://www.woodenmodelboat.com/model/woodpro/all/USS_boston.htm. Gianhien

USS Sterett web site, http://destroyerhistory.org/goldplater/ns_sterett/

US Wars.com, *Battle of Lacolle Mills, Internet source:* http://www.mywarof1812.com/battles/121120-lacolle-mills.html

US Wars.com, http://www.mywarof1812.com/leaders/chauncey-isaac/

Vallar, Cindy, http://www.cindyvallar.com/barbarycorsairs.html

Bibliography 223

Vatican Radio, 7/25/2014 as reported by Reuters. http://en.radiovaticana.va/news/2014/07/25/worlds_muslim_leaders_condemn_attacks_on_iraqi_christi ans/1103410

Wabarakathuhu, A.S.A.W.R.: http://islamicresponse.blogspot.com/2008/07/symbolism-and-allegory-in-quran.html.

Walbert, David, Spain and America: From Reconquest to Conquest, NC Digital History, http://www.learnnc.org/lp/editions/nchist-twoworlds/1677

War of 1812, http://www.eighteentwelve.ca/?q=eng/Topic/94, Ridler, Jason, bio of Roger Hale Sheaffe,

White House History, http://wayback.archive.org/web/20081026204715/http://www.oldandsold.com/articles31n/white- house-history-11.shtml.

William Henry Harrison. (2015). The Biography.com website. Retrieved 09:58, Mar 20, 2015, from http://www.biography.com/people/william-henry-harrison-9329968#presidency-and-sudden-death

Wilson, Scott: http://abcnews.go.com/blogs/politics/2014/07/star-spangled-banner-myths-debunked/

Wikipedia-cited source: Colonial Society of Massachusetts, 1907, page 366

Wikipedia, http://en.wikipedia.org/wiki/Andrew_Sterett#Resignation

Wikipedia, http://en.wikipedia.org/wiki/AndrewSterett

Wikipedia, http://en.wikipedia.org/wiki/Duchy_of_Parma

Wikipedia, http://en.wikipedia.org/wiki/Henry_Dearborn

Wkipedia: http://en.wikipedia.org/wiki/History_of_the_United_States_Navy

Wikipedia, http://en.wikipedia.org/wiki/Jesse_Elliott#cite_note-4

Wikipedia, http://en.wikipedia.org/wiki/USS_Adams_(1799)

Wikipedia: http://en.wikipedia.org/wiki/History_of_the_United_States_Navy

Wikipedia: http://en.wikipedia.org/wiki/Revenue_Marine

Wikipedia, http://en.wikipedia.org/wiki/Samuel_Barron_(1765%E2%80%931810)

Wikipedia, http://en.wikipedia.org/wiki/Stephen_Decatur

Wikipedia: http://en.wikipedia.org/wiki/Timeline_of_the_French_Revolution1783

William and Mary special collections database, Earl Gregg Swem Library, James Barron Papers, http://scdb.swem.wm.edu/?p=collections/findingaid&id=6725&q=&rootcontentid=176236

Wilson, Scott (quoting University of Michigan Associate Professor of Music, Mark Clague) http://abcnews.go.com/blogs/politics/2014/07/star-spangled-banner-myths-debunked/

Wordpress.com: barrseitz (blogger) http://barbarywars.wordpress.com/timeline/

Documents/ Letters/Articles

Documents 1-40: 1776-1818 (Peace Treaty with Algiers 1815) Washington: Government Printing Office, 1931 (spelling edited by author)

National Archives Founders On Line: http://founders.archives.gov/documents/Jefferson/01-36-02-0394

National Archives Founders On Line: http://founders.archives.gov/documents/Madison/02-04-02-0533

National Archives Microfilm M 625, Naval Records Collection, 1775-1910, William Eaton to James Cathcart 4 August 1802.

Philadelphia Inquirer, Oct 25, 2011, article by Colimore, Edward, Proceedings of the United States Naval Institute, volume 32, 1906. Original U. of Minnesota digitized October 23, 2013.

US Army Command and General Staff College, FT. Leavenworth, 1994, Master's Thesis, King, Maj. David M.

US Naval Institute, Naval History and Heritage Command, Andrew Morris to William Eaton, July 21, 1802

* * *

APPENDIX A

THE ORIGINAL SIX FRIGATES OF THE CONTINENTAL NAVY AND THEIR FATE

SHIP	FATE
United States	Broken up 1865
Constellation	Broken up 1853
Constitution	Still in Commission
Congress	Broken up 1834
Chesapeake	Captured by British 1813, Broken up 1820
President	Captured by British 1815, Destroyed 1818 [472]

USS United States:
1. *USS United States* was the first of the heavy frigates authorized by the Naval Act of 1794 and was launched on May 10, 1796, from Philadelphia.[473] She was designed by renowned naval architect of the time Joshua Humphreys who lived up to his reputation by building ships that were fast enough to escape British ships of the line yet had the firepower to best any vessel of its size. Launching a ship, however, did not mean that it was ready for sea and when peace was settled with the Dey of Algiers, it triggered a clause in the original authorization by Congress to halt construction of the frigates.[474]

---

472 The Mariners Museum, https://www.marinersmuseum.org/sites/micro/usnavy/04/04d.htm
473 ibid.
474 Hickman, http://militaryhistory.about.com/od/shipprofiles/p/ussus.htm

When President George Washington convinced Congress to provide funds to finish building three of the frigates closest to being completed, a Continental Navy veteran and a hero of the revolution, John Barry, was recalled and given a commission to supervise the completion of one of the new frigates, which he accomplished by the spring of 1798, 15 months later.

In August and September of that year Commodore John Barry captured two French privateers, *Sans Pareil* and *Jalouse*,[475] but lost the two prize ships, which apparently escaped, in a storm off Cape Hatteras on the way home. Barry continued his service chasing privateers and recovering merchant ships during the Quasi-War with several interruptions for the ship's repair. In 1801, when peace had been made with France, the ship went in ordinary (the modern term is "in mothballs") in Washington, D.C. until late 1809 when orders were given to refit her for sea.

Captain Stephen Decatur took command of her in June 1810, and sailed her down the Potomac for the refitting in Norfolk. Author Samuel Waldo had this to say in Decatur's biography: *"Commodore Decatur, in 1810, was ordered to take command of the frigate, United States, which was again fitted for sea and put in commission. Exhilarating indeed must have been the reflection, that he was now the sole commander of the noble frigate in which he commenced his Naval career in the humble capacity of midshipman."*[476]

While he was in Norfolk refitting the *United States*, Decatur met the British captain of *HMS Macedonian*, James Cardin. They became friends and Decatur bet his new friend a beaver hat that if they ever met in battle he would best him. Sure enough, that came true. On October 25, 1812, Decatur's lookouts on the *USS United States* spotted the *Macedonian* just south of the Azores, and after an hour and a half hour battle resulting in the *Macedonian's* masts being disabled, Captain Cardin struck

---

475 ibid.
476 Waldo, page 163.

his colors. The *Macedonian* suffered 104 casualties compared to the *United States'* 12.

The initial action report from the *Macedonian* indicated 36 KIA and 68 WIA. Later, the report was revised to 89 KIA and 15 WIA after 53 of those wounded had died. Decatur's action report was filed on October 30, 1812, in a letter to Secretary of the Navy, Paul Hamilton:

"USS United States at Sea
October 30, 1812

"The Hon. Paul Hamilton

"Sir – I have the honor to inform you that on the 25th inst. being in LAT 29 N LON 29.30 W we fell in with, and after an action of an hour and a half, captured his Britannic's Majesty's Ship Macedonian, commanded by Captain John Cardin, and mounting 49 carriage guns (the odd gun shifting). She is a frigate of the largest class, two years old, four months out of dock and reputed one of the best sailors in the British service. The enemy being to windward, had the advantage of engaging us at his own distance, which was so great, that for the first half-hour we did not use our carronades; and at no moment was he completely within the effect of our muskets or grape – to this circumstance and a heavy swell, which was on at the time, I ascribe the unusual length of the action.

"The enthusiasm of every officer, seamen and marine on board this ship on discovering the enemy – their steady conduct in battle, and precision of their fire, *could not be surpassed.*

Where all met my fullest expectations, would be unjust of me to discriminate. Permit me, however, to recommend to you my First Lieutenant, Wm. H. Allen. He has served me upwards of five years, and to his unremitted exertions in disciplining the crew, is to be imputed to the obvious superiority of our gunnery exhibited in the result of the contest.

"Subjoined is a list of the killed and wounded on both sides. Our loss, compared the enemy will appear small. Amongst our wounded you will observe the name of Lieutenant Funk, who died in a few hours after the action – he was an officer of great gallantry and promise, and the service has sustained a great loss in his death.

"The Macedonian lost her mizzen mast, fore and main top masts and mean yard, and was much cut up in her hull. The damage to this ship was not such as to render return into port necessary, and had I not deemed it important that we should see our prize in, should have continued our cruise.

"With the highest consideration and respect, I am your obedient humble servant,

[Signed] "Stephen Decatur"

[List of killed and wounded was attached]

After the victory Decatur was once again welcomed home as a hero and awarded medals and and many honors. After all the hoopla, the *USS United States,* along with the *Macedonian* and the *USS Hornet,* left New York Harbor on May 24, 1813. A week later on June 1, they ran into a formidable British blockade of ships and were driven into the safe port of New London, Connecticut, where they spent the rest of the War of 1812. In 1814, Decatur was transferred to command the *USS President* as previously described. In 1815 the *USS United States* was attached to the second US Mediterranean Squadron. She was the flagship of Commodore Bainbridge's squadron, and was under the command of Captain John Shaw. When Bainbridge came home, Shaw took over as Commodore of the Mediterranean squadron until he was relieved by Commodore Isaac Chauncey. The ship came home from the Mediterranean in 1819 and was in ordinary in Norfolk until 1823. She then underwent refitting and had multiple peacetime assignments, up until 1849, when she once again went in ordinary until the opening shots of the Civil War in 1861.

The Confederate Navy refitted her, although she was in desperate shape, and used her as a block ship. She was then recommissioned as *CSS United States* near Hampton Roads, and later deliberately sunk as an obstacle in the Elizabeth River, which would force any union ships, if they didn't run into the obstacle, to sail in range of Confederate guns. After the war she was raised by union forces, condemned, and broken up in 1865-66.[477]

USS Constellation:
2. The *USS Constellation* was built at the Sterett Shipyard, Baltimore, Maryland, and launched on September 7, 1797. Named after the original 15 states represented by a constellation of stars in the original U.S. flag, the ship was commissioned in June 1798 with Thomas Truxton commanding.

    She started out escorting merchant vessels off the Atlantic coast, but transferred to the Caribbean where she got her baptism of fire against the French ship, L'Insurgente in the famous battle fought off Nevis, West Indies, on February 9, 1799. She had many other successes during the Quasi-war and actually recovered three American merchant ships in May 1800. Storm damaged while anchored in Delaware Bay in April 1801, the *Constellation* required extensive repairs. *Constellation* served well in the first Barbary War sailing with Commodores Robert Morris, Samuel Barron, and John Rodgers. After the war she was placed in ordinary (meaning in mothballs) until 1812. After extensive repairs in 1813 she traveled to Hampton Roads near Norfolk, Virginia, where she was effectively blockaded by the British for the duration of the War of 1812.

    The U.S. Naval Historical Center, Dictionary of Fighting Ships tells the rest of the original *Constellation's* history best:

    "In the wake of the War of 1812, naval action resumed against the Barbary powers that had enriched themselves considerably during the struggle with England. Constellation, attached to the Mediterranean Squadron under Commodore Stephen Decatur, sailed from New York on May 20, 1815 and joined in the capture of the Algerian frigate Meshuda on 17 June 1815. Treaties of peace

---
477 Hickman: http://militaryhistory.about.com/od/shipprofiles/p/ussus.htm

soon ensued Algiers, Tunis and Tripoli. Constellation remained with the squadron under Commodores William Bainbridge, Isaac Chauncey, and John Shaw to enforce the accords, returning to Hampton Roads only in December 1817.

"Except for brief periods under repair in 1828-29, 1832, 1834-35, and 1838-39, Constellation's career through the mid-point in the 19th century proved varied and colorful. From 12 November 1819 to 24 April 1820 she served as flagship of Commodore Charles Morris on the Brazil Station, protecting American commerce against privateers and supporting the negotiation of trade agreements with South American nations. On 25 July 1820, she sailed for the first time to Pacific waters where she was attached to the Squadron of Commodore Charles Stewart. She remained thus employed for two years, protecting American shipping off the coast of Peru, an area where disquiet erupted into revolt against Spain.

"In 1827, Constellation acted briefly as flagship for the West India Squadron on a twofold mission involving the eradication of the last of the pirates and the interception of slavers operating in the area. In August 1829, she cruised to the Mediterranean to watch over American shipping and to collect indemnities from previous losses suffered by U.S. merchantmen. While enroute to her station, she carried the American ministers to France and England to their posts of duty. Returning to the United States in November 1831, she underwent minor repairs and departed again for the Mediterranean in April 1832 where she remained until an outbreak of cholera forced her to sail for home in November 1834.

"In October 1835, Constellation sailed for the Gulf of Mexico to assist in crushing the Seminole uprising. She landed shore parties to relieve the Army garrisons and sent her boats on amphibious expeditions. Mission accomplished, she then cruised with the West India Squadron until 1838 serving part of this period in the capacity of flagship for Commodore Alexander Dallas.

"The decade of the 1840s saw Constellation circumnavigate the globe. As flagship of Captain Kearny and the East India Squadron, her mission, as assigned in March 1841, was to safeguard American lives and property against loss in the Opium War, and further, to enable negotiation of commercial treaties. Enroute home in May 1843 she entered the

Appendix A   231

Hawaiian Islands, helping to keep them from becoming a British protectorate, and thereafter she sailed homeward making calls at South American ports.

"Ultimately laid up in ordinary at Norfolk from 1845 to 1853, *Constellation* was broken up there in 1853."[478]

USS Constitution
3. The *USS Constitution* was built in Boston's Edmund Hartt's shipyard and launched on October 21, 1797 under the command of Captain Samuel Nicholson, a Revolutionary War veteran who had served under John Paul Jones, and who supervised the *Constitution's* construction.

"At the outset of the War of 1812, USS Constitution had already won all of her engagements in two wars: the Quasi-War with France (1798-1801) and the Barbary Wars (1801-1805). During the War of 1812, to the surprise of both the Americans and the British, she defeated four English warships, Upon returning to Boston from each victory at sea, the ship and her sailors were honored with parades and public adoration, and her legend grew into the national icon that "Old Ironsides" remains to this day.

"USS Constitution was among the 22 commissioned warships of the United States' 18-year- old Navy, compared to more than 80 British vessels on station off America's eastern seaboard in 1812. While the American fleet boasted many successes during the War of 1812, their actions had little impact on the outcome of the war.

"Objective analysis of the War of 1812 must conclude that the victories of Constitution had no Most Fortunate Ship. The losses suffered by the Royal Navy were no more than pinpricks to the great fleet: they neither inspired its battle readiness nor disrupted the blockade of American ports. What Constitution did accomplish was to uplift American morale spectacularly and, in the process, end forever the myth that the Royal Navy was invincible.

---
478 Naval Historical Center, dictionary of fighting ships: history.navy.mil/research/histories/ship-histories/danfs

"Throughout the next four decades following the War of 1812, USS Constitution secured numerous bloodless victories until she was taken out of active service in 1855. However, she is best remembered for that unparalleled string of successes two centuries ago, and she has never fired a round in combat since February, 1815, during her battle with HMS Cyane and HMS Levant.

"Although a peace treaty between the United States and England was signed on Dec. 24, 1814 in Ghent, Belgium, and ratified on Feb. 15, 1815, sporadic battles between the two erupted for the next several months. The War of 1812 marks the last time America and Great Britain were on opposing sides of an armed conflict, and the beginning of the former's rise to joining the latter as the world's premiere maritime superpower."[479]

Constitution Chronology:[480]
March 27, 1794 – The Naval Armament Act authorizes the construction of six frigates.
1794-1797 – Under construction at Edmund Hartt's Shipyard, Boston
October 21, 1794 – *Constitution* launched
July 22, 1798 – Sails from Boston to Caribbean on first cruise
1798-1801 – Quasi-War with France, West India squadron flagship
1801-1803 – In ordinary (mothballs) and repair in Boston
1803-1805 – Barbary War I, Mediterranean Squadron flagship
1805-1807 – Continues as Mediterranean Squadron flagship
1807-1809 – In repair in New York
1809-1810 – Flagship of North division Coast Guard duty
1810-1811 – North division command, Commodore Isaac Hull
August 1811 – February 1812 European cruise to England France and Holland
War of 1812 – August 19, 1812. Defeats *HMS Guerriere*
December 29, 1812 – Defeats HMS Java

---

[479] Naval Historical Center, dictionary of fighting ships: http://www.history.navy.mil/browse-by-topic/ships/uss-constitution- americas-ship-of-state/history.html
[480] USS Constitution Museum: http://www.ussconstitutionmuseum.org/collections-history/discover-constitutions-history/chronology/

February 20, 1815 – Defeats *HMS Cyan & HMS Levant*
1816-1821 – In ordinary and repair in Boston
1821-1824 – Mediterranean Squadron flagship
1824-1828 – Mediterranean Squadron
1828-1831 – In ordinary, Boston
1831-1835 – Undergoes refit in Boston
March-June 1835 – Voyage to France with Minister to France, Edward Livingston
1835-1838 – Mediterranean Squadron flagship
1838-1841 – Pacific squadron flagship
1842-February 1843 – Home Squadron flagship
May 1843 – September 1846 around the world cruise
1846-1848 – In ordinary and repair, Boston
1848-1851 – Mediterranean Squadron (Pope Pius visits the ship in 1849)
1851-1853 – In ordinary and repair, New York
1853-1855 – African squadron monitoring slave trade
November 3, 1853 – Captures her last prize *H.N. Gambril*
1855-1860 – In ordinary and refit to school ship Portsmouth, NH
1860s – School ship U.S. Navy Academy & Newport Rhode Island
1871-1872 – In ordinary, Philadelphia, refitted 1873-1875

In 1877 the *Constitution* became a training ship, transported exhibits to Paris in 1878 for the *Exhibition Universelle*, and basically served as a training ship and exhibit for many years thereafter. She still serves as an historical exhibit based at the Charleston Navy Yard, Boston, and is the oldest commissioned U.S. Navy warship still afloat.

USS Congress (not to be confused with the one built in 1841 and destroyed during the Civil War)
4. The *USS Congress* was built in Portsmouth, New Hampshire and launched on April 15, 1799, under the command of Captain James Sever. Her first assignment involved protecting American merchant shipping during the Quasi-War with

France, but on her maiden voyage just six days out she lost her mast to storm damage and returned to the states.

After repair she departed again for the West Indies on July 26, 1800. Three days later on August 29 she recovered the merchant brig *Experiment,* which had just been taken by a French privateer. In April 1801, she was placed in ordinary in Washington, D.C.

Two years later, in April 1804, under the command of Captain John Rodgers. She left Norfolk for the Mediterranean joining Commodore Sam Barron's squadron for the next year. She returned to the States in November 1805 under the command of Stephen Decatur carrying the Tunisian Ambassador to the United States, Sidi Soliman Mellimelli and his attendants.[481] She spent the next seven years in ordinary at Washington, D.C. until 1811.

USS Congress was recommissioned in late 1811, just before the War of 1812 was declared. She spent most of the War of 1812 in the North Atlantic with Commodore John Rodgers' squadron and later off the Cape Verde islands and the coast of Brazil. All told, she captured only four enemy ships in eight months, one of the longest cruises of the war.[482] In December, 1813, she returned to Portsmouth, Virginia and was in ordinary until October 1822. She then operated under the command of Captain James Biddle chasing pirates until April 1823. She also ferried United States ministers to Spain and Argentina. In 1824, *Congress* was placed in ordinary in Washington for repairs. She was stationed in Norfolk until 1829 as a receiving ship and then placed in ordinary again. A survey in 1834, found her unfit for repair and she was broken up at the Gosport Navy Yard, Portsmouth, Virginia by order of the Commissioner of the Navy.[483]

---

481 Thomas Jefferson Encyclopedia, http://www.monticello.org/site/research-and-collections/tunisian-envoy

482 Toll, Ian, Six Frigates, page 420, W.W. Norton & Company, Inc., New York, London

483 Ibid, page 474.

USS Chesapeake
5. The *USS Chesapeake* was launched from the Gosport Navy Yard (now called Norfolk Navy ship yard or NNSY) in Portsmouth, Virginia on December 2, 1799. Although Joshua Humphrey had originally designed the ship, she was modified by Josiah Fox to where it was an entirely different design above the keel. She was also one of the six frigates that had interrupted construction due to the "halt construction" clause of Congress' funding when a peace accord was reached with Tripoli.

When finally commissioned, *Chesapeake* put to sea on May 22, 1800, under the command of Samuel Barron. She was the smallest of the original six frigates. During the Quasi-War with France, she captured a French privateer, *La Jeune Creole,* on New Year's Day 1801, after a chase lasting more than two days.

During the first Barbary War, she was the flagship under the command of Commodore Richard Valentine Morris. Having sustained storm damage on the way to Gibraltar, she arrived on May 25 and didn't leave until August 17, after repairs were made. If you recall, Morris was to replace Commodore Dale, who had commanded the first Mediterranean Squadron and subsequently resigned from the Navy under much criticism after his return to the States.

Morris was also the Commodore who was accompanied by his wife and son during the voyage, dilly-dallyed his way around the Mediterranean, (his squadron was accused of "dancing and wenching" by William Eaton), was suspended from the command, and later dismissed from the Navy.

Chesapeake returned to the United States under Captain James Barron, (Sam Barron's brother) in April 1803, when Morris transferred his flagship to the *USS New York*. *Chesapeake* remained in reserve in ordinary until January 1807, when Captain Charles Gordon took command and began to prepare her for sea duty. Gordon was under orders to join Commodore James Barron's Mediterranean Squadron as the flagship when the ship was ready. On June 22, she departed.

Three British ships were lying in ambush, *HMS Melampus, HMS Bellona* and *HMS Leopard*.

The ships were under orders from their fleet commander in Halifax, British Vice Admiral George Cranfield Berkeley, to recover impressed sailors who were American citizens and considered deserters from the British Navy.

The Navy Board of Inquiry that investigated the *HMS Leopard* affair disciplined not only Commodore Barron and Captain Gordon, but also Marine officer, Lieutenant Hall. Gordon was reprimanded as was Lieutenant Hall, but Commodore Barron apparently as the senior officer was held most responsible and found guilty of *"neglecting on the probability of an engagement to clear his Ship for action."*[484] James Barron was suspended from the service for a period of five years.

As previously noted, the *Chesapeake – Leopard* affair caused considerable anger amongst United States citizens and was probably the triggering event for President Jefferson to invoke Congress to pass the Embargo Act of 1807, which crippled the U.S. economy at the time.

During the War of 1812, *Chesapeake*, after her repairs, was commanded by Captain Samuel Evans who captured several British ships. In ill health, Evans requested relief of command which was granted in May 1813, when James Lawrence took command.

Leaving Boston Harbor on May 31, *Chesapeake* was challenged by *HMS Shannon*, and took the worst in an exchange of two broadsides. Lawrence was wounded in the initial exchange of fire and later killed by rifle fire during the battle. Captured by the British Navy, *Chesapeake* was repaired and placed into service as *HMS Chesapeake*. In July, 1819, she was sold to a timber merchant in England and broken up for sale the next year.

---

484 Wikipedia

USS President:
6. *USS President* was the last of the original six frigates to be built. She was launched from New York Harbor April 10, 1800 under the command of Silas Talbot. In August of that year she began patrols during the Quasi-War and was able to recapture several merchant vessels. In May of 1801, she became Commodore Richard Dale's flagship of the first Mediterranean squadron. Her Captain at that time was Samuel Barron, who also had her command for the second tour of the Mediterranean in 1804.

Before the War of 1812, in May 1811, while under the command of John Rodgers she exchanged fire with *HMS Little Belt*, a ship that Rodgers mistook for the *Guerriere*, which was suspected of harboring impressed U.S. sailors. The incident resulted in multiple casualties for the *Little Belt* including some KIA, and became known as the *Little Belt Affair*. It was said to be responsible for increasing tensions leading up to the declaration of the War of 1812.[485] She then spent several months in skirmishes under the command of John Rodgers, captured several merchant ships, and one warship, the *HMS Highflyer*.

In January 1815, Stephen Decatur took command of the *USS President* after she had spent nearly a year in port blockaded by the British. Trying to escape the blockade from New York Harbor, Decatur ran her aground damaging her keel. Decatur himself tells it best in his own words in this letter to the Secretary of the Navy (B.W. Crowninshield):

"At Sea January 18 aboard H.B.M.S. [His British Majesty's Ship] Endymion

"Sir – this painful duty of detailing to you the particular causes which preceded and led to the capture of the late United States frigate President, by a squadron of his Britannic Majesty's ships (as per margin) has devolved upon me. In my communication of the 14th, I made known to you my intention of proceeding to sea that evening. Owing to some mistake of the pilots, the ship, in going out, grounded on a bar, where she continued to strike heavily for an hour and a half. Although she had broken

---
485 Wikipedia.

several of her runner – braces, and had received such other material injury as to render her return to port desirable, I was unable to do so from the strong westerly wind that was then blowing. It being high water, it became necessary to force her over the bar before the high tide fell; in this we succeeded by 10 o'clock, when we shaped our course along the shore of Long Island for 50 miles, and then steered [Southeast by East].

"At 5 o'clock, three ships were discovered ahead; we immediately hauled up the ship and passed 2 miles northward of them. At daylight, we discovered four ships in chase, one on each quarter and two astern, the leading ship of the enemy a razee[486] commenced a fire upon us, but without effect. At meridian, the wind became light and baffling; we had increased our distance from the razee, but the next ship astern, which was also a large ship, had gained and continued to gain on us considerably; we immediately occupied all hands to lighten ship, by starting water cutting the anchors, throwing overboard provisions, cables, spare spars, boats and every article that could be got at, keeping sails wet from the Royals down. At 3, we had the wind quite light; the enemy, who had now been joined by a brig, had a strong breeze and were coming upon us rapidly. The Endymion (mounting 50 guns, 24 pounders on the main deck) had approached us within gunshot, and had commenced a fire with her bow guns, which we returned from our stern. At 5 o'clock she maintained a position on our starboard quarter, within half-point blank shot, on which neither our stern nor quarter guns would bear; we were now steering [East by North], the wind [North West]. I remained with her in this position for half an hour, and hope that she would close with us on our broadside, in which case I had prepared my crew to board, but from his continuing to yaw his ship to maintain his position, it

---

[486] Naval Warfare in the Age of Sail, http://mysite.du.edu/~jcalvert/hist/naval-war.htm.

A ship of the line had three decks, usually a deck of long guns, and then two decks of carronades. A razee, from French, rasée, meaning shaved, had had the top gun deck removed for better handling.

became apparent that to close was not his intention. Every fire now cut some of our sails or our rigging. To have continued our course under these circumstances, would have been placing it in his power to cripple us, without being subject to injury himself, and to have hold up more to the northward to being our stern guns to bear, would have exposed us to his raking fire. It was not dusk when I determined to alter my course for the purpose of bringing the enemy abeam, and although their ships astern were coming up fast I felt satisfied that I should be enabled to throw him out of the combat before they could come up, and was not without hopes that if the night proved dark, (of which there was every appearance) that I might still be enabled to effect my escape. Our opponent kept off at the same instant we did, and commenced at the same time. We continued engaged steering South, with steering sails set two hours and a half, when we completely succeeded in dismantling her. Previously, to her entirely dropping out of action, there were intervals of minutes, when the ships were broadside and broadside, in which she did not fire a gun. At this period, (half past 8 o'clock) although dark, the other ships of the squadron were in sight and almost within gun – shot. We were of course compelled to abandon her. In resuming our former course, for the purpose of avoiding the squadron, we were compelled to present our stern to our antagonist – but such was his state, though we were thus exposed and within range of his guns for half an hour, that he did not avail himself of this favorable opportunity of raking us. We continued this course until 11 o'clock, when two fresh ships of the enemy (the Pomona and Tenedos) had come up. The Pomona had opened fire on her larboard bow, within musket- shot; the other two cables' length astern, taking a raking position on our quarter; and the rest (with the exception of the Endymion) within gun-shot. Thus situated, with about one fifth of my crew killed and wounded my ship crippled, and more than a four-fold force opposed to me, without a chance of escape left, I deemed it my duty to surrender.

"It is with emotions of pride [that] I bear testimony to the gallantry and steadiness of every officer and man I had the honor to command on this occasion, and I feel satisfied to the fact of their beating a force equal to themselves, in the presence, and almost under the guns of so vastly superior a force, when it was almost self-evident, that whatever their exertions might be, they must ultimately be captured, will be taken as evidence of what they would have performed, has a force opposed to them been in any degree equal.

"It is with extreme pain that I have to inform you that lieutenants Babbitt, Hamilton, and Howell, fell in the action. They have left no officers of superior merit behind them.

"If, Sir, the issue of this affair had been fortunate, I should have felt it my duty to have recommended to your attention Lieutenants Shubrick and Gallagher. They maintained through the day the reputations they had acquired in former actions.

"Lieutenant Twiggs of the Marines displayed real zeal; his men were well supplied and their fire comparable, so long as the enemy continued within musket range.

"Midshipman Randolph, who had charge of the forecastle division, managed it to my entire satisfaction.

"From Mister Robinson, who was serving as a volunteer, I received essential aid, particularly after I was deprived of the services of the master, and the severe loss I had sustained in my officers on the quarter deck.

"Of our loss in killed and wounded, I am unable at present to give you a correct statement; the attention of the surgeon being so entirely occupied with the wounded, that he was unable to make out a correct return when I left the President, nor shall I be able to make it until our arrival in port, we having parted with the squadron yesterday. The enclosed list, with the exception I fear of being short, will be found correct.

"For twenty-four hours after the action it was nearly calm and the squadron was occupied repairing the crippled ships. Such of the crew of the President that were not badly wounded, were put on board the different ships; myself and a part of my crew were put on board this ship. On the 17th we had a gale from the Eastward, when this ship lost her bowsprit, fore and mainmast, and mizzen topmast, all of which were badly wounded, and was in consequence of her disabled condition, obliged to throw overboard all her upper deck guns; her loss in killed and wounded must have been very great. Ten were buried after I came on board (36 hours after the action) the badly wounded such as [those who] are obliged to keep their cots, occupy the starboard side of the gun deck from the cabin bulkhead to the main mast. From the crippled state of the President's spars, I feel satisfied she could not have saved her masts and I feel serious apprehensions for the safety of our wounded left on board.

"It is due to Captain Hope to state that every attention has been paid by him to myself and officers that have been placed aboard his ship, that delicacy and humanity could dictate.

"I have the honor,

[signed] Stephen Decatur"[487]

After the surrender, Captain Hope sailed the *Endymion* and the *President* to Bermuda where the British Navy repaired both ships and renamed the USS *President* as the HMS *President* and put her into the British fleet service until 1818 when she was condemned and destroyed. They must have admired her construction, however, since they built an identical ship to her exact specifications, kept the name and kept her in service until 1903 when she was finally sold for salvage.[488]

* * *

---

487 Waldo, pages 228-233
488 Wikipedia, HMS President: http://en.wikipedia.org/wiki/HMS_President_(1829)

APPENDIX B

"Treaty of peace[489] concluded between The United States of America and his Highness Omar Bashaw Dey of Algiers

"ARTICLE 1st
"There shall be from the conclusion of this treaty, a firm inviolable and universal peace and friendship between the President and citizens of the United States of America on the one part, and the Dey and subjects of the Regency of Algiers in Barbary, on the other, made by the free consent of both parties and upon the terms of the most favored nations; and if either party shall hereafter grant to any other nation, any particular favor or privilege in navigation or commerce it shall immediately become common to the other party, freely when freely it is granted to such other nation; but when the grant is conditional, it shall be at the option of the contracting parties to accept, alter, or reject such conditions, in such manner as shall be most conducive to their respective interests.

"ARTICLE 2d
"It is distinctly understood between the contracting parties, that no tribute either as biennial presents, or under any other form or name whatever, shall ever be required by the Dey and Regency of Algiers from the United States of America on any pretext whatever.

"ARTICLE 3rd
"The Dey of Algiers shall cause to be immediately delivered up to the American Squadron now off Algiers all the American citizens now in his

---

489 Source/credit for these articles of the peace treaty are noted at the end of Appendix B. Multiple spelling errors of the original documents have been corrected by this author with the exception of the words cruise/cruizer which is spelled cruize/cruizer, common spellings for the 1800s.

possession, amounting to ten more or less, and all the subjects of the Dey of Algiers now in the power of the United States amounting to five hundred more or less, shall be delivered up to him, the United States according to the usages of civilized nations requiring no ransom for the excess of prisoners in their favor.

"ARTICLE 4th
"A just and full compensation shall be made by the Dey of Algiers to such citizens of the United States, as have been captured, and detained by Algerine cruizers [sic] she commenced a fire of, (sic) or who have been forced to abandon their property in Algiers in violation of the 22d article of the treaty of peace and amity concluded between the United States and the Dey of Algiers on the 5 September 1795.
"And it is agreed between the contracting parties, that in lieu of the above, the Dey of Algiers shall cause, to be delivered forthwith into the hands of the American Consul residing in Algiers the whole of a quantity of bales of cotton left by the late Consul General of the United States in the public magazines in Algiers; and that he shall pay into the hands of the said consul the sum of ten thousand Spanish dollars.

"ARTICLE 5th
"If any goods belonging to any nation with which either of the parties are at war should be loaded on board of vessels belonging to the other party, they shall pass free and unmolested, and no attempt shall be made to take or detain them.

"ARTICLE 6th
"If any citizens or subjects belonging to either party shall be found on board a prize vessel taken from an Enemy by the other party, such citizens or subjects shall be liberated immediately, and in no case or on any presence whatever shall any American citizen be kept in captivity or confinement, or the property of any American citizen found on board of any vessel belonging to any nation with which Algiers may be at War, be detained from its lawful owners after the exhibition of sufficient proofs of American citizenship, and American property, by the Consul of the United States residing at Algiers.

"ARTICLE 7ᵗʰ
"Proper passports shall immediately be given to the vessels of both the contracting parties, on condition that the vessels of war belonging to the Regency of Algiers on meeting with Merchant Vessels belonging to citizens of the United States of America, shall not be permitted to visit them with more than two persons besides the rowers; these only shall be permitted to go on board without first obtaining leave from the (commander of said vessel, who shall compare the passports and immediately permit said vessel to proceed on her voyage; and should any of the subjects of Algiers insult or molest the commander or any other person on board a vessel so visited, or plunder any of the property contained in her, on complaint being made to the Consul of the United States residing in Algiers, and on his producing sufficient proofs to substantiate the fact, the Commander or Rais of said Algerine ship or vessel of war, as well as the offenders shall be punished in the most exemplary manner.

"All vessels of war belonging to the United States of America, on meeting with a Cruizer (sic) belonging to the Regency of Algiers, on having seen her passports, and Certificates from the Consul of the United States residing in Algiers shall permit her to proceed on her Cruize (sic) unmolested, and without detention. No passport shall be granted by either party to any vessels but such as are absolutely the property of Citizens or subjects of the said contracting parties, on any pretense whatever.

"ARTICLE 8ᵗʰ
"A citizen or subject of either of the contracting parties having bought a prize vessel condemned by the other party, or by any other nation, the certificates of condemnation and bill of sale shall be a sufficient passport for such vessel for six months, which, considering the distance between the two countries is no more than a reasonable time for her to procure passports.

"ARTICLE 9ᵗʰ
"Vessels of either of the contracting parties putting into the ports of the other and having need of provisions, or other supplies shall be furnished at the market price, and if any such vessel should so put in from a disaster at sea and have occasion to repair, she shall be at liberty to land, and

re-embark her cargo, without paying any customs, or duties whatever; but in no case shall she be compelled to land her cargo.

"ARTICLE 10th

"Should a vessel of either of the contracting parties be cast on shore within the territories of the other all proper assistance shall be given to her, and to her crew; no pillage shall be allowed. The property shall remain at the disposal of the owners, and if reshipped on board of any vessel for exportation, no customs or duties whatever shall be required to be paid thereon, and the crew shall be protected and succored until they can be sent to their own country.

"ARTICLE 11th

"If a vessel of either of the contracting parties shall be attacked by an enemy within cannon shot of the forts of the other, she shall be protected as much as is possible. If she be in port she shall not be seized, or attacked when it is in the power of the other party to protect her; and when she proceeds to sea, no enemy shall be permitted to pursue her from the same port within twenty four hours after her departure.

"ARTICLE 12th

"The commerce between the United States of America and the Regency of Algiers, the protections to be given to merchants, masters of vessels, and seamen, the reciprocal right of establishing consuls in each country, the privileges, immunities and jurisdictions to be enjoyed by such consuls, are declared to be upon the same footing in every respect with the most favored nations respectively.

"ARTICLE 13th

"On a vessel or vessels of war belonging to the United States of America anchoring before the City of Algiers, the consul is to inform the Dey of her arrival when she shall receive the salutes, which are by treaty or custom given to the ships of war of the most favored nations on similar occasions, and which shall be returned gun for gun: and if after such arrival so announced, any Christians whatever, captives in Algiers make their escape and take refuge on board of the said ships of war, they shall not be required back again, nor shall the Consul of the United States, or commander of the said ship be required to pay anything for the said Christians.

"ARTICLE 14th
"The Consul of the United States of America shall not be responsible for the debts contracted by the citizens of his own country unless he gives previously written obligations so to do.

"ARTICLE 15th
"As the Government of the United States of America has in itself no character of enmity against the laws, religion, or tranquility of any nation, and as the said States have never entered into any voluntary war, or act of hostility, except in defense of their just rights on the high seas, it is declared by the contracting parties that no pretext arising from religious opinions shall ever produce an interruption of harmony between the two nations; and the consuls and agents of both nations, shall have liberty to celebrate the rights of their respective religions in their own houses.

"The consuls respectively shall have liberty and personal security given them to travel within the territories of each other, both by land, and by sea, and shall not be prevented from going on board of any vessel they may think proper to visit; they shall likewise have the liberty of appointing their own dragoman, and broker.

"ARTICLE 16th
"In case of any dispute arising from the violation of any of the articles of this treaty no appeal shall be made to arms, nor shall war be declared, on any pretext whatever; but if the consul residing at the place where the dispute shall happen, shall not be able to settle the same, the government of that country shall state their grievance in writing, and transmit the same to the government of the other, and the period of three months shall be allowed for answers to be returned, during which time no act of hostility shall be permitted by either party; and in case the grievances are not redressed, and war should be the event, the consuls, and citizens, and subjects of both parties respectively shall be permitted to embark with their families and effects unmolested, on board of what vessel or vessels they shall think proper. Reasonable time being allowed for that purpose.

"ARTICLE 17th
"If in the course of events a war should break out between the two nations, the prisoners captured by either party shall not be made slaves, they shall not be forced to hard labor, or other confinement than such as may be necessary to secure their safe keeping, and they shall be exchanged rank for rank; and it is agreed that prisoners shall be exchanged in twelve months after their capture, and the exchange may be effected by any private individual, legally authorized by either of the parties.

"ARTICLE 18th
"If any of the Barbary powers, or other states at war with the United States shall capture any American vessel, and send her into any port of the Regency of Algiers, they shall not be permitted to sell her, but shall be forced to depart the port on procuring the requisite supplies of provisions; but the vessels of war of the United States with any prizes they may capture from their enemies shall have liberty to frequent the ports of Algiers for refreshment of any kinds, and to sell such prizes in the said ports, without paying any other customs or duties than such as are customary on ordinary commercial importations.

"ARTICLE 19th
"If any citizens of the United States, or any persons under their protection, shall have any disputes with each other, the consul shall decide between the parties, and whenever the consul shall require any aid or assistance from the government of Algiers to enforce his decisions it shall be immediately granted to him. And if any dispute shall arise between any citizens of the United States, and the citizens or subjects of any other nation having a consul or agent in Algiers, such disputes shall be settled by the consuls or agents of the respective nations; and any dispute or suits at law that may take place between any citizens of the United States, and the subjects of the Regency of Algiers shall be decided by the Dey in person and no other.

"ARTICLE 20th
"If a citizen of the United States should kill wound or strike a subject of Algiers, or on the contrary, a subject of Algiers should kill wound

or strike a citizen of the United States, the law of the country shall take place, and equal justice shall be rendered, the consul assisting at the trial; but the sentence of punishment against an American citizen, shall not be greater or more severe, than it would be against a Turk in the same predicament, and if any delinquent should make his escape, the consul shall not be responsible for him in any manner whatever.

"ARTICLE 21st
"The Consul of the United States of America shall not be required to pay any customs or duties whatever on anything he imports from a foreign country for the use of his house & family.

"ARTICLE 22d
"Should any of the citizens of the United States die within the Regency of Algiers, the Dey and his subjects shall not interfere with the property of the deceased, but it shall be under the immediate direction of the consul, unless otherwise disposed of by will; should there be no Consul the effects shall be deposited in the hands of some person worthy of trust until the party shall appear who has a right to demand them, when they shall render an account of the property; neither shall the Dey or his subjects give hindrance in the execution of any will that may appear.
"Done at Algiers on the 30th day of June A. D. 1815.
(Signed) "OMAN BASHAW (L. S).
"Whereas the undersigned William Shaler a Citizen of the United States, and Stephen Decatur Commander in chief of the U. S. naval forces now in the Mediterranean, being duly appointed Commissioners by letters patent under the signature of the President, and Seal of the U. S. of America, bearing date at the City of Washington the 9th day of April 1815 for negotiating and concluding a treaty of peace between the U. S. of America, and the Dey of Algiers.
"Now Know Ye that we William Shaler and Stephen Decatur commissioners as aforesaid, do conclude the foregoing treaty, and every article, and clause therein contained, reserving the same, nevertheless for the final ratification of the President of the United States of America, by and with the advice and consent of the Senate

"Done on board of the United States Ship Guerriere in the bay of Algiers on the 3d day of July in the year 1815 and of the independence of the U. S. 40th.

(Signed) "WE SHALER
"STEPHEN DECATUR."
Source: Treaties and Other International Acts of the United States of America.
Edited by Hunter Miller
Volume 2
Documents 1-40: 1776-1818
Washington: Government Printing Office, 1931.

Digital version (spelling edited by author from original) courtesy of the Lillian Goldman Law Library Yale University in memory of Saul Goldman, Avalon Project.
  Internet source: http://avalon.law.yale.edu/19th_century/bar1815t.asp

ABOUT THE AUTHOR

Franklin Hook, MD

Franklin Hook is a retired physician and radiologist. A U.S. Navy and Army veteran, he commanded the 311th Evacuation Hospital during the first Persian Gulf War.

His military career includes three years of active duty with the navy, including one year of sea duty, and service as an Army Reserve officer. Currently, he lives in Hot Springs, South Dakota. He is a member of the American Legion, as well as a lifetime member of the VFW.

Dr. Hook is a graduate of Stanford University and the Sidney Kimmel Medical College of Jefferson University in Philadelphia. He is also an associate professor of radiology (retired) at the University of North Dakota School of Medicine.

He is the award-winning author of Never Subdued, a true narrative history of the Philippine-American War, Desert Storm Diary, and Pinky, the story of an aerial combat ace on Guadalcanal. He has written a number of medical articles for various journals, and one medical textbook on CD-ROM.

INDEX

10 Commandments of Muslim Diplomacy, xiii, 167-8, 180-83
4th infantry Regiment. 111

Abdrahaman, Sidi Haji, xxvii, xliv-lv, 10
Abellino, an American privateer 168-70
Abū Muslim rebellion xxvi
Act for the protection of commerce, 23, 158-9
Abrogation
    Of marriage troth xix
    Of treaties xxxix, xli 153
Adams, Abigail, 12, 191
Adams, John, ix, xxxiv, xxxvi, xliv, xlv. 5-6, 10-11, 191, 201-02
Aga, Hassan, 85
Agha, Omar, 167-68
Al Andalus, xx-xxi
Alauite Dynasty, 31
Alexandria, 69-70, 73, 77-6, 88, 203
Alfred, a US Merchant ship, 65
Algiers, xxviii-xxix, xxxi, xxxvi, 15-16, 28-9, 31-8, 41-6, 52, 158-69, 171-80, 195, 204, 225, 230, 243-50
Allegory, xi-xii, 223
Allen, Gardner W., xxviii, xxx, 214-15, 219
Allston, Joseph, 98
Almohad, xxii
Almoravid, xxii
Alpujarras, xxiv

Amherstburg, see Fort
Anacreontic Song, 155
Anti-Semitism, xxvi-xxvii
Appleton, Thomas, 43, 65
Aragon, ix-xx
Armstrong, John, 121, 144-45
Armstrong, Karen, xxii-xxvii, 188
Atheism, xxvii
Azamba, Umar, xii

Bainbridge, William, 16, 29-30, 51-7, 124, 160-62, 177-79, 181-92, 218, 228-30
Baltimore Riot 1812, 109-10
Barbarossa, Horuk (Oruk) xxviii-xxix,
Barbarossa, Khair-ed Din, xxviii-xxix
Barklay, Robert H., 132, 139-40
Barreaut, Captain, xliii
Barron, James, 16, 29, 35, 42, 48, 50, 59, 105-06, 192, 195, 197, 210, 224, 235-36
Barron, Samuel, 30, 61-6, 69, 82, 85-7, 193, 223, 229, 234-37
Barron's Book of Signals, 48, 50
Barrseitz, an internet blogger, 31
Bassa, Hamud (Bey of Tunis), 37, 43
Bastinadoes, 19
Battle of Burnt Corn, 147
Battle of Châteauguay, 144-47, 218, (under Laferty)

Battle of Crysler's Farm, 144-46, 217, (under Hickman)
Battle of Horseshoe Bend, 149-52, 217, (under Hickman)
Battle of Lake Erie, xvii, 130, 136, 140, 177, 198, 219 (under Navy Dept.)
Battle of Queenston Heights, 119
Battle of the Thames, 141, 207 (under Procter)
Battle of Tippecanoe, 107-08, 198, 213, 220
Battle of York, 126-29, 207-08, 215, 220
Bayard, James A., 6
Beane, Dr. William, 154-56
Beaumont, Dr. William, 128
Bell, William, 133
Beltran de la Cueva, xxii
Ben Ghazi, xlv, 73
Ben Unis, Hadji Unis, 34
Berkeley, George Cranfield, 105-06, 236
Bermuda Triangle, 178, 216
Betsy, a US merchant ship, xlv, 30, 77, 162
Bielinski, Stefan, 119, 216
Blennerhassett, Harman, 101-02
Blodgett, Dr. Brian, 108, 216
Boarding House, Conrad & McMunn, 3, 6-10
Bomba, 81-2
Bourbon family, 40
Breese, a Navy Chaplain, 138
Brock, Isaac, 113-19, 126, 208
Brodnick, Roxane, xiii, xiv
Brown, Jacob (Col. or Gen.), 146
Brown, Noah & Adam, 134

Burr, Aaron, 3-6, 64, 89-102, 105, 144, 193, 196, 199, 206, 211, 221
Burr-Hamilton Duel, 91-94

Cádiz, xxiii
Cairo, 69-71, 95
Caldwell, Lieut. James, 62-3
Caller, James, 147
Campbell, Hugh, 29-30, 52-3, 162-63
Canard River, 114
Cape Palos, 161
Caramelli, Hamet see Karamanli
Cardinal Cisneros, see Cisneros
Carronades, 58, 131, 136, 139, 227, 238
Cartagena, 165-66
Cass, Lewis, 114
Castile, xix-xx, xxii-xxiii
Catalano, Salvatori, 58
Cathcart, James, 10-11, 13-15, 27-8, 34-8, 42, 46-7, 193-95, 224
Caughnawaga see Kahnawake
Charles IV of Spain, 39
Charles V of Spain, xxiv
Châteauguay River, 144-45, 211, 218
Chauncey, Isaac, 42, 63, 126-32, 135, 140, 179, 210, 222, 228, 230
Cherokee, 148-52
Chesapeake-Leopard Affair, 105-06, 192, 236
Chippewa see Ojibwa
Christians, ix, xxi-xxviii, xxx, 71, 185-87, 246-47
Cisneros, Cardinal, xxiv
Clague, Mark, 154-55, 224
Claiborne, Ferdinand L., 149
Clare, Israel Smith, 53, 69, 214

Clark, William, 9, 62
Coast Guard, xxxiv, 232
Colden, C.D., 117
College of William and Mary, xliv, 4, 192, 224
Columbus, Christopher, xxiv
Comb, Selim, 78
Congressional Gold Medal, 161, 197, 206
Connant, 78
Constantinople, xxix, 54, 160
Cornells, James, 147-48
Corps of Discovery Expedition, see Lewis & Clark
Crawford, Michael J., xiv, xlvi, Creek 147-50
Creek War, 148
Crockett, Davy, 149
Cutters, definition, xxxiv
Cuyahoga, a U.S. Merchant ship, 113

Dale, Richard 10, 14-21, 25-8, 32, 42, 51, 54, 62, 222, 235-37
Dale, Sam, 149
Danielson, Eli, 69, 77-8
Davis, Dr. George, 37, 47, 56, 62, 202-03
De Salaberry, Charles, 123, 145
Dean, John, 114, 110
Deane, Silas, xxxix
Dearborn, Henry, 23, 26, 117-18, 122-23, 126-29, 143, 195, 206, 211, 222-23
Decatur, James, 62, 169
Decatur, Stephen, xv-xvi, 39, 54-59, 62, 66, 98, 124-25, 154-96, 209, 213-15, 221, 223, 226-50
Declaration of Independence, 5, 8, 110, 202
Democratic-Republican, xxxvii, 5-6, 64

Derna, 61, 68, 73, 82-9, 110, 157, 199, 203
Derne, see Derna
Detroit, 111, 113-16, 121, 126, 130-32, 136-40, 198, 200, 207, 214
Detroit River, 111, 113-15, 207
Dhimmi, xxi, xxiii, xxv-vi
Dobbins, Dan, 130-34
Don Juan of Austria, xxix
Doria, Admiral Andrea, xxix
Dorsey, John, 62-3
Downs, John. 164-67
Duel, 57, 69, 92-4, 192-93, 195, 197, 199, 202
Duke of Parma, 39-40

Eaton, William, xiii, 28, 31-8, 46, 61-3, 66-78, 81-9, 95-101, 110, 195-99, 202, 215, 221, 224, 235
Eckford, Henry, 131
Edict of Expulsion, xxiii
Edwin, a U.S. merchant ship, 157
Egypt, xx, xxvii, 69-71, 73, 76-7, 88
Electoral College, 5-6, 64, 92, 198, 201
Elliott, James D., 179, 197-98, 223, 130-40
Embargo Act of 1807, 106-07, 236
Erie, xvii, 129-36, 140, 177, 198, 215, 219
Estedio, an Algerian ship, 165-66
Eustis, William. 121-22

Farnese family, 40
Farquhar, Richard, 69-78
Federalist, xxxvii, 3, 5-6, 8, 17, 64, 89, 92, 95, 107, 109-10, 191, 196, 205

Ferdinand V (of Spain), b 1451, xxi, xxvi
Ferdinand, of Aragon, see Ferdinand V (Spain)
Ferdinand V, Duke of Parma, b 1751, 39-40
Fermoso, Angelo, 85
First Nation see Indian Confederacy
Force Act, 107
Fort Amherstburg, 111, 114, 117, 122, 126, 133, 144
Fort Detroit, see Detroit
Fort Malden, 111
Fort McHenry, 154-56, 207, 217
Fort Meigs, 129, 140
Fort Mims Massacre, 148
Fort Niagara, 128, 144
Fort Stephenson, 140
Fowler Jr., William M, 28
Fox, Emmet, xi-xii
Franklin, Benjamin, ix, xxxv, xxxix, 3, 31, 157
Fremont-Barnes, Gregory, 36, 215
Frenchtown, 121
Fulton, Robert A, ix-xvi, 214
Fundamentalism, xxvi-xxvii, 185, 188

Gallatin, Albert, 23, 124-25
Gawalt, Gerard W., xxxi
Genet, Edmond C, xii
Genoa, xxiv, xxix
George, Nicolo, 85
Gerry, Elbridge, xxxvii-xxxviii
Gibraltar, 15, 20, 28-31, 35-8, 41-8, 50-1, 56, 157, 160-62, 177, 235
Gordon, Charles, 106, 162, 235

Gormez, Mehmet, 187-88, 216
Granada, xxi-iv, xxvii-viii

Hajji Ali, Bey of Algiers, 158
Hambleton, a Navy purser, 138
Hamilton, Alexander, ix, xxxiv, 92-4, 193, 199
Hamilton, Paul, 124, 131-32
Hammida, Rais (Admiral), 162-66
Hampton Roads, 30, 220, 229-30
Hampton, Wade, 144-46, 215
Hancock, John, 114
Hannings, Bud, 164-66, 211
Harrison, William Henry, 105, 107-08, 121-22, 140-41, 198, 223
Heitman, Francis Bernard, 67, 217
Hemings, Sally, 7, 202
Henry IV, of Castile, xxii
Hickey, Donald R, xiii, 111, 121-22, 125-28, 140-41, 143-44, 146-47, 149, 152, 162, 212, 215
Hickman, Kennedy, 42, 89, 106, 108, 144-47, 151-52, 217, 225, 229
HMS Amazon, 55
HMS Detroit, 132, 135, 139
HMS Guerriere, (captured, the USS Guerriere), 159, 163-76, 199, 232, 237, 250
HMS Java, 161, 179, 205-06, 232
HMS Lady Prevost, 139
HMS Leopard, 105-06, 192, 236
HMS Little Belt, 237-39
HMS Queen Charlotte. 116, 136, 139-40
HMS Serapis, 15, 26
HMS Shannon, 136, 236
Hollis, Iran, 28, 214, 217

INDEX 257

Holy Roman Emperor, see Charles V
Hook, Paul, xiv, 16, 124, 134
Hoople's Creek, 146
Houston, Sam, 149, 151-52, 221
Hull, William 110-11, 113-18, 121-22, 126, 144, 198, 200, 206, 221
Hull, Isaac, 42, 44, 54, 66-8, 74, 81-5, 110, 125, 199-200, 210, 232
Humphreys, Joshua, xlii, 225
Humphreys, Salisbury, 106

Iberian Peninsula, xx-xxvi
Impressment, xlvi, 105, 109, 157
Indian Confederacy, 107-08, 113
Isabella, of Portugal, xix
Isabella, of Spain, xix, xxii
ISIS, xxv, 122, 186-87
ISIL, 187-88, 216
Israel, Joseph, 63-4
Istanbul, see Constantinople

Jackson, Andrew, 143, 149-52, 200-01, 209, 213, 216, 219
Jamace, Bernardo, 85
Janssens, Jean Claude, 165, 167, 218
Jay Treaty, xxxv, xlvi
Jay, John, xi-xii, xiv, xxxv
Jefferson, Martha, 6-7, 202, 222
Jefferson, Thomas, xxiv, xliv, 7-14, 25, 95
Jews, ix, xi, xxi-xxvii, 185
Jizya, xxii, xxv-vi
Joan of Portugal, xxvi
Jones, Jacob, 165, 169
Jones, John Paul, xxxi, 15, 26, 231
Jones, Richard B, 169-71, 175-76

Jones, William, 132
Juana, xxii

Kahnawake, 123, 145
Karamanli, Hamet, 14, 31, 33-8, 61, 66-89, 196, 202
Karamanli, Yusuf, xvi, 10-11, 13-15, 19, 31-8, 44-5, 56, 62-3, 66-74, 81, 85-6, 89, 157. 160, 169-71, 196, 202-03, 216
Kentucky Militia, 121
Key, Francis Scott, 154-55, 203-04, 207, 217
Khorāsān, xxvi
Kibbe, Ephraim, 98
King Louis XVI, xxxii, xxxv, 39
King of the Two Sicilies 45, 166, 169
King, Maj. David M., 87
Kingston, 125, 144
Knoll, Denys, 126-29, 131-36, 215
Koran xi-xii, xxvii, xliv, 10

Lacolle River, 123, 222
Lafferty, Renee, 145, 147, 218
Lake Champlain, 144-45, 211
Lardas, Mark, 56-8,, 213
Laulewasikau see Tenskwatawa
Laurens, Henry, xi
Lawrence, James, 135, 236
Lear, Tobias, 9, 45, 52, 66, 85-6, 88-9, 157-58, 196, 202 204, 222
Lee, Arthur, xxxix
Leghorn, 40-1, 43-6, 63
Legion of the United States, 59, 65
Lepanto, Greece, xxx
Levedo, Spedo, 85

Lewis & Clark, 9, 62
Lewis, Captain, 159, 164, 177
Lewis, Meriwether, 9, 11, 23, 221
Lincoln, Levi, 23
Linder, Doug, 100-02
L'Insurgente, a French frigate, ii, xlii-iii, 17, 30, 210, 229
Livingston, Robert R, 29, 39, 41, 233
Livorno, see Leghorn
London, Joshua, 35, 44-6, 66, 215
Long, David Foster, 33, 213
Louisiana Purchase, 9, 40-1, 215
Lucca, Capt., 85
Luigi, Pierre, 40

Mackenzie, Alexander Slidell, 136, 139-40, 213
Mackinac, 114, 129
Madani, Iyad Ameen, 187
Madison, Dolley, 12, 204
Madison, James, xxxiii, xlv, 5, 7-15, 23-38, 46, 61, 65-6, 107-09, 116-19, 124, 130, 144, 152, 156, 158-61, 166-7, 178-79, 200, 204, 218-19, 224
Malaga, 47-8
Malcomson, Robert and Thomas, 127-28, 219
Malta, xxix, 14-17, 27-8, 31-3, 41-6, 54-5, 63, 79, 83, 153, 198
Mann, George, 69, 78, 84
Marquis Circello, 174
Marshall, John, xxxvii, 3, 5, 11, 91, 95, 99-102, 196, 205
Martin, Daniel, 105
Mastico, a Tripolitan ship, 54, 57-8

Mathurins, Order of, xxxii
McKee, Christopher, 54-5, 210, 213
McKenzie, Alexander, xvii
McNeill, Daniel, 29
McQueen, Peter, 147
Meade, George, 130-32
Meshuda, a Tripolitan ship, 30, 42-3, 162-66, 178, 229
Messina, Sicily, xxix-xxx, 45, 47, 65, 173-76
Mexico, 96-7, 193, 101, 212
Miller, James, 114
Minor, Benjamin, & Wells, JD, 166, 215, 219
Miranda, Francisco de, 97
Mirboka, a Moroccan ship, 51-2
Mississauga, 126-27, 146
Mississippi Militia, 147-48
Mohamed IV, 31
Moniac, Sam, 147
Monroe, James, 41, 124, 167,
Monticello, xiii, 3-4, 6, 9-11, 27, 46, 202, 221, 234
Monticello Reserve Ale, 9-10, 221
Montréal, 122-23, 127, 144-46, 206, 211
Moors, xx-xxi, xxiv-v, xxxii, 220
Moran, Edward, 59
Moranos (Morranos), xxiv-vi
Moriscos, xxiv-v
Morocco, ix, xxxi-ii, xxxv, 16, 31, 45, 51-2, 162-63
Moros, ix-x, xx, xxxii, 68
Morris, Andrew, 32-3, 224
Morris, Richard, 28-38, 41-52, 56, 126, 146, 162-3, 205, 210, 224, 229-30, 235

INDEX

Murabitun, xxii
Murray, Alexander, 29-31
Muslim exodus from Spain, xxvii-viii
Muslims, ix-xxxii, 166, 179, 171-82, 186-89
Mutiny, 81, 113, 161
Muwwahidun, xxii

Naples, 45, 47, 173-74
Napoleon Bonaparte, xxxviii, xliii, xlvi, 39, 41, 116, 197
Natelson, Rob, 153
National Intelligencer, 3
Naval Act of 1794, xxxiii-vi, xxxix, xliii, 225
Naval Historical Center, xlv, 216, 219, 229, 231-32
Navy Board of Commissioners, 208
Navy, Continental, xxxi-xxxiv, 15, 54, 225-26
Neale Benedict, 167, 177-78
New Orleans, 29, 39-41, 97, 152-53
Niagara, 117, 119, 128-29, 143-44
Nihilism, xxvii
Noah, Mordechai, 168
Norderling, Johan, 166

O'Bannon, Presley, 68-9, 77-8, 81, 84, 88-9
O'Brian, Bernard, 85
O'Brien, Richard, 31-2, 38, 46
Ojibwa, 127
Old Hickory, see Jackson, Andrew
Omar the Terrible, see Agha
Ontario, 114, 126-27, 129-33, 140, 207-08
Ottoman Empire, xxiv-xxvii, 70, 72

Parable, xi-xii
Parker, Philip S., 117
Pasha, Ali, xxx
Paulina, an Algerian brig, 35-6, 170
Paullin, Chas, 35-6, 38, 43-4, 47, 51-2, 213
Peace commissioners (1782), xl
Peck, Pascal, 77-8, 81
Pensacola, 147-48
Perry, Oliver Hazard, xvii, 121, 129, 132-33, 135-40, 179, 197-98, 205-06, 213, 220
Pershing, John, xxxii, 182
Peters, George, 154
Philip III, xxiv
Pierce, Cromwell, 128
Pike, Zebulon, 122-23, 127-28, 206-07
Pinckney, Charles Cotesworth, xxxvii, 64
Pinckney, Thomas, 5
Pope Paul III, 40
Porcile, Countess Maria Anne, 30, 35, 96
Portugal, ix-xxvii, 195
Preble, Edward, xiii, 48-59, 62-6, 87, 98, 126, 162-63, 169, 173, 180, 188, 206, 210, 213-14, 217
Presque Isle, 130-34
Press Gangs, see impressment
Prevost, Sir George, 116
Privateers, xxxvi-xlvi, 125, 226, 230
Procter, Henry, 140-41, 207
Prophet, The, 108
Purdy, Robert, 145

Quasi-War, xv-xlii, 17, 30, 42, 49, 54, 107, 161, 198, 205, 210, 226, 229, 231-37
Quebec City, 116

Queen Charlotte, a Canadian ship, 116, 136, 139-40
Qur'an see Koran

Raisin River, 121-22, 207
Ransom, xvi-xliv, 32, 34-6, 46, 75-7, 148, 158, 173, 244
Ratford, Jenkins, 105-06
Red Eagle, see Weatherford, William
Red Sticks, 147-52
Redbeard, see Barbarossa
Reign of Terror, xxxviii-xli
Revenue-Marine, xxxiv-vi
Richelieu River, 123, 211
Ridler, Jason, 111, 127, 223
Roco, 78
Rodgers, John, 29, 34-8, 43-54, 63, 66, 86-7, 124-26, 162-63, 188, 193, 207-08, 210, 213, 221, 229, 234, 237
Rosetta, 69-70
Rous, Rais Mahomet, 18-19
Ruffini, Silvia, 40

Sacket's Harbor, 130, 145
Salaberry, Charles de, 123, 145
Sandwich, 114
Saragosa see Syracuse
Sewall, Lewis, 148
Shaker, William E., 167
Sharp, Robert, xiv
Sharples, James Senior, 118
Shaw, John, 29, 179, 228, 230
Sheaffe, Roger Hale, 127-29, 208, 220
Shubrick, John Templer, 167, 179, 240
Side boys, 49, 138
Skelton, Bathurst, 6, 202

Skinner, John, 154-56
Smith, George C., 157
Smith, Jean Edward, 91
Smith, Robert, 23, 205, 209-10
Smith, Samuel, 151
Somers, Richard, 47-51, 56, 63-4, 158, 179, 220
Spellberg, Denise A., xliv, 215
St. Lawrence River, 116, 144-46, 211
Star Spangled Banner, 154-55, 207, 218, 224
Sterett, Andrew, 16-20, 29, 35, 42, 209-10, 222-23, 229
Stewart, Charles, 58, 230
Stewart, David O., 93-4
Strachan, John, 105, 129
Suleiman, Emperor, 51-2, 163, 188
Syracuse, Sicily, 56-7, 202
Syren see USS Siren

T'garn'sls, 139
Taiib, al, & Mahamat, Arab Sheiks, 79
Tallapoosa River, 150-51
Talleyrand, xxxvii-viii
Tangiers, 51
Tecumseh, 107-08, 113-14, 122, 141, 147, 207, 216
Tennessee Militia, 149, 151, 201
Tenskwatawa, 108-09
Thomas, David, 84
Thor, Brad, xxxi
Thorburn, Mark, 115-16, 221
Tillotson, Robert, 117
Tohopeka, see Tallapoosa
Toll, Ian W., xiii, 210, 214, 234
Torah, xi, xiii

INDEX

Toronto, 114, 126, 129, 154, 186, 207-08, 215
Treaty of Alliance, xxxiv-xliii
Treaty of Ghent, Belgium, 156
Treaty of Granada, xxiii
Treaty of Paris, xxxiv-xl
Treaty of San Ildefonso, 39-41
Treaty of Tripoli, 159
Tripoli, xxv-xlv, 161-63, 168-79, 191, 196-97, 202-06, 213, 215, 230, 235
Tripoli, the ship, 17-20
Truxton, Thomas, ii, 17, 30, 48, 54, 98, 210, 229
Tucker, Spencer (et al), 23, 44, 159, 162, 165, 178, 203, 213-15
Tunis, xxviii-xxxv, 16, 19, 28, 31-8, 41-7, 61-2, 70, 87-8, 96, 168-71, 177-80, 196, 230, 234
Tuscany, 30, 39-40, 46
Twelfth Amendment, 64
Two Sicilies, 47, 75, 170, 173

Umar ben Muhammed, see Agha
Umayyad, xxvi
USS Adams, 29-30, 43-4, 52, 132, 162-3, 205, 223
USS Allegheny, 158
USS Amelia, 135
USS Argus, 54, 66
USS Bonhomme Richard, 15, 26
USS Boston, 29, 222
USS Chesapeake, 28-30, 35, 41-2, 106, 136, 235
USS Constellation, ii, xlii, 17, 29-31, 162-63, 210, 229
USS Constitution, xxiii, 161, 199, 231-33

USS Enterprise, 16-20, 29, 35-6, 42-7, 54, 57, 110, 199
USS Epervier, 159, 164-67, 177-78
USS Essex, 16, 29, 161
USS Firefly, 159
USS Flambeau, 159
USS Franklin, 31
USS George Washington, 29
USS Guerriere, 159, 163-76, 199, 232, 237
USS Hornet, 81-5, 228
USS Independence, 177
USS Intrepid, 54, 57-8, 63-4, 220
USS Java, 205
USS John Adams, 29-35, 43-4, 48, 63, 126
USS Lawrence, 131-35
USS Macedonian, 165, 169
USS Nautilus, 82
USS New York, 29, 35, 41-3, 48, 54, 235
USS Niagara, 131-36
USS Ontario, 163, 197
USS Perseverance, 38
USS Philadelphia, 16, 30, 51-3, 59, 87, 160
USS President, 16, 19, 42, 61-3, 159-61, 228, 237
USS Retaliation, 161
USS Siren, 58
USS Spark, 159, 165
USS Spitfire, 159, 165
USS Torch, 159, 165
USS United States, xxviii, 54, 125, 177, 225-28
USS Vixen, 56

Valladolid, xix-xxiv
Van Buren, Martin, 117, 198

Van Rensselaer, Solomon, 119
Van Rensselaer, Stephen, 119
Vengeance, a French frigate, 17
Vergennes, Fr, Foreign Minister, xl
Vincent, John, 129
Virginia militia, 6-8

Wabarakathuhu, xii, 223
Wadsworth, Henry, 63-4
Waldo, Samuel Putnam, 172, 177, 166-69, 215, 221, 226, 241
Wales, John, 202
Ware, William, 105
Washington, George, xxxii-xlv, 5-11, 24, 78, 89, 111, 143, 199, 204, 211, 214, 226

Weatherford, William, 148-49, 152
Weehawken, N.J., 94
Wheelan, Joseph, 19, 214
White House, burning of, 153-54, 204
Wilson, Scott, 154-56
Wilton, John, 84-5
Winchester, James, 121-22

XYZ Affair, xxxvi-xli

Yarnall, John, 167, 177

Zacks, Richard, xiii, 69, 78, 81, 85, 89, 107, 215
Zahara de la Sierra, xxiii

Made in the USA
Charleston, SC
30 July 2015